An
UNFINISHED
AGENDA

An

UNFINISHED AGENDA

My Life in the

PHARMACEUTICAL INDUSTRY

K. ANJI REDDY

PORTFOLIO
PENGUIN

PORTFOLIO
Published by the Penguin Group
Penguin Books India Pvt. Ltd, 7th Floor, Infinity Tower C, DLF Cyber City,
Gurgaon 122 002, Haryana, India
Penguin Group (USA) Inc., 375 Hudson Street, New York, New York 10014, USA
Penguin Group (Canada), 90 Eglinton Avenue East, Suite 700, Toronto,
Ontario, M4P 2Y3, Canada
Penguin Books Ltd, 80 Strand, London WC2R 0RL, England
Penguin Ireland, 25 St Stephen's Green, Dublin 2, Ireland (a division of Penguin Books Ltd)
Penguin Group (Australia), 707 Collins Street, Melbourne, Victoria 3008, Australia
Penguin Group (NZ), 67 Apollo Drive, Rosedale, Auckland 0632, New Zealand
Penguin Books (South Africa) (Pty) Ltd, Block D, Rosebank Office Park,
181 Jan Smuts Avenue, Parktown North, Johannesburg 2193, South Africa

Penguin Books Ltd, Registered Offices: 80 Strand, London WC2R 0RL, England

First published in Portfolio by Penguin Books India 2015

ISBN 9780670087808

Typeset in Dante MT Std by Eleven Arts, Delhi
Printed at Replika Press Pvt. Ltd, India

A PENGUIN RANDOM HOUSE COMPANY

To the memory of my parents

'One day you must tell me your full and complete story, unabridged and unexpurgated. We will set aside some time for it, and meet. It's very important.'

Maneck smiled. 'Why is it important?'

Mr. Valmik's eyes grew wide. 'You don't know? It's extremely important because it helps to remind yourself of who you are. Then you can go forward, without fear of losing yourself in this ever-changing world.'

Rohinton Mistry
A Fine Balance

CONTENTS

FOREWORD

Dr Anji Reddy was father and father-in-law to us. For over twenty-five years, we also worked closely with him in the pharmaceutical business he founded. For us, reading his memoirs is like reliving the past. We hear his voice, regaling us with one anecdote after another and his uninhibitedly joyous, full-throated laughter. We remember his infectious enthusiasm as he recounted the breath-taking progress of science and the promise that it held for the future. We recall being enthralled by the grand vision he had for the business we were in, and the impact we could make. We remember, too, his fortitude when faced with disappointments as well as his marvellous ability to put them firmly behind him and look ahead with characteristic optimism.

Dr Reddy was a voracious reader of science as is evident from his memoirs, but many other things, big and small, kept him absorbed. He had an abiding interest in literature and films in Telugu, the language of his schooling. The music that moved him most was in Telugu, particularly 'Nagumomu ganaleni', a composition of the saint-poet Tyagaraja. He had a surprising collection of art, some of which unsurprisingly found its way to the discovery research facility. But all these and more were peripheral to his main interest and find no mention in his story. The molecules of medicine were at the centre of his universe and his memoirs are mainly about them—first about producing the known ones, and then the quest for discovering new ones, with engaging detours along the way.

Despite the modest circumstances of his early life, which Dr Reddy briefly and unselfconsciously recounts, he had the self-confidence to pursue his interests, without the benefit of counselling and the awareness that is taken for granted today. It was the same self-confidence, and the excitement spawned by the accomplishments of science, that set him off on his entrepreneurial journey.

And what a journey it has been!

Dr Reddy started off at an entry-level position at Indian Drugs and Pharmaceuticals, a pioneering public sector undertaking at Hyderabad and some years later struck out on his own. His entrepreneurial story mirrors that of the pharmaceutical industry in India. How did an industry that lacked the technology and the means to make the most basic of drugs become a pharmacy to the world? Dr Reddy himself made no small contribution to this transformation, but his account also provides fascinating vignettes of others who shaped the course of the industry.

Dr Reddy's pioneering efforts led to many milestones being achieved by the company that bears his name. All of them delighted Dr Reddy, some more than others. One of the most significant resulted from his decision to slash the prices of drugs in a new class of antibiotics, the fluoroquinolones, in the early 1990s. It shook up the industry. More medicines followed at prices which were within the reach of a large number of people in need of them. The competition was forced to respond. The pricing paradigm of medicines in India changed irreversibly and they became affordable. No other milestone better sums up his understanding of the purpose of the business he was in. It is no wonder that he constantly reminded us of George Merck's dictum that medicines are for people, not for profits. And as Merck also said, the better we remembered that, the better were our profits. In the years that followed, the rapid increase in volumes resulted in record profits for the company.

Affordable medicine is not just a question of pricing. To remain sustainable, it requires innovation to make medicines efficiently and economically. Dr Reddy's early innovations were all about that, at a time when it was not the norm it now is in Indian industry. Never one to rest on his laurels, Dr Reddy shifted his attention in the mid-1990s to the highest level of innovation in the industry, that of discovering new medicines. It was an unthinkable aspiration for the Indian pharmaceutical industry at that time. Nothing deterred him—not the sceptics, the uncharted waters, the expense or the risk.

Against all odds, several new molecules were discovered and one of them, balaglitazone, a novel insulin sensitizer for the treatment of diabetes, was licensed to Novo Nordisk for clinical development on 1 March 1997. It was a historical first for the Indian pharmaceutical industry and was cherished the most by Dr Reddy. Everything went swimmingly for a while and an even more potent insulin sensitizer, ragaglitazar, was discovered. The discovery was remarkable, for it was not just a potentially more useful treatment for diabetes than balaglitazone, but it was also a 'first-in-class' molecule, with an entirely novel structure, an extraordinary outcome for a fledgling discovery programme. Ragaglitazar too was licensed to Novo Nordisk, but it stumbled at the final hurdle. It was the biggest disappointment in Dr Reddy's life. We vividly recall that even at this dark time, one of his first concerns was how he could soften the blow and rally the scientists who had laboured in the discovery.

This setback, though huge, did not quell the innovator in Dr Reddy. It was not just the compulsive quest for discovery, the defining characteristic of a true innovator, which kept him going. He was also driven by his overwhelming belief in the purpose of medicine. As he argues in his memoirs, new medicines must be affordable to be useful and this demanded a new model of drug discovery research. His unflinching resolve was born of this conviction. He, therefore, persisted in his quest, with his personal funds. This was his unfinished agenda.

Just last month, we were poignantly reminded of Dr Reddy's lasting commitment to research. He writes in his memoirs that the patent for balaglitazone was the first and the last one where he was named an inventor. It was of course in the context of Dr. Reddy's Laboratories. On 30 September 2014, a patent was issued in the United States for novel pyridine carboxylic acid derivatives, which could be useful in the treatment of Alzheimer's disease. Dr Reddy was named the co-inventor.

The application for the patent had been made in 2010, about a year and a half before he became very ill.

Discovery research was not the only interest that consumed Dr Reddy for the last two decades of his life. Another was his substantial involvement with initiatives to better the lives of people who were underprivileged, which he recounts in the concluding part of his memoirs. We were struck by the fact that he never once used the word philanthropy. We do not think it was a conscious decision. It probably never occurred to Dr Reddy to think of it that way. If anything, he regarded it as a debt he was discharging for all the good that fortune had favoured him with.

Dr Reddy never said it in so many words, but we do think now that he did not see the larger purpose of his pharmaceutical business as very different from that of the social enterprises he had set up. Both of them aimed to better the lives of people.

Above all, we remember Dr Reddy's irrepressible zest for life. When he was diagnosed with cancer of the liver, we grieved. We also worried about how he would deal with it. Knowing him as we did, we ought not to have been apprehensive.

Dr Reddy understood the prognosis better than most people. He did not dread the inevitable. Instead, he put it quickly and firmly behind him. He turned his attention to what he could do in the limited time available to him. One of the things he decided to do was to write his memoirs. Nearly a year later, and barely a week before he passed away, he read the first version, hastily printed, from cover to cover, in a hospital bed. He seemed to be overcome with emotion as he held the book in his hands, but that was for just a few moments. He looked up and joked one last time. 'My life is in my hands,' he said, and smiled. If he had not been so tired, we would have heard his full-throated laughter.

Dr Reddy penned his memoirs with the same zest that he had for life and everything that interested him. We hope you will enjoy reading them.

Hyderabad

25 November 2014

K. Satish Reddy

G.V. Prasad

1 THE MOON IS THE LIMIT

The first ever photograph on the moon,
20 July 1969

Neil Armstrong/Courtesy of NASA

Hyderabad, 20 July 1969

For days, the newspapers have been full of reports of man's first attempt at a moon landing. America, upstaged earlier by Russia in its attempt to conquer space, has recaptured the initiative, redeeming the promise made by its young President, John F. Kennedy.

The world is gripped with a sense of wonderment at what science can accomplish. Scientists are walking tall. It does not matter whether one works on rocket propulsion at NASA or with a beaker in a distant laboratory in a Third World town—we are all frontiersmen of science.

It is night and I am taut with tension. I cannot sleep and turn on the radio. Television is unheard of in Hyderabad in 1969 and, besides, I cannot afford one. But it does not matter. The Voice of America announcers have been doing a fine job delivering a live commentary and describing the countdown to the moon landing. I listen with rapt attention, eyes closed, trying to picture the craft approaching the lunar landscape, settling down, the figure stepping out in a white spacesuit, the first voyager to the moon!

Seven hours later Neil Armstrong's voice comes across, quavering a little over the static, his message simple and yet so profound: 'That's one small step for man, one giant leap for mankind.'

How does the son of a turmeric farmer who hasn't yet had his first plane ride react to something like this? Men climb aboard a spaceship, travel to outer space, land on the moon—and hope to return safely to earth. What will science accomplish next? How powerful America is!

Since my first days at university in Bombay (now Mumbai), I have been fascinated with the USA—its railroads, its massive cars, its cities and universities, the way the nation encourages talent, and even the way Americans greet each other—with a 'Hi!'

One of my biggest indulgences at university was an annual subscription to *Time* magazine, while I was living on a monthly allowance of 110 rupees sent by my father. I remain a loyal reader. *Time* chronicles America for me week after week. It seems to have a ringside view of every major event and maps every key social trend. Quite often, it treats the titans of our age in an irreverent way that fascinates me. I look forward to their moon-landing issue.

Apollo 11 has landed. As I sit alone in the living room of my tiny Hyderabad flat, my mind churns with emotions—pride, hope, joy and a new confidence that it is not wrong or foolish to dream. America has shown the world that a grand vision can be realized with great science. Surely, there is a lesson in this for individual enterprise.

Of course, it doesn't happen all at once. There are bills to be paid, testy bosses to handle and a young family to nurture. But the emotions unleashed by Armstrong's historic feat whirl around in my head. The idea that I should venture into uncharted territory takes hold.

The records say Dr. Reddy's Laboratories was established on 24th February 1984. The truth is, the company was born on the day Armstrong stepped out of the astronauts' bay of *Apollo 11* on to that cold lunar landscape.

2   STEPPING STONES

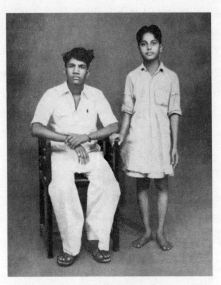

My first photograph: *With my friend*
Bolla Krishna Reddy (seated)

While Neil Armstrong's landing on the moon galvanized my entrepreneurial instincts in one electrifying moment, it took quite some time for me to figure out that I wanted to be in the pharmaceutical industry. I have often been asked whether anything in my childhood had heralded my career or shaped my future, but the truth is that there was no such thing. It was as much by chance as by choice.

I was born in my father's house facing the railway tracks in Tadepalli, a small town of perhaps 10,000 people, ten kilometres south of Vijayawada in Andhra Pradesh. My father, Kallam Venkat Reddy, was a well-to-do turmeric farmer and my mother, Nagabullemma, was from Nutakki, a fertile and relatively prosperous village about thirteen kilometres away on the banks of the River Krishna. I was born on 10th August 1941, but my father put down my date of birth as 2nd January 1939 in my school records. In those days, it was not unusual to enter an earlier date of birth in the school records for male children. There was a minimum age requirement for passing out of school and many parents believed that the earlier one finished school, the more of a head start one would get in life.

My parents had different personalities. My father was soft-spoken and unassertive, thoughtful and methodical in his ways, and took a long time to come to any decision. I cannot recall his ever being in a hurry to sell his turmeric crop, but when he did do so, he invariably got a good price. My mother, confident with the wisdom that comes from shouldering responsibilities early in life, was the decision-maker in the family. I would like to think that I owe my business instincts to my father and my penchant for making quick decisions to my mother.

My father had less than six years of schooling and my mother had neither been to school nor had she learnt how to read and write.

My schoolmates, teachers and staff at Nutakki: *I am the shortest, standing second from left in the rear row*

However, they were clear that I needed a good education. That was their greatest gift to me.

I moved to Nutakki, my mother's village, enrolled in class five and stayed with my grandmother for the next six years of schooling. The instruction was in Telugu, the regional language of Andhra.* Nowadays, schooling in the local language is looked down upon, but I never felt at a disadvantage. I was not a particularly serious student—I played the fool as much as any other boy of my age, yet I topped my class every year as I was attentive and had a retentive memory.

After school came a two-year intermediate course. In those days, the world view of students in villages or small towns was very limited. When it came to a choice of subjects in the intermediate course, I was inclined to study history, mainly because my cousin had done so. Luckily for me, my cousin did not think it was a good idea and persuaded me to study science instead. I got admission to the intermediate course at the Hindu College in Guntur, a town less than thirty kilometres from Tadepalli, with botany, physics and chemistry as my subjects.

My years in Hindu College were unhurried and carefree. Every teacher had his own distinctive style of teaching, which often gave rise to irreverent humour. Our botany lecturer had a habit of referring to every plant first by its botanical name and then by its Telugu name. Botanical names were always in Latin, a language chosen in the eighteenth century by Carl Linnaeus, the Swedish originator of the system of nomenclature for plants. Linnaeus was so dedicated to his system that he even 'Latinized' his name to Carolus. We were blissfully devoid of any such dedication to botany and did not know any Latin, so the irreverent ditty in honour of our botany lecturer was made up in a mixture of English and Telugu. Something must have rubbed off on me, however—I still look up the botanical name whenever I come across a natural product used as a drug.

* Editor's note: The state of Andhra Pradesh was bifurcated into Telangana and Andhra Pradesh on 2 June 2014.

The English lecturer in our intermediate course was particularly good in the language and he made it a point to teach only in English. This was hard for us to follow as we had done our schooling in Telugu, so we requested that he give us explanations in Telugu. He obliged, but his Telugu was so high-flown that it was as incomprehensible to us as English, and he soon got what he wanted from us—a request that he revert to English in his classes. In the process, I became adequately proficient in English.

When I finished my intermediate course, my father took me to the Agricultural College at Bapatla, a town about eighty kilometres from Tadepalli. Agriculture had been my family's traditional occupation and it probably did not occur to my father that I might like to do anything different. I had no intention, however, of being a farmer, and set about securing admission to the BSc course in Andhra Christian College at Guntur.

Our physics lecturer in the intermediate course in Hindu College was an inspiring teacher and I got interested in the subject. Logically, I should have followed up with a bachelor's degree in physics, but for a reason I cannot recall, I chose chemistry as my major and physics and botany as minors; my favourite subject was physical chemistry.

There were only three chemistry teachers in Andhra Christian College. One of them was Dr Varadanam, a PhD from Andhra University—the only doctorate in the entire college. He had perfected the art of teaching by rote—every chemical formula would be repeated in a rather curious fashion. For example, if he wished to write the formula of propyl alcohol on the board, he would first write the formula for methyl alcohol, erase the methyl and write the formula for ethyl, erase it and finally write the formula for propyl. In sync with his writing, he would be saying 'methyl, ethyl, propyl' like a mantra. Whether one liked it or not, the repetitive recitation of formulae registered in one's head.

Andhra Christian College, better known as AC College, had been established in 1885 by Protestant missionaries; admission to it was much sought after. An American, Swavely, was the principal, and he

Andhra Christian College, Guntur: *The chemistry bug bit me here*

spoke with an American twang that the students found quite strange. One of the things Swavely did not like was students loitering aimlessly in the verandas of the college, and they scattered at his approach. If he chanced upon an unwary student, he would ask him sternly, 'Why are you wandering in the veranda?' Needless to say, he was dubbed the 'Veranda Principal', which was quite unfair considering his other sterling qualities. Several prominent people in Andhra Pradesh have graduated from AC College, including three chief ministers. I was fortunate to have studied there: it laid the foundation for my future learning.

I did quite well in my examinations and my parents were supportive of my studying further. I knew of two options—Delhi University under Prof. T.R. Seshadri, who was famed for his knowledge of the chemistry of natural products, and the University Department of Chemical Technology (UDCT) in Bombay. Both institutions were much in demand and there was only one seat available in each for students from south India. My classmate P. Srinivasa Rao stood first in the university and was a gold-medallist; I came second. I knew that it was pointless for us to compete with each other. So I struck a deal with him—he would have the first choice and I would not apply to the institution he preferred. In turn, I suggested that he should not apply to the second one so I had a better chance there. Srinivasa Rao said that Bombay was too expensive for him and he chose to go to Delhi. So I went to UDCT. Though the course they offered led to a Bachelor of Science (Technology) degree, it was really a postgraduate course that one could apply for only after obtaining a bachelor's degree in science.

Strangely enough, I joined the textile chemistry course in UDCT, but I soon realized I was more interested in pharmaceuticals. Luckily for me, when I asked for a change, they allowed me to shift. The formal name of the course was quite a mouthful: it was called the Technology of Pharmaceuticals and Fine Chemicals.

Established in 1933 with the generous support of textile magnates in Bombay, UDCT was industry-oriented from the start, focusing initially on textile chemistry. Prof. K. Venkataraman was the first Indian director of UDCT. During his nineteen-year-long tenure, the institution became one of the leading centres of science and technology in the country. His *Chemistry of Synthetic Dyes* was published in 1952 and later translated into fourteen languages, including Chinese. Prof. Venkataraman also went on to become the first Indian director of National Chemical Laboratory (NCL).

When I was at UDCT, students had to write a dissertation in the summer and these were often industry assignments, such as developing a new process. It was quite exciting. Students worked sixteen hours a day—they knew that if they succeeded, they would get a job with the company that had given them the assignment.

There were connections to the pharmaceutical industry too. UDCT had set up a pilot plant to make a tuberculosis drug for Pfizer. I was fascinated by it and that was probably when the idea of getting into the pharmaceutical industry got into my head. I used to joke that one day I would build a factory like Pfizer. However, the person who inspired me most was M.L. Khurana, professor of pharmacy and a giant of a pharmacist. His teaching of pharmaceutical chemistry was masterly and

I retained my notes from his lectures for a long time. Prof. Khurana's students found positions in industry and research the world over and several of them have made outstanding contributions to pharmaceutics. The Indian Pharmaceutical Association instituted an award in his memory; I was privileged to receive the award in 1988 and deliver the memorial lecture in honour of my icon.

UDCT was a breeding ground for entrepreneurs. Mukesh Ambani, now chairman of Reliance Industries, Indravadan Modi, founder-chairman of Cadila Healthcare, and V.G. Rajadhyaksha, former chairman of Hindustan Lever (as Unilever was then known), all graduated from UDCT. So did Homi Sethna, who became chairman of the Atomic Energy Commission, and R.A. Mashelkar, former director general of the Council of Scientific and Industrial Research. UDCT is now a full-fledged university and has been renamed the Institute of Chemical Technology.

After I finished my BSc (Tech), instead of building a factory like Pfizer, I landed a job at the Indian Institute of Technology (IIT), Bombay, as a junior technical assistant in the department of chemistry. IIT Bombay had been set up a few years earlier and Prof. N.R. Kamath, who had been a professor at UDCT, had joined IIT and become its deputy director. After six months at IIT, I met him and said I wanted to work in the industry. He gave me an introduction to H.J.V. Krishna, the head of the steroid plant of Glaxo. Krishna was helpful. He said, 'Mr Reddy, I don't have a job for you, but would you like to do a PhD?' I said, 'Yes.' He offered, 'Dr Doraiswamy is a friend of mine and he's looking for bright boys like you. Would you like to join him?' I said that I would and he gave me a letter of introduction.

Though I was keen on working in the industry, I enrolled in the PhD programme in 1963 at NCL in Pune, primarily because I had no better opportunity. A doctoral student got a junior research fellowship of 250 rupees per month. It was a lot of money for me. Dr L.K. Doraiswamy was a chemical engineer and my PhD was in chemical engineering, not chemistry. My thesis was on the kinetics of oxidation of toluene and I co-authored a paper with Dr Doraiswamy based on my thesis which was published in the journal *Chemical Engineering Science* in 1969. About a decade ago, I checked out of sheer curiosity, and was quite pleased to see that the paper was still being cited some thirty years after its publication.

My first publication, however, was on a different subject. Dr Doraiswamy had given me a problem which had nothing to do with the topic of my thesis. He said, 'Anji Reddy, do some work on liquid diffusivity. Though the fundamental theoretical equation is the Stokes–Einstein equation, it does not hold good under all conditions. There is a need for an empirical equation. Here is the data. Your job is to fit these into an equation and compare the calculated results with the actual data.'

I should have been daunted by the task. It was Einstein himself who had derived the equation for his PhD dissertation. There were perhaps another half a dozen empirical equations, the most significant being the Wilke–Chang correlation, a semi-empirical modification of the Stokes–Einstein equation. My task was to better this. It involved a lot of computation. There was only one calculator in NCL, which was the size of a large typewriter and always busy. Instead of waiting for my turn with the calculator, I developed a framework with a slide rule and went to the calculator only for the final computations. I got an equation that fitted the data well, so I wrote up a paper and went back to Dr Doraiswamy. He was quite surprised at the speed with which I had completed the assignment and thought it merited publication. Though he had come up with the suggestion of working on an empirical equation, he was diffident about its significance. He sent the paper to the journal *Industrial & Engineering Chemistry Fundamentals*, not as a full-fledged article, but as a letter.

Dr Doraiswamy got a prompt response from the editor. 'This is a very good equation. It fits in where the Wilke–Chang correlation fails.' The editor was interested in publishing it as a full-fledged paper and suggested some additions and modifications. I rewrote the paper and it was published in February 1967. The equation came to be known as the Reddy–Doraiswamy equation. By the end of the year, we had received 150 communications regarding the equation, one of them from the US Atomic Energy Commission. Years later, I asked my son-in-law Prasad, who had done his chemical engineering at Illinois, 'Do you know this equation?' Pat came his reply, 'Of course. It's an empirical equation.'

Alongside work on my thesis, I was interested in a project going on at NCL for making a tobacco extract for some people in Guntur, the town where I did my BSc, which is located in the midst of a well-known tobacco-growing area. The extract was used to make a cardiovascular drug. I kept track of the project and the idea of doing something in the industry grew on me.

When I finished the experimental work for my thesis, I had an offer for a postdoctoral fellowship from the Norwegian University of Science and Technology at Trondheim. But by that time, a manufacturing plant of Indian Drugs and Pharmaceuticals Limited (IDPL) had come up in Hyderabad with Russian collaboration. It was a big project of national importance. One of my classmates from AC College had joined IDPL. I asked him about opportunities there and he wrote back, 'They will soon advertise for applications. You should respond to the advertisement.' I did, and was called for an interview to Hyderabad for the position of senior scientific assistant.

I had been warned that one member of the interviewing committee, Dr H.L. Bami, was a terror—and he lived up to his reputation at the interview. The first question he asked me was about my PhD dissertation. His response was typical. 'Kinetics of toluene? Kinetics is in the sky, we are on earth,' he snarled. I did not know what to make of this and kept quiet. Luckily for me, the rest of the interview went well and Raja Rao, the chief technologist, seemed to be positive. I learnt later that it was on Raja Rao's insistence that I was selected; Bami was not in favour. After an agonizing wait, I received my letter of appointment and was posted to the Quality Control department.

My work in Quality Control soon turned out to be anything but humdrum analysis. Raja Rao was extraordinarily good at making processes work. Processes to make chemical substances are first developed in a laboratory to yield gram quantities. Quite often, there are glitches in scaling up to commercial quantities and occasionally the processes do not work at all. Raja Rao created a scale-up facility to iron out these

My life in the pharmaceutical industry began here

problems and chose a team of four people to execute this task. He picked me to be one of the four.

The processes took a long time to complete and the facility worked 24/7; each of us in the team worked one shift. It was hard work. The night shifts were irksome, more so because I travelled to work on a battered Vespa scooter. In those days, Vespa scooters were in great demand and there was a long waiting list to get a new one, so many people bought a used one like I did. The headlight on mine was not bright, and it was quite a temperamental vehicle.

I was once on a night shift and as was the usual practice, I first read the process log and looked for instructions on the next step. I found to my surprise that the instruction was to add alkali. I was taken aback as the logical next step would be to use alcohol. Raja Rao would have given the process instructions and I was sure that the mistake was not his, but that of the previous shift in-charge. I could have woken up Raja Rao and asked him what to do. Instead, I went ahead and used isopropyl alcohol. The following morning, I rang up Raja Rao and told him what was in the log—Raja Rao threw a fit and I enjoyed the moment. He was relieved when I told him I had used alcohol and that the experiment had been completed successfully. Raja Rao's confidence in me grew after this. He taught me the tricks of the trade, for which I am enormously grateful.

Dr L.K. Behl was the works manager of IDPL at that time. Dr Behl was from Himachal Pradesh and a DSc from Germany. He spoke neither English nor German well and I cannot comment on his Punjabi, but he was a practical man and genuinely interested in the growth of IDPL. Raja Rao once met with an accident and was bedridden for a while. In his absence, Dr Behl gave me the responsibility for scaling up a new product. The material which was supposed to be white came out off-white. I therefore added a final recrystallization step to the process that I got from R&D (research and development) and the material came out white. I cleared the process for production with this additional step. The head of R&D was not amused. He said the material met specifications without recrystallization and complained to Dr Behl that I had added an unnecessary step that increased costs. Dr Behl called me in for an explanation. I showed him the off-white and white samples. I then told him that the product was intended for Warner Hindustan which was importing the material and I did not want IDPL material to be inferior to the imported one. Dr Behl saw my point of view. IDPL was not only cost-conscious but also committed to producing high-quality products.

Dr Behl also had an eye firmly on profits. IDPL had developed a process for sulphamoxole and I was asked to work on the costing. The costs were really low compared to the prevailing price of imports as the process that had been developed was very efficient. The Drug Price Control Order had come into effect by then and prices had to be determined on a cost-plus basis. Since our costs were low, prices would be slashed. I took the cost sheets to Dr Behl. He had a simple solution: 'Multiply the costs by two.' Forty years later, my son Satish still struggles to comply with the Drug Price Control Order; but he does not resort to Dr Behl's simple solution.

Dr Behl went on to become general manager and then chairman and managing director of IDPL. The political environment of Delhi, however, ruined both him and IDPL. He made politically expedient but financially disastrous decisions. I cannot but feel unhappy about this since IDPL was where I gained the experience and the confidence to become an entrepreneur in the bulk drug industry. No other institution could have prepared me better.

3 A SCIENTIFIC BUSINESS

Uniloids, 1976: *Metronidazole was manufactured here from basic raw materials for the first time in India*

It is hard to believe now, but when I decided to become an entrepreneur in 1973, there were few signs that Indian pharmaceutical companies would serve the needs of the nation. Foreign companies, which had grown rapidly since our independence, had a dominant market share of 70 per cent. Household remedies, vitamins and the like accounted for over a quarter of their revenues from drugs. Indian companies were lagging far behind in technology, financial resources and marketing skills.

Glaxo and Pfizer were the leading foreign companies at that time with annual revenues of over 200 million rupees each from drugs, followed by Ciba. In the second rung, with about half their revenues were Merck, Sharp & Dohme, Hoechst and Geoffrey Manners which made the famous Woodward's Gripe Water. Following in their wake were more than forty other companies with 40 per cent or more of foreign equity.

The pricing of steroids and other drugs by foreign companies put them outside the reach of many patients. Prices remained high for many years either because these companies had a monopoly in certain drugs or because of their slick marketing and liberal distribution of free samples to doctors, which Indian companies could not match. The general impression was that foreign companies profiteered and repatriated fat dividends and technical fees to their parent companies. Unsurprisingly, the government did not consider foreign companies dependable partners for the development of the nation. Consequently, the policy environment was not conducive for their growth. The government issued policy directions in 1970, specifically preventing foreign companies from increasing their capacities. The new Patents Act, which abolished patents for medicines, came into force in April 1972. This was a major blow to foreign companies as they held all the patents and enjoyed the resultant monopoly. Worse was to follow. In 1973, companies with more than 40 per cent foreign equity were required to ensure that their Indian shareholding was not less than 26 per cent within a specified period of time. All this worked against foreign companies taking a long-term view; their focus was on repatriation of profits in the short term. One could hardly expect them to invest resources to manufacture new drugs in the country at affordable prices, even assuming that they could get licences.

The 'licence raj' was reigning supreme then and was stifling not just for foreign companies but for large Indian industrial houses too. Some businesses ignored licence restrictions or found ways around them. Licensed and actual capacities had to be disclosed in a company's annual statement of accounts. One such disclosure of licensed capacity had an asterisk, which was rather curiously annotated with a terse footnote: 'Irregular capacity now regularised'. I wondered how this was possible.

There were other instances of some kind of a racket, with licences being sold in dubious deals.

There were many questions in Parliament about the licensing policy and the government was worried about the lack of indigenous capability and drug shortages. It appointed a committee headed by Jaisukhlal Hathi, an eminent parliamentarian, to recommend measures to improve the situation. The Hathi Committee Report was submitted in 1975 and widely discussed in Parliament and the press. The report painted a vivid picture of the fairly limited size of the pharmaceutical industry. Around 116 units in what was called the 'organized sector'— those licensed by the government—produced 750 million rupees of 'bulk drugs' and 3.7 billion rupees of 'formulations'. In addition, more than 2500 small-scale units were believed to exist for which the Hathi Committee had no data, but it estimated that they might add another 20 per cent to the value of formulations and 50 million rupees to the value of bulk drug production. The term 'bulk drug' is perhaps peculiar to India—the common term in many other countries is 'active pharmaceutical ingredient'. The active pharmaceutical ingredient, as the name implies, is responsible for the therapeutic effect and is formulated with other substances to produce the finished dosages or 'formulations' that are available in pharmacies—tablets, capsules, syrups, injections, ointments, and so on.

The Hathi Committee was concerned about the dominance of foreign companies in the Indian pharmaceutical industry. They said harsh things about these companies and recommended even harsher measures. The sentiment against foreign companies was so high that a section of the committee urged nationalization of the industry. Fortunately, the fear of drug shortages and evidence of diffusion of technology from foreign companies carried the day and none of the draconian recommendations was implemented.

Another aspect that bothered the Hathi Committee was the limited production of bulk drugs in the country. It bemoaned the fact that only 64 of the 116 units in the organized sector produced bulk drugs. Foreign companies accounted for about a quarter of the value of production and Indian companies in the private sector for about 40 per cent, the leading ones being Ranbaxy, Cipla and Unichem. Most of this production was from the penultimate stage and for captive consumption. There was little enthusiasm for producing bulk drugs from basic raw materials and making them available to formulators of finished dosages. Alembic was one of the few companies in the private sector that went down this difficult path—it was the first Indian company to manufacture penicillin and a company in Calcutta (now Kolkata), Standard Pharmaceuticals, followed suit.

The total value of production of bulk drugs in the country in 1973 was 240 million rupees and the public sector produced about a third of that. The significance of the public sector producing bulk drugs from basic raw materials should never be understated. IDPL and Hindustan Antibiotics manufactured several life-saving medicines including penicillin, streptomycin and sulpha drugs and made them widely available at affordable prices. Their pioneering efforts made a difference to the health of the people in the 1970s and '80s and spawned the growth of the bulk drug industry in the country.

The government tried to force pharmaceutical companies into manu-facturing bulk drugs, rather than importing them for formulations. The ministry of petroleum and chemicals, which was the administrative ministry for pharmaceuticals, had decreed that no manufacturer with a turnover of more than 20 million rupees could produce new formulations unless it also manufactured the bulk drugs required for them. The Hathi Committee recommended that manufacturers producing bulk drugs in excess of their licensed capacity should be forced to part with half their excess production to other formulators. It also wanted to put an end to the ploy of foreign companies producing bulk drugs from imported penultimate intermediates and recommended that they be compelled to produce them from starting materials within a period of three years.

I was sceptical about the implementation of all these coercive measures, most of which seemed to be putting a stop to the growth of foreign companies or large Indian business houses. It seemed to me that the key to increasing availability of bulk drugs was in creating new manufacturing capacity, developing efficient manufacturing processes and fostering a commitment to the highest quality. Coercion did not appear to be an effective means to this end.

From my perspective, government policies seemed to favour the setting up of a bulk drug manufacturing business. Imports, which could have crippled a new business, were restricted and licences to set up medium-scale manufacturing units were granted relatively easily. I knew that there were just fifteen units in the organized sector that produced only bulk drugs, but that there were several thousand formulators. Competition was therefore relatively lower in bulk drugs than in the formulations segment. However, technology was hard to come by, which clouded the prospects for bulk drug manufacturers without a robust technology base.

Clearly, there was a huge demand for bulk drugs and I was confident of my technical abilities. I decided to set up a bulk drug business. This was a big decision and fraught with risk. In the early 1970s, few people abandoned the security of a job in a public sector undertaking and jumped into the uncertain world of business, but I took the plunge in 1973, six years after I had joined IDPL.

I zeroed in on metronidazole for my first product. It was discovered in the laboratories of Rhône-Poulenc in France in the early 1960s and marketed with the brand name of Flagyl to treat vaginal itching. It was licensed to Searle in the USA and did well in the market as it had good tissue penetration and did not cause diarrhoea like other antibiotics. The market for metronidazole expanded rapidly in the late 1960s after it was found to be effective against a wide range of infections caused by anaerobic bacteria—bacteria that do not need oxygen for growth.

One of the bacteria that metronidazole was found to be lethal against was *Entamoeba histolytica*, which causes amoebiasis, or dysentery, with blood and mucus in stools. Infectious *E. histolytica* is excreted in the faeces and then spreads through contaminated food or drinking water. Defecation in agricultural fields contaminates vegetables which are often eaten raw. Unwashed hands, open drains and drinking water contaminated with sewage are also major causes for infection. Amoebiasis was widely prevalent in India and the demand for metronidazole was increasing by leaps and bounds. The great Mughal emperor Akbar is said to have died of dysentery in 1605. We have not been able to contain a preventable disease even after 400 years.

May & Baker marketed metronidazole as Flagyl in India, under licence from its parent, Rhône-Poulenc. It made the bulk drug for captive consumption from imported penultimate intermediate. May & Baker made about 7–8 tonnes per annum, though it was licensed for only 600 kilos, but did not sell the bulk drug to other formulators. Domestic demand from other formulators was met by the import of about 25 tonnes of metronidazole, canalized through the State Trading Corporation of India (STC). IDPL had done some feasibility studies for the manufacture of metronidazole, but encountered problems and eventually abandoned the effort. It was not an easy product to make at that time. The Hathi Committee recognized the importance of indigenous availability of metronidazole and recommended the acquisition of foreign technology for its manufacture.

I applied for a manufacturing licence for metronidazole and got one for 10 tonnes per annum. I registered a new company in Hyderabad and named it Uniloids. I found three others to invest in the company and obtained sanctions for loans. My entrepreneurial journey had begun.

I was not the first private sector bulk drug manufacturer in Hyderabad. Dr Karanth used to manufacture bulk drugs on a modest scale even when I was in IDPL. Dr Karanth had been a student of Paul Karrer. Karrer was Swiss, had won the Nobel Prize in 1937, and had written the celebrated *Textbook of Organic Chemistry*, which is followed throughout the world. Dr Karanth developed into a brilliant chemist. He was also a perfectionist. If he found a dirty beaker, for example, he would be furious and wash it himself! Whatever Dr Karanth manufactured was world-class. He supplied some of his products to IDPL and on one occasion, his material was rejected by my colleague. I warned my colleague that the material could never fail as it was supplied by Dr Karanth and he should repeat the analysis. He ignored my advice. Very soon, Dr Karanth heard of this and stormed into the lab demanding that the analysis be repeated. He then performed the analysis himself, while my colleague looked on, and demonstrated that his material was meeting specifications.

My first step was to set up a laboratory to develop the process for manufacturing metronidazole from basic raw materials. I finalized the process sitting in the library at the Regional Research Laboratories at Hyderabad, now called the Indian Institute of Chemical Technology. There was an irksome procedure before one could use the library, but I was fortunate to have been granted the permission to do so. Some years later, I went to Stanford in the heart of Silicon Valley in California. I stayed there for a week with a friend who worked with Hewlett Packard. He dropped me off every morning at the Stanford University library on his way to work. I found an article, five pages long. I spotted a Xerox machine in a corner and wondered if I could have it photocopied. I went up to the lady at the desk and asked hesitantly if I could photocopy it and offered to pay for it. 'What do you mean by pay,' she said, 'you can have it with the compliments of the Stanford library.' I was surprised and it must have shown on my face. She added, 'You seem to be from India.' It struck me that many Indians using an American university library for the first time would have been similarly surprised at how well-organized and accessible libraries in American universities are. This is one among many reasons why Indian scientists wish to study and work in the USA.

The few people who were with me in Uniloids were very hard-working and I worked in the laboratory with them whenever needed. The process development of metronidazole progressed well till the final stage. The product was made, but there was a huge problem with the melting point caused by the traces of an intermediate material that stubbornly remained as an impurity. I observed, however, that the impurity was soluble in ammonia and this was a vital clue that I passed on to the chemists working on the process. I thought the problem would be solved in the nick of time—the lab was being inaugurated by the chairman of the Industrial Development Bank of India (IDBI) in four days. IDBI had loaned us the money to set up the laboratory and the plant, so I wanted to have the product ready and make a good impression. It was a race against time.

I called the lab the day before the inauguration and asked if the product was ready. It was, but it was still yellow and the melting point was not satisfactory. I was quite annoyed. It had been three days since the answer to the problem had been found. There was no time for discussion. I barked out an order on the phone—'Wash it in weak ammonia'—and hung up.

I had to be in office on the day of the inauguration. The chairman of IDBI came and in the evening we went to the lab. The first thing I heard was that the process had been completed and the product was white, without the yellow tinge that even the imported material from Italy had. The melting point was what it should be. Metronidazole had been developed for the first time in India!

The lab was formally inaugurated that evening. It was lit up nicely and festive marigolds were strung in profusion. The chairman of IDBI started his speech. On an impulse, I slipped out and had another good look at the lab. I thought it was beautiful. I came back to my chair, anxiously wondering if the chairman had noticed my absence. I recalled a movie I had seen years ago at Eros theatre in Bombay—*Fanny*, starring Maurice Chevalier and Leslie Caron. The story was about an old, very rich merchant in Marseille who had fallen in love with an eighteen-year-old who sold fish with her mother at the waterfront. The girl's mother was invited to the house of the merchant and a swank limousine was sent to fetch her. On the way, the woman caught a familiar scent and hopped out of the car to follow her nose. She was delighted at what she saw and exclaimed, 'Oh, my beautiful fish!' To each his own, I thought and, smiling to myself, switched back to the speech.

The inauguration went off without a hitch, but the early years were a struggle. Orders came in and were executed, but we were always short of cash. I travelled a lot. Once when I needed to go to Bombay, I was sick of the train journeys and decided to travel by air, but there was no money in the company. I did something that I would rather forget. My mother had given me 1000 rupees as a gift for my daughter when she was born. It was a sizeable sum in those days and I had kept it in a bank deposit for her. I withdrew the money and bought a plane ticket.

I needed to go to Bombay as we did not have money to pay salaries the following month. Delaying salaries was the worst thing that could happen and I could not allow that situation to come about. I knew that Servotech in Bombay, a firm that had supplied our equipment, had surplus cash so I asked for a loan of 400,000 rupees. One of the partners of Servotech was willing to loan me the money, but the other was agreeable only if I could furnish a bank guarantee that I would repay it in three months. The interest he wanted was 10 per cent—40,000 rupees—per month! I was dumbstruck, but had to agree. My financial partner approached Andhra Bank and a deputy general manager, who trusted us, issued the guarantee. We got the money. We also repaid it, with the agreed interest. I redeposited 1000 rupees in my daughter's bank account, but without any interest. I never was in such a situation again.

One day I got a telegram from Yusuf Hamied, the chairman of Cipla—there was no fax those days. 'Congratulations on successfully making metronidazole. We have some 2-Methyl. Would you be interested in converting it? Please tell us when you will come to Bombay next.' 2-Methyl-5-Nitroimidazole was the penultimate compound and needed only to be alkylated to give metronidazole. The conversion was a cinch for us.

Yusuf Hamied had worked with no less a person than Lord Alexander Todd at Cambridge for his PhD. Todd was the colossus of chemistry in his time; his work on the nucleic acids—DNA and RNA—and the synthesis of adenosine triphosphate was pathbreaking. He won the Nobel Prize in 1957 for his work on proteins. Students from all over the world flocked to Todd at Cambridge; he was nicknamed 'Almighty Todd'.

Yusuf Hamied must have been good at chemistry, as Todd had

accepted him as a student, but he did not choose to make the metronidazole bulk drug himself. I was sure that he had imported the intermediate for conversion merely because he wanted to satisfy the condition of his licence to manufacture formulations—the government had a policy permitting the manufacture of 50 million rupees of formulations for every 10 million rupees of bulk drugs manufactured. Manufacturing bulk drugs was considered a 'dirty' business, so Yusuf probably wanted somebody else to do it.

On the other hand, I wanted the business. So the morning after I got his telegram, I went to Bombay. I remember staying at the Ambassador Hotel and Yusuf sent a Mercedes to fetch me. I said to myself, this man has style! I was ushered into his office as soon as I arrived and we got down to business right away. We did not have calculators in those days but I needed only a few minutes with pen and paper to offer him a price for the conversion. We discussed it, agreed on a price and signed a contract. A fortnight later, he sent me the material and within two weeks I sent him the finished product. I gained a valuable customer in Cipla and a good friend in Yusuf.

The easy availability of the bulk drug from Uniloids spurred a number of formulators to introduce their own brands of metronidazole into the market. May & Baker's Flagyl was the brand leader. J.B. Chemicals & Pharmaceuticals, an established Indian company in Bombay also had a popular brand, Metrogyl, and it bought the bulk drug from us. Metrogyl remains the company's leading brand. Soon enough, there were a number of other followers and many of the brands ended with a 'gyl', though some of them were short-lived. I heard of a medical representative in Hyderabad, perhaps influenced by the tradition of Urdu verse, who resorted to rhyme to increase the recall of his brand. He would go to a doctor and recite a couplet which went something like this:

This gyl may come and that gyl may go
But Metron will go on and on

He was prophetic. Metron continues to be sold by Alkem Laboratories.

Though Uniloids was the number one metronidazole company in the country, I was acutely conscious that it was a one-product company. There were a number of other bulk drugs waiting to be produced. I wanted to operate on a bigger scale. However, my financial partners and I developed some differences on how the business should be run. I thought the time had come to part ways. I cashed out of the business and embarked on the next phase of my entrepreneurial career.

4 A LARGER CANVAS

Standard Organics, 1983. *(From left)* M.P. Chary, me, C.C. Reddy;
Union leader Satyanarayana (extreme right)

The success of metronidazole at Uniloids demonstrated the viability
and the potential of the bulk drug business. It also reinforced my belief
that efficient processes could be developed indigenously to meet global
quality standards. I saw no reason to tinker with a successful approach
and decided to replicate it in my second venture, Standard Organics.
The crucial decision was of course the choice of the first product. This
time, I chose sulphamethoxazole.

Sulphamethoxazole has an interesting history. Though it was
discovered by a Japanese company, Shionogi, in 1958 and licensed to

Hoffmann-La Roche, perhaps the world's largest manufacturer of sulphonamide compounds at that time, it was not a significant drug on its own. Curiously, there was a similar lack of enthusiasm for trimethoprim, another anti-bacterial drug discovered just a year earlier by Burroughs Wellcome, and not even marketed. Bacteria require folate for replication, but they need to synthesize it for themselves as they cannot absorb folic acid from dietary intake. It was known that some sulpha drugs inhibited an enzyme required for folate synthesis and thus 'starved' the bacteria to death. Both sulphamethoxazole and trimethoprim inhibited folate synthesis, but at different stages of the pathway, so it was thought that the combination would be particularly effective against bacterial infections. It took a decade, however, for scientists at Hoffmann-La Roche to file a patent for the combination of sulphamethoxazole and trimethoprim, after it was found to be effective against sulphonamide-resistant strains of bacteria. The combination was approved for marketing in the USA in 1973 with the brand name Bactrim.

Meanwhile, Burroughs Wellcome also filed for a patent for the combination—the British name was co-trimoxazole—and launched the combination product in the UK in 1968. They launched the product in many other countries with the brand names Septra, Septrin and Septran. Rather than litigate the patents, Hoffmann-La Roche and Burroughs Wellcome settled on an arrangement which allowed both companies to market the combination drug.

The combined might of Hoffman-La Roche and Burroughs Wellcome made co-trimoxazole a global blockbuster for both companies. In India too, Septran did very well. The commercial success of the product was the compelling reason for its choice as the first product for Standard Organics. I was confident that the success of the relatively new addition of co-trimoxazole to the sulpha family would be sustained and demand would explode if the bulk drug became available at reasonable prices.

Older sulpha drugs were considered essential medicines and widely used in India. Even in the mid-1970s, IDPL produced the largest tonnage of sulpha drugs in the country—about 700 tonnes per annum—but they did not make sulphamethoxazole. In the private sector, Cibatul, May & Baker, Ciba Geigy and German Remedies were large players with substantial capacities for a number of the older sulpha drugs. The country was nearly self-sufficient in sulpha drugs and imports had fallen dramatically. Given all the experience available in the country for manufacturing sulpha drugs and the signs of decline already visible in the sales of older ones, I knew I had to be among the first in the market with sulphamethoxazole and be particularly efficient to ward off the competition that would soon follow.

I had set up a process development laboratory even before I parted from Uniloids. It was in Dwarakapuri Colony in Hyderabad, very close to my home. We developed sulphamethoxazole from basic raw materials for the first time in the country. STC was importing sulphamethoxazole bulk drug and rationing it out at 400 rupees per kilo. There was a thriving trade in sulphamethoxazole—I wonder how traders got hold of the product despite all the import restrictions and sold it at 600–900 rupees per kilo! Demand boomed as more and more formulators introduced the product. There was no shortage of buyers but my main target was Burroughs Wellcome. Their sales of Septran had grown rapidly. Their biggest problem was sourcing the bulk drug from STC. I thought they would be happy to source the drug from a domestic manufacturer.

I tried repeatedly to get an appointment with the managing director but could not get past his secretary. I could not understand why he was reluctant to give me a hearing and this irritated me. I knew Burroughs Wellcome was buying sulphamethoxazole from traders at prices much higher than mine. I went to Bombay and called the managing director of Burroughs Wellcome again. I got the usual run-around from his secretary, but this time I lost my cool and asked, 'How many times do I need to call to get to speak to him? I am a manufacturer, a private manufacturer, offering to sell sulphamethoxazole at 600 rupees a kilo and he continues to buy it from traders at higher prices. Tell him that this is the last call from me and if he does not meet me today, he will face the consequences.'

The outburst must have had an effect. I still remember that trip to Bombay—it was for the first time that I was staying in a hotel with a phone in the bathroom and discovered its advantages! The managing director called me when I was in the shower. I answered the phone and after the preliminaries he said, 'Please meet me at the factory at 11.30.' I rushed to the factory and made my pitch. I told him I was manufacturing sulphamethoxazole, not from the penultimate intermediate, but from acetone, the basic raw material. I thought he would be impressed; he thought it was a joke. He asked me how much I could ship immediately. I told him that I could airlift a tonne of material. This stunned him and he got a purchase order issued for one tonne at 600 rupees per kilo. I supplied the material promptly and never had a problem getting orders from Burroughs Wellcome after that. The orders were rather peculiar—the quantities were always specified as 'two tonnes *or more*'. This breakthrough was the turning point for Standard Organics.

Demand exploded as I had anticipated and a number of players came into the sulphamethoxazole business. Some of them were manufacturers of bulk drugs, but it seemed to attract all kinds of people. One of them was Gharda Chemicals, a company founded by Keki Gharda, a PhD in chemical engineering from Michigan who had been my professor at UDCT. He taught general chemical technology and his examinations were in the American mould where no amount of 'mugging' or learning by rote helped. One had to understand the fundamentals. I still remember an exam where the question involved stoichiometry, a topic that deals with the relative mass of the reactants and products in chemical reactions. I got the answer right and so did one or two others in a class of about a hundred. Everybody else failed and threatened to boycott the next exam. I felt that the threat was unfair—nobody can call himself a chemist without understanding the fundamentals of stoichiometry.

Gharda set up Gharda Chemicals in the mid-1960s to manufacture dyestuffs and pesticides, among other things. He made a Bayer product and sold it at half their price, driving Bayer's product out of the market. It was a warning shot across the bows. A decade later, global giants operating in India were pressurizing the government for licences to manufacture synthetic pyrethroids and other pesticides in India. A public hearing was held on this issue and lawyers for the multinational companies claimed they were very difficult and hazardous to manufacture. At the end of the hearing, Gharda spoke up and stunned the multinationals by asserting that the technology was nowhere near the complexity they claimed and he could make the same products at 60 per cent of their price. He was not talking in the air. He was innovative and had developed a number of products with new processes that crashed costs and enabled him to remain very profitable despite slashing prices. He competed successfully with major multinationals, including Dow Chemicals, Monsanto and DuPont. Ironically, Gharda had been awarded scholarships by each one of them when he was doing his doctoral research. He is eccentric, but brilliant at his work, honest and charitable. Among other things, he has built an impressive engineering college in Khed, about 220 kilometres from Mumbai, which does not charge capitation fees.

I followed Gharda's progress in the media as he was my teacher and he followed mine as I had been his student. At some point, he toyed with the idea of entering bulk drugs. He knew I was making sulphamethoxazole and thought I was overcharging Burroughs Wellcome. He knew the executive director of Burroughs Wellcome and I was told he offered to sell it to them at 400 rupees a kilo, but his samples failed. There may have been some truth to this story; some years later, when I was making ciprofloxacin, he wrote a letter accusing me of charging an exorbitant price for it. He said I would soon have to discontinue production as he had developed a new process to make a product far cheaper than mine. I was quite annoyed but did not want to respond directly. I asked our then managing director M.P. Chary to write to him conveying my regards as I was his student and point out that manufacturing bulk drugs involved human safety. Consequently, manufacturing processes and specifications were complex, and this pushed up costs. I also conveyed the message that prices of ciprofloxacin would crash, not because of his product, but because of the intense competition that would inevitably set in. I did not receive any further communication, and Gharda's ciprofloxacin did not get any further than his pilot plant. Though Gharda's bulk drug foray was not successful, he is a revered man in his field. More than a decade after the ciprofloxacin communication, I called on him in Mumbai to pay my respects. Despite his age, he was working at full steam, brimming with ideas and sparkling conversation. He was, of course, as eccentric as ever.

Prabhakar Reddy was another interesting entrant into the sulphamethoxazole business. A medical graduate turned actor, he was usually cast as a villain in Telugu films. At that time, sodium metal, a hazardous starting material for the manufacture of sulphamethoxazole, was in short supply. Alkali Metals, a company in Hyderabad founded by Dr Y.V.S.S. Murthy, was one of the few that manufactured sodium metal. It took courage to make it. Dr Murthy was our sole supplier and he was running to full capacity. Prabhakar Reddy tried to persuade him to cut down our supply and divert it to him. Dr Murthy told him that I was making sulphamethoxazole while he was cavorting in a film studio and we continued to get the supplies we needed.

Pyrazinamide was another drug we manufactured at Standard Organics. Its development makes an interesting story. This drug is never used alone, but always in conjunction with other drugs such as isoniazid and rifampicin to treat tuberculosis. The classical process for the manufacture of pyrazinamide is a 'dirty' process in terms of chemistry—sluggish and inefficient, with some messy waste products. As I searched the literature for better processes, I came across a synthetic scheme for the manufacture of a carboxylic acid derivative from DAMN, diaminomaleonitrile, an interesting starting material. I recognized the carboxylic acid derivative as the intermediate in the conventional process for the manufacture of pyrazinamide. The synthetic scheme held out the promise of an efficient process. I searched for sources of DAMN and found one in Japan. It turned out that the Japanese company was manufacturing acrylonitrile and hydrogen cyanide was a waste product in that process. Hydrogen cyanide, commonly known as prussic acid, boils at a little above room temperature and is poisonous. The Japanese company converted this waste product to DAMN to facilitate its disposal. I asked for a quote and it worked out to a landed cost of 700 rupees a kilo. Pyrazinamide was selling for 1300 rupees a kilo at that time, so I thought it would be profitable to manufacture it from DAMN. I ordered one kilo to develop the process.

We developed an elegant process for pyrazinamide from DAMN for the first time in the world on an industrial scale. Like all good chemistry, the process was simple. I was quite pleased at this development as hydrogen cyanide has extraordinary connotations. At one extreme, it was used as a horrific poison to take away life in Nazi extermination camps; at the other, it has been speculated that it had a role to play billions of years ago in the origin of life as a precursor of amino acids. Whatever may have been its past, we were now putting hydrogen cyanide waste to good use to make a drug that would help in treating tuberculosis, a poor-country disease. Much of the incidence and most of the deaths due to the disease occur in low- and middle-income countries, mainly India and some parts of Asia and Africa. Incidentally, China and Brazil have made rapid strides in tuberculosis control; there must be something we can learn from them.

I asked the Japanese company how much of DAMN they had in stock. They had 357 kilos. Normally, suppliers charge a higher price for development supplies as the quantities are small. In this case, however, the Japanese company would not budge from the price at which it had supplied the first quantity of one kilo. I had no choice—I ordered its entire stock and more at the price it wanted. The Japanese were quite curious about this sudden demand. Their representative visited me twice and tried to find out what I was doing with the material but I did not give him any information. They figured it out in due course and started selling it to Lupin, which still is one of the leading manufacturers of anti-tuberculosis drugs. Supplies of DAMN became erratic sometime later and I had to discontinue the process eventually. I was quite surprised, however, that the Japanese never developed the process to make pyrazinamide from DAMN. I wondered if it had something to do with tuberculosis not being prevalent in Japan or whether their famed skills for process improvements had not permeated the bulk drug industry.

The Japanese certainly have a good track record in discovering new drugs. They have a word for continuous improvement, *kaizen*, which is now part of management vocabulary. There is also another Japanese word, *shokunin*, which literally means craftsman, but is more than that. It connotes the mastery of any profession and pride in perfection. Some years ago, a Japanese restaurant was in the news for earning three Michelin stars. It was located in a basement with just ten seats, but the eighty-five-year-old chef and owner was uncompromising in his quest for the perfect sushi every single day—a true shokunin. Process development for bulk drugs, which is so amenable to continuous improvement, ought to have been a natural field of endeavour for the Japanese to excel in. Surprisingly, this is one field where India has an advantage, though it is now being seriously challenged by China.

Hyderabad has a reputation of being the bulk drug capital of India. Dr Karanth was a bulk drug shokunin. M. Narayan Reddy was another. He was with me in Standard Organics and was keen on manufacturing sulphamethoxazole. He set up a company, Virchow Laboratories, with the one million rupees he had been gifted as dowry. He is now the largest manufacturer of sulphamethoxazole in the world and his customers include Hoffman-La Roche and GSK. The key to Narayan Reddy's success was his unflagging zeal in constantly improving the cost effectiveness of the manufacturing process. He developed a continuous process, which is the most efficient in the world for the manufacture of sulphamethoxazole. Even the Chinese don't seem to be able to make it more economically. Raja Rao, my mentor at IDPL, was an early votary of the continuous process for the manufacture of bulk drugs. He would have been proud of Narayan Reddy's achievement. Dr A.V. Rama Rao is another remarkably skilled chemist. After graduating in chemical technology from Bombay University, he went on to do his PhD under Prof. Venkataraman at NCL in Pune. I was to follow in his academic footsteps some ten years later. Dr Rama Rao worked at NCL after his PhD and somewhere along the way, he took a sabbatical to join Prof. E.J. Corey's lab at Harvard University as a postdoctoral fellow. Later, he became director of the Regional Research Laboratories at Hyderabad and, after his retirement, he set up Avra Laboratories.

Such was Dr Rama Rao's mastery of chemistry that he could come up with ideas for novel synthetic schemes while having a casual conversation. I once visited him at his home in Pune and mentioned that I was contemplating developing an improved manufacturing process for ibuprofen, a widely used painkiller. During the course of the conversation, he outlined a possible novel scheme for its synthesis. Coincidentally, the novel synthesis of ibuprofen involved a nitrile group—the same group that allowed a facile reaction to convert DAMN in the process of manufacture of sulphamethoxazole. Though we had a tough time developing the process, we eventually succeeded in making the purest ibuprofen in the world. I knew people would be sceptical of the quality we had achieved and sent samples to a testing laboratory in Michigan in the USA. The report came back confirming our own test results.

A German trader interested in sourcing ibuprofen from us came to Hyderabad. He met me and asked, 'Can you match the quality of Boots?' I was quite irritated, but kept my cool and pulled out the test report which compared the quality of ibuprofen made by Boots, Ethyl Corporation and us. I said, 'You can go through this. As you can see, my ibuprofen is 99.8 per cent pure, while that of Boots' is only 99.3 per cent. Both meet the required standards. But if you want me to match the purity of the Boots' product I will need to add an impurity.' I was so annoyed that I did not want to deal with him. I told him that companies abroad seem to have a preconceived notion that we make substandard drugs in India, but one day, perhaps, we would make drugs purer than those in Germany.

Many years later, in 2001, I was honoured as the 'Technology Businessman of the Year' by Pune Vyaspeeth. Mukesh Ambani was the chief guest. I talked about the ibuprofen incident in my acceptance speech. After the talk, Mukesh Ambani leant towards me and said, 'Sir, your speech was inspirational.' He was then vice chairman and managing director, Reliance Industries Limited, the flagship of the Reliance Group which had become the largest in the country that year with revenues of over 600 billion rupees. Mukesh had led the creation of the world's largest grass-roots refinery at the Jamnagar complex, which also housed the world's largest paraxylene and polypropylene plants. In India, age is respected and it is common to address an elder as 'Sir', but even so, I was touched to be told that what I had said was inspirational by a man who was himself inspirational.

I had met Mukesh earlier when I was travelling to London. Chirayu Amin, the chairman of Alembic, was on the same flight and so was he. Chirayu introduced me to Mukesh saying, 'Dr Reddy is our guru. Whatever he does, we follow.' I was tickled at this compliment coming from a person whose father had established India's first penicillin plant in 1961 and had added vitamin B_{12} and erythromycin to Alembic's portfolio within a decade.

Chirayu was being generous, but our efforts at bringing new bulk drugs to the market quickly and efficiently were being increasingly recognized. Though IDPL had shown the way in the late 1960s by commencing the manufacture of bulk drugs on a large scale, the technology for the development and manufacture of the new bulk drugs was largely the preserve of multinationals and other companies in Europe, particularly Italy and Spain. This was a matter of national concern. In 1973, the Hathi Committee dolefully noted India's limited capacity and capability to make bulk drugs. Within a decade, however, indigenous production of bulk drugs had grown nearly five-fold and the private sector had made a notable contribution. This, in turn, led to rapid growth in the availability of finished dosages for a wide range of diseases.

By the early 1980s, Hyderabad accounted for 90 per cent of the bulk drugs produced in south India. Standard Organics was at the forefront of this remarkable growth and accounted for about three-quarters of the production in the private sector at Hyderabad. Apart from sulphamethoxazole and pyrazinamide, we developed and commercially manufactured trimethoprim, ampicillin, amoxicillin and tinidazole, among other bulk drugs and sold them to a large number of formulators. Standard Organics became the number one bulk drug manufacturer in the private sector in the country. But, more importantly, its success established beyond doubt the capability of Indian enterprise to develop efficient processes for commercial manufacture of bulk drugs to global quality standards. The Indian Chemical Manufacturers' Association (ICMA; now the Indian Chemical Council) honoured me with the Acharya P.C. Ray Award for the 'Development of Technology Indigenously'—the first time it was awarded to a person in the bulk drug industry. There were several pioneers before me who had made remarkable contributions to the pharmaceutical industry, but it gave me no small satisfaction that I had played a part in the growth of the Indian bulk drug industry.

I wanted to do more. Many of my customers making finished dosages were not passing on the benefits of a lower bulk drug price to consumers. I felt there was something wrong with this approach as many drugs were not affordable. I thought the market would be much larger and revenues higher, if prices were reasonable. I discussed this with some of my customers, but the response was cold or downright condescending. I started thinking seriously about the formulations business. We had started a formulations business in Standard Organics and a marketing manager from Cipla joined us to run this, but the scale of operations was small. I knew there was no way in which I could succeed if I copied the business model of multinationals or the major Indian companies. Why would physicians prescribe the brand of a relatively unknown company? I had to think of something new, which would give me an advantage over the established players in the formulations business.

5 DR. REDDY'S IS BORN

Dr. Reddy's first bulk drug plant: *The commercial manufacture of methyldopa commenced here in 1985*

It may come as a surprise to most people that when Dr. Reddy's Laboratories was incorporated on Friday, 24th February 1984, it was not intended to be a manufacturing business. Though I was still with Standard Organics at the time, both C.C. Reddy and I had other businesses too. A consultancy business had come my way entirely by chance. I incorporated a new company to undertake this business and named it Dr. Reddy's Consultancy Services Private Limited. It was only later, when I needed to start a pharmaceutical business all over again, that the name was changed to Dr. Reddy's Laboratories. This was the third time I had started a pharmaceutical business, but this time I was determined not to take on co-investors who would have a say in running it.

At Uniloids, I had three co-investors. None of them had a background in pharmaceuticals and I had to work really hard to set it up and then build up the business. It took nearly three years after I left IDPL in 1973 to set up Uniloids and develop the first product. Later, I also tested the waters by marketing some formulations. It was difficult to walk away from Uniloids, which was largely my own creation, particularly when it had started doing well. However, things were coming to such a pass that I knew I would have to take this decision sooner rather than later.

In 1979, I began what became a lifelong habit. I began my day with a long walk which was not only invigorating but also gave me time to think. On several of those walks, I pondered over the deteriorating situation in Uniloids. Finally, I told myself that I would sink with my co-investors if I continued with them, and decided to part ways. Around that time, I embarked on setting up another company promoted by Uniloids to manufacture bulk drugs and acquired some land at Patancheru, near Hyderabad. I named the new company Standard Organics, made the project plan and was on the verge of obtaining the financing from the Andhra Pradesh Industrial Development Corporation (APIDC) when I decided to talk to my co-investors and make them an offer: 'Sell me Uniloids and I will pay you for it; or, if you want Uniloids, you need not pay me any money, but give me Standard Organics.' My co-investors were quite happy to keep Uniloids which was a profitable, running business and leave the uncertainity of a new project to me.

I did not have the money to implement the Standard Organics project on my own. I needed a co-investor. This time, I offered a 50 per cent stake to C.C. Reddy, a friend and classmate in Bombay University. C.C. Reddy was in the textile business in Nigeria, but we had kept in touch. He had come back and was scouting around for business opportunities, so he accepted my invitation to invest in Standard Organics. He had also started another company called Dexo Labs with

Ramachandra Reddy and, as a reciprocal gesture, offered me a stake in this company which I accepted.

It was all very good in the beginning. Within a few years, however, our relationship started cooling. Even in the early days, the progress of Standard Organics was attracting attention and I was in the news off and on. I suspect this was one of the contributing factors, and C.C. Reddy's family and friends, including Ramachandra Reddy, were probably adding fuel to the fire by saying I was hogging the limelight. Whatever the reason, C.C. Reddy called me one day and said that it was not good for a company to have three partners. I got the message and asked him if he wanted to buy me out. That was exactly what he wanted, so I sold my stake in Dexo Labs and we continued together in Standard Organics.

C.C. Reddy and I disagreed increasingly on the way the company ought to be run. Standard Organics was doing quite well by then and had just received a very large export order that I did not even know about. Without telling me about the order, C.C. Reddy said he wanted me to sell my shares to him and exit. I did not want to—unlike Dexo Labs, it was I who had started Standard Organics. I somehow kept things going for a while despite the tension between us. However, after a while, I had had enough and called C.C. Reddy over for a drink on the lawns of the Sailing Annexe of the Secunderabad Club. I referred to the issues between us and told him that it was best we parted ways. I suggested two options: either I could buy him out or he could. C.C. Reddy disdainfully ignored what I had said and looked around—there was a huge tree on the lawn and a number of crows roosted there in the evenings. He said sarcastically in Telugu, *'ikkada kaakulu ekkuvuga unnai'* (There are too many crows here). I felt quite insulted that he did not think my offer was even worth a response and it was at that moment that I decided to walk out. Soon thereafter, I sold my shares to C.C. Reddy at a price lower than what I thought they were worth.

No partnership can succeed without a shared vision of the business and this was the root cause of my partnerships breaking down in both

Uniloids and Standard Organics. I had established both these companies, but I had been one of four shareholders in the first and a 50 per cent shareholder in the second. Both in Uniloids and Standard Organics, there were two managing directors—I was one and the other was the co-investor who had a say in management. For my third and most ambitious foray, I wanted to be the unquestioned head, the chairman of the company.

It was then that I decided to use Dr. Reddy's Consultancy Services Private Limited as the vehicle for my third foray without wasting further time and energy in setting up a new company. I recalled that exactly three weeks before Dr. Reddy's Consultancy Services was incorporated, the space shuttle Challenger had blasted off under the command of Vance Brand, who was on his third mission into space. For the first time in history, two of the astronauts under his command ventured out of the Challenger without a tether—I wondered how it felt to be completely free to soar in infinite space without a safety net. The Challenger returned safely to earth on the eighth day. It seemed to be a good augury for my third foray as an entrepreneur along with M. Purushothama Chary and Murali K. Divi, two very competent people with whom I had worked earlier.

I had known Chary from the days we were together in IDPL. He was a graduate in science and had not done a course in chemical engineering, but he had an amazing ability to get production up and running once the process came out of the lab. He had joined me in Uniloids and had followed me to Standard Organics where he was the works manager. Chary was extremely industrious, led by example and was thoroughly dependable. As I had anticipated, he did not think twice about accepting my invitation to join me in the new venture I was contemplating—he told me he would be with me in whatever I decided to do.

Murali Divi had worked with me in Uniloids and went to the USA for his master's degree. He was a very good chemist and, like Chary, worked extraordinarily hard. He had the kind of zeal that makes for a successful entrepreneur. Going to the USA was a big event in the 1970s and I had gone to the airport to see him off. It was at the airport that he asked me whether I had any contacts in America and I suggested he get in touch with of one of my classmates working there. He contacted my friend and landed a job in the same company. One day, even before I had set up Standard Organics, he called me from America and said he wanted to come back to India. I offered him a job in Standard Organics and he accepted. However, there was constant friction between Chary and Divi while they were at Standard Organics.

When I decided to leave Standard Organics, I wanted both Chary and Divi in my team. The problem was there couldn't be a team with both Chary and Divi on it. I therefore thought of having two separate companies, one with Chary and the other with Divi. I also wanted them to have a stake in the business so they could profit from the enormous effort they would put into building it. I offered each of them a 25 per cent stake in the company they would work in.

I appointed Chary as the first managing director of Dr. Reddy's. As a matter of fact, the name, Dr. Reddy's Laboratories was suggested by him, when I was thinking of changing the name Dr. Reddy's Consultancy Services to something more suitable. I did not jump at the idea initially, but it grew on me gradually. After all, some of India's greatest companies bore the names of their founders, the most famous being the Tata Iron and Steel Company Ltd, as it was called when it was incorporated in 1907. But Chary's initial contribution was more than just the name—he also suggested we make methyldopa.

The choice of methyldopa was a departure from the pattern I had followed in Uniloids and Standard Organics. In both these companies, I had started off with a product that was manufactured for the first time in the country from basic raw materials, metronidazole in Uniloids and sulphamethoxazole in Standard Organics. I had always been disinclined to tread the beaten path and manufacture what others were already making. Methyldopa was being manufactured at IDPL and it was common knowledge that it was having a problem in doing so. A major problem was that the glass-lined reactors in which the product was manufactured were good only for six months or less and the costs were therefore unviable. Chary and I both knew that IDPL had decided to shut down production of methyldopa. I thought this would be a shame as methyldopa was an important drug used for the treatment of high blood pressure, at a time when the other alternative widely available in India was reserpine—a drug used both as an antihypertensive and as an antipsychotic. Reserpine was initially isolated from the root of *Rauwolfia serpentina* or Indian snakeroot (*sarpagandha*), which had been known for centuries in traditional Indian medicine as an antidote for snake bites and a treatment for fever as well as some painful intestinal conditions. As an antihypertensive, however, it had numerous side effects and its use had largely diminished after Merck introduced methyldopa under the brand name Aldomet in the USA in 1962. Merck marketed the product in India too.

Other classes of antihypertensive drugs had also been developed. Merck had discovered thiazide diuretics and Sir James Black in Imperial Chemical Industries (ICI) had discovered propanolol, the first of the beta blockers. Methyldopa had its share of problematic side effects and was beginning to lose out to these new and more tolerable drugs, but it had its uses too. Even today, it is often used to treat hypertension in pregnant women because it is known not to harm the foetus. Moreover, a lot of hypertensive patients in India were being treated with methyldopa. I thought it was a good commercial opportunity as there would be a vacuum in the market if IDPL discontinued the product and Merck would be happy to source the bulk drug from a domestic manufacturer in the private sector. Additionally, given all the restrictions that existed on imports at that time, I was apprehensive about the availability of Aldomet if the bulk drug was not going to be indigenously available and the consequent distress to patients. It was also a challenge to manufacture methyldopa economically and safely, so I did not think there would be too much of competition to contend with. I asked Chary to go ahead with setting up a plant to manufacture methyldopa even as I commenced work on redeveloping the process. The first thing

I did was to set up a lab. This time, I rented premises in Anand Nagar, conveniently close to my home in Hyderabad.

The year 1984 was terrible for India. Social and political unrest disrupted normal life. The separatist movement in Punjab had built up to a feverish pitch and in June 1984 Prime Minister Indira Gandhi ordered troops to storm the Golden Temple where Jarnail Singh Bhindranwale, the leader of the separatist movement, was holed up with well-armed militants. Bhindranwale made his last stand at the Akal Takht building in the temple, the seat of temporal power of the Sikhs, before he died in a hail of bullets. The sight of bullet marks on their most sacred shrine and the bombed-out Akal Takht fired Sikh anger like never before. Mrs Gandhi's own Sikh bodyguards, whom she had retained against security advice, mowed her down in October. The next day her surviving son, Rajiv Gandhi, was sworn in as prime minister. Widespread reprisals against the Sikh community and senseless violence paralysed much of the nation for weeks.

Between the storming of the Golden Temple in June and her death in October, Mrs Gandhi erred again. N.T. Rama Rao, an extraordinarily popular film actor, founded the Telugu Desam Party and led the fledgling party to a landslide victory in Andhra Pradesh in 1983. The Congress party had been in power ever since the state had been formed in 1956. Stung by this electoral reversal, Mrs Gandhi struck back. Quite ironically, on Independence Day, 15th August 1984, Rama Rao was ousted as chief minister in a shameful fashion, when he was undergoing heart surgery in the USA. People were outraged and angry demonstrations paralysed the state. Mrs Gandhi was compelled to backtrack and reinstall Rama Rao as chief minister within a month. The state legislature was dissolved and the Telugu Desam Party swept to power with an overwhelming majority. Rama Rao was triumphantly back as chief minister for a second term.

Like most Indians, I was deeply troubled by all this. It was also difficult to keep things moving at the pace I wanted in the middle of this turmoil. We were on a tight budget and delays could mean catastrophic overruns in cost. We managed somehow to keep things on course.

In November 1984, the Andhra Pradesh State Financial Corporation sanctioned a term loan of 3 million rupees and the APIDC also came in with a term loan of 4.47 million rupees. Canara Bank, which by then had been added to our list of bankers, gave us a working capital limit of 5.8 million rupees as well as a limit for Letters of Credit. We did not have a lot of money but, together with the 2.5 million rupees of equity, we had enough.

Project implementation picked up pace. Nearly 80 per cent of the civil works had been completed. I felt that the plant could be commissioned in March 1985. Optimism crept back into our world; Rajiv Gandhi, our new prime minister, was like a breath of fresh air in the hitherto murky world of politics.

And then the Bhopal gas tragedy happened.

On the intervening night of 2nd–3rd December 1984, a tank containing methyl isocyanate, used to manufacture pesticide, overheated at the Union Carbide factory in Bhopal, capital of the state of Madhya Pradesh in central India. Water leaking into the tank probably triggered a violent runaway reaction, building up pressure and possibly rupturing the tank. About 30 tonnes of methyl isocyanate spewed into the air in less than sixty minutes and formed a cloud of poisonous smoke that began to rise from the leaking tank, then drifted in the slow northerly wind over the rooftops and headed into the town.

The worst affected was a shanty colony that had sprung up across the road from the Union Carbide factory. The squatter colony had been illegal to start with, but politicians eyeing a vote bank had turned it into an authorized settlement, which meant an instant escalation of property values for the settlers. Most of the residents had locked up and gone to bed when the gas seeped under their doors and came in through the windows. Eyes began to sting, people began to cough.

By the time the cloud of poisonous fumes had passed through the town, more than 3700 people were dead or would die in the weeks to come, according to the official count. Thousands more would be incapacitated for life, their lungs so damaged that they would be unable to take more than a step or two at a time before exhaustion set in. Overall, more than half a million people suffered injury from the gas leak according to official estimates. It was the worst industrial tragedy since machines were invented by man. It capped a horrible year for India.

Those of us who had anything to do with chemicals were particularly troubled by Bhopal. It was a grim reminder of the responsibility we carried as manufacturers who stored, processed and manufactured chemical compounds. For the uninitiated, chemicals became a word that aroused suspicion and fear.

My landlord in Anand Nagar where I had my office-cum-lab was a sardarji, a turban-wearing follower of the Sikh faith who was also a neighbour. I had seen his turban popping up over the compound wall occasionally, gravely eyeing the drums of chemicals that came into the lab, but he had never said anything till the day of the Bhopal gas tragedy. The day after the disaster, he came into the office with a clear and simple message: I want you out of here. I did not argue with him.

Chary put in enormous effort in accelerating completion of the plant. We produced our first methyldopa in July 1985. This would have been a creditable achievement even in normal times, but was quite extraordinary in the face of so many disruptions. Exports began within a year of commencement of production. Dr. Reddy's was the first Indian company to export methyldopa to West Germany and subsequently to other European countries.

On a parallel track, I was also progressing on the project with Divi. Cheminor had got off to a quick start following the acquisition of a loss-making firm with a bulk drug manufacturing facility. The acquisition saved a lot of time and I put Divi in charge of it as managing director. Cheminor's first product was ibuprofen, which was introduced in the Indian market in 1984 itself. Ibuprofen was discovered by Boots in the early 1960s; it was initially approved for marketing as a treatment of rheumatoid arthritis in the UK in 1969 and later in the USA in 1974. Its use as a painkiller was growing rapidly all over the world, including in India. Though the bulk drug was being manufactured in India, I thought

Bulk drugs for the world: *P.V. Venugopal (right) showing a foreign buyer around Cheminor's first manufacturing plant*

the rapidly increasing demand would offer global opportunities if it could be manufactured cost-effectively.

Wanting to improve on the existing process, I passed on the pointer that Dr A.V. Rama Rao had given me to Divi and left it to him to do the rest. As it turned out, it was no easy task and Divi had to struggle for months. Batch after batch failed, but Divi persisted with dogged determination and finally succeeded. He was that kind of a person.

Ibuprofen was then marketed in several countries across the globe. I had, however, set my sights on the most lucrative market of all—the United States of America. Obtaining approval for marketing the drug in the USA was necessarily a time-consuming process and Divi worked with his trademark intensity to accelerate progress.

In the meanwhile, I stepped on the gas in Dr. Reddy's.

6 GROWTH PANGS

Making a pitch to investors, 1986: *Despite tense moments, our maiden issue was fully subscribed on the first day*

Dr. Reddy's and Cheminor made their maiden public issues in the second half of the 1980s. Sometime thereafter, serious organizational issues surfaced dramatically in both Dr. Reddy's and Cheminor. Fortunately, both the companies emerged much stronger because of the crises they went through. Accepting investment from the public brings with it a responsibility to build a strong and enduring organization. This is an onerous task that often remains on the 'to-do' list of start-ups amidst all the pressures and excitement of growth, but if neglected can sometimes have disastrous consequences.

The initial plant capacity of Dr. Reddy's was a case of cutting the coat according to the cloth available. I had allocated 2.5 million rupees towards the equity of the initial project and I could leverage this with debt to finance a project for 14.5 million rupees. This got me to a bulk drug capacity of 24 tonnes per annum. As soon as this capacity was commissioned in June 1985, I started thinking about how I could finance the doubling or trebling of the capacity for bulk drugs and also establish a formulations unit. The process for manufacturing methyldopa had been established on a commercial scale and I was confident that demand would grow exponentially. The market was ours for the asking.

I made some quick calculations—the cost of the expansion would be 25–30 million rupees. After the initial investments in Dr. Reddy's and Cheminor, all that I had left was 2.5 million rupees. I could put that into Dr. Reddy's as further equity, but it would not go far. I could hardly turn back to the financial institutions for further loans—they would want to wait and evaluate our performance. I would have got homilies but no money.

The capital markets had been fairly dormant for several decades, but interest in them was picking up in the 1980s. In 1984, V.P. Singh, who was finance minister, announced some reforms in the annual budget, including the abolition of estate duty and the reduction of taxes, which were widely welcomed. The stock market responded positively. The market for public issues, or the 'primary market' as it was then called, was expanding. I knew that I could make a public issue of equity but could not have issued it a premium without substantial reserves and a track record of profitability. We had neither at the time as we had just started production. In those days, there was no Securities and Exchange Board of India (SEBI) and public issues were regulated by the Controller of Capital Issues. New companies were permitted only to issue equity at par and the premium allowed on issues by established companies was usually low, despite their track record.

Public issues of good companies were usually oversubscribed and allotments were made by picking lots—it was really a lottery. Because public issues were generally undervalued, there was often a handsome profit on listing the shares, but it was always a chance, given the lottery-like allotment. As a result, the first question about public issues in those days was, 'What are the chances of allotment?' People seemed to pay little attention to what the company was all about or why it should be profitable if they thought they could get a good allotment and profit on its listing.

I did not want to issue equity at par or at a low premium. While looking for solutions, I turned to Kamlesh Gandhi, a stock broker who ran a financial consultancy business. We had met when I was with Standard Organics. I discussed my problem with him. He came up with a proposition to raise 10 million rupees in equity and 15 million rupees in non-convertible debentures. Of this amount, I would subscribe 2.5 million rupees in equity, so that I would hold 40 per cent of the post-issue equity.

The non-convertible debentures would carry 15 per cent interest per annum and be redeemed in equal annual instalments from the seventh to the tenth year. In those days, interest rates were high and there were several options to earn similar or higher rates of interest without tying up the money for seven to ten years. So why should the public subscribe to them when the profit was in equity? The answer lay in linking the equity issue to that of debentures. Applicants for every 100 shares of 10 rupees in the public issue would be required to apply for 20 non-convertible debentures with a face value of 100 rupees. So for 1000 rupees of equity, one had to apply for 2000 rupees of debentures. The plan banked on the public appetite for better chances of allotment of debenture-linked equity issues and the profit that would be anticipated on the equity. And as a sweetener, a 5 per cent premium was offered on redemption of the debentures.

I asked Kamlesh Gandhi to go ahead with the plan. I also invited him to be on the board of directors of Dr. Reddy's and Cheminor. I asked V.S. Vasudevan, who had worked with me earlier in Standard Organics, to head finance in Dr. Reddy's and handle the public issue.

Vasudevan was a competent chartered accountant but, more than that, he was a problem solver and just the right man for the job. He continued to head the finance function in Dr. Reddy's for more than two decades thereafter.

The public issue opened on 24th May 1986 for non-resident Indians and on 5th June for the Indian public. The issue was subscribed 1.1 times by the evening and we closed the issue. I was lucky. The very next day there was an announcement that debenture-linked equity issues would no longer be permitted.

The equity was listed on the Bombay Stock Exchange (BSE) in August 1986. I was now accountable not just to myself and the employees of Dr. Reddy's, but also to investors from the public. I was very pleased to chair the annual general meeting of the company in 1987, the first after the public issue, and announce a 20 per cent dividend. The shares of the company were appreciating on the bourses and it was all very satisfying.

Meanwhile, Cheminor was doing well. It had a capacity of 600 tonnes per annum and, quite predictably, I wanted to more than double it. I planned to construct a greenfield plant as I was sure we would want to expand capacity soon. We finalized a site at Pydi Bhimavaram, near the seaport of Visakhapatnam, 600 kilometres north-east of Hyderabad. The project cost was estimated at 210 million rupees and we needed money again. It was time for Cheminor to make a public issue.

Kamlesh Gandhi's company, Champaklal Investment and Financial Consultancy Company, had managed Dr. Reddy's earlier public issue along with Canara Bank, who were also Dr. Reddy's bankers. The Cheminor issue was managed by Champaklal, the merchant banking divisions of the Industrial Credit and Investment Corporation of India and ANZ Grindlays, Canbank Financial Services and SBI Capital Markets. Five managers for an issue of 55 million rupees!

This time, we issued fully convertible debentures but the conversion was to be staggered over a period of time and at a premium over the face value of the equity. We were also able to raise loans of 107 million rupees from financial institutions and banks. Internal accruals met the rest of our needs. The issue was made in November 1989 and we pressed ahead with the implementation of the project, even as we ramped up production in our existing facility in Hyderabad.

Disaster struck in 1990, soon after the public issue. There were complaints that Divi had packed the Visakhapatnam unit with his relatives. Some inquires were made. I had no option but to ask him to leave and I paid him for his shares. I also had to sort out the mess that Cheminor was in.

In my hour of need, I turned to Prasad.

Prasad had married my daughter Anuradha in 1985. He is the son of Harishchandra Reddy who is in the construction and hotel business—he started the Green Park chain of hotels. Prasad had an impressive academic career. He graduated in chemical engineering from the Illinois Institute of Technology at Chicago where he won the Outstanding Senior Student Award from the Chicago Chapter of the American Institute of Chemists. He went on to do his MBA from Purdue where he was on the Dean's List. He came back to Hyderabad in 1983 and joined his father's construction business. After he married Anuradha, he set up Benzex Labs to make sulphamethoxazole, but by that time it was a commodity and not profitable for a start-up. Dr. Reddy's needed additional capacity and I made him an offer to buy Benzex. He exited the business in 1986 and went back to construction, but continued to be on the board of directors of both Dr. Reddy's and Cheminor.

I needed somebody who was competent and whom I could trust implicitly. Prasad fitted the bill perfectly. I persuaded Prasad to accept my offer of becoming the managing director of Cheminor, and put up the proposal for ratification by the board of directors of the company.

I thought this would sort the problems but I was in for a shock. Little did Prasad realize what he was letting himself in for. Many years later, Prasad recalled this experience in an internal communication:

Cheminor was a fairly successful operation, having pioneered the launch of some very important bulk actives in India like Ibuprofen, Ranitidine and Diltiazem. It was a profitable business and seemed to have all the ingredients for success. But my journey began with a big bang!

The day I joined, about 200 out of a total staff of 300 resigned as they were fiercely loyal to my predecessor and many of them were members of his family. Imagine the situation: while the board was selecting me to lead Cheminor, I was pulled out of the meeting and informed that two-thirds of our employees had resigned. Chaos followed in the manufacturing units, and there was a sense of panic amongst the senior team. I hardly knew the company, and there I was facing my first crisis!

Prasad did a wonderful job of calming the panic and rallying the senior management. That month, Cheminor set several new records for production. Prasad then set about changing the culture of the organization and introduced transparent processes and systems so that the situation would never recur.

Satish, my son, was at Purdue University then, completing a degree in medicinal chemistry. He had also secured admission to the master's programme at Columbia University and was planning to do a PhD in central nervous system diseases. Satish was not yet twenty-three but my weekly phone calls to him left me in no doubt that he had flowered into a mature youth, his feet firmly on the ground. Living in Purdue had done him much good and he had a feel of the world outside Hyderabad.

Purdue is a university town. The nearest cities are Indianapolis, 65 miles away, and Chicago, which is about 100 miles distant. At that time, it had about 400 Indian students. There are probably more of them now because Indians are one of the largest student groups in America. When Satish arrived there, one of his first tasks was to open a bank account, which he had never had before. He found rooms and furnished them himself. When he looked around though, he felt a little embarrassed. The Indian students showed tremendous industry. Rather than depend on remittances from their parents, they got scholarships and teaching assistantships. Some celebrated their first paychecks earned by working part-time.

Satish could have shrugged and continued living a carefree student life, with no shortage of money. Instead, he did something that filled me with pride as a father. Within six months, he got himself a teaching assistantship, earning 800 dollars a month. What was more, he moved out of his private apartment into cheaper university dormitories and bought himself an inexpensive car, a Mazda 323. His personality was changing: he had learnt to budget.

There were other things that would open Satish's eyes. Coming out of India, where respectful behaviour towards elders, particularly teachers, was the norm, Satish was agape when, on his first day in class, the lecturer strolled in with a can of Coke in his hands. Around him, students sat casually in their seats, some with their feet up. The relaxed atmosphere was a shock to him. But the way the teachers explained concepts and problems, interspersed with humour, made learning fun. From class, the library was a short distance away and Satish found it soon enough. There was also a public library which he visited on weekends. I worried sometimes that Satish did not have enough fun as a student.

It pained me deeply to ask Satish if he would consider returning to India. Prasad was under great strain and could use help. Besides, Satish could understudy Prasad and me, and it would be useful to see if he had an aptitude for the business. I did not need to press him too hard. Satish had already guessed that things were not quite right in the business. Our phone conversations were usually filled with laughter and talk of my hopes for the company. But, he had a growing feeling that at the other end of the line his father was a tense and worried man.

Satish returned to Hyderabad at the end of 1990 and began work at Dr. Reddy's early in the New Year. I didn't want to rush him. He was inducted into the board as executive director two years later in January 1993. I thought it would be best if his interest in the business came from his own instincts.

Dr. Reddy's was not in great shape internally, although sales and profits were rising. There were discipline issues. A worker had slapped his plant manager one day, yet this act of gross indiscipline was condoned because administrative action led to a strike and production suffered. When it came to trying to increase productivity, workers would stoutly oppose any move and get away with it. Absenteeism was rampant. The Congress party and a group sympathetic to the communists got involved in a wage settlement. Labour issues began to affect business.

And then came the bombshell.

B. Parthasaradhi Reddy, who had headed R&D at Dr. Reddy's for a long time, announced that he was leaving the company. Parthasaradhi had several complaints, most of them relating to how badly he was being treated by Chary. I was taken aback. I thought I had been a mentor to the man. As is my wont, I had given him full freedom to operate. I had given him a sense of ownership in the business and, just as Chary and Divi had been given substantial stakes in the business in return for their commitment, Parthasaradhi too had been well looked after. I was, in fact, considering his induction to the board.

I asked Satish to handle the issue but Parthasaradhi would not be swayed. What was worse, he was taking most of my senior research scientists with him to start a new company. As we learnt eventually, his plan was to compete with us in the very business in which we were most profitable: omeprazole, the number one money-spinner then and now for Dr. Reddy's. Possibly, indications that he would have a board position hastened the announcement of his departure; that would have made it more difficult for him to leave and start a competing business.

Parthasaradhi, however, said nothing about his plans. Instead, he stormed into Satish's office, raging against Chary and went on about how unfair the managing director had been to him. He declared to a completely nonplussed Satish that he was leaving the company, though with great reluctance, and promised that he would ensure everything was in safe hands. Parthasaradhi said that he was only taking a small team with him, no more than twenty people, unlike Divi, who sought to leave with most of the workforce.

Satish did not know what to say. His knowledge of the production process was limited. Parthasaradhi assured him that the plant technicians who had chosen to stay were competent enough to do the job. Most of them had no qualifications beyond a graduate degree in chemistry. The only technical officers with any expertise were M.S.N. Reddy, an assistant manager, and S. Venkatraman. At that time, MSN had been with Dr. Reddy's for less than half a year. Both of them stood by us during those difficult days.

Satish went to the plant the next day and pieced together the full picture. The staff that stayed back revealed that Parthasaradhi and his team had developed a lower-cost process for omeprazole and intended to manufacture it. At Dr. Reddy's, our route to omeprazole began with a raw material called collidine, which was very expensive. That did not matter as long as there was no competition. But Parthasaradhi had developed a cheaper route, using lutidine as raw material. Now, they were planning to walk away and attack the core of our business by marketing cheaper omeprazole.

It was late evening when Satish returned from the factory with the news. I was told about all this the next morning as I sat eating steamed rice idlis, my favourite breakfast. I could see that he was very disturbed. It was a growing-up lesson for him. I considered the situation as dispassionately as I could. I knew I had only myself to blame. I had been too trusting for long. For this reason, there was little archiving, few standard management procedures. I had allowed people to build private fiefdoms that were now poised to threaten my very existence as a businessman. If I did not act fast, the game was as good as over because Dr. Reddy's decline would start the day Parthasaradhi entered the market. I was not going to let that happen.

Satish faced the challenge head-on. He marshalled the available resources and organized the redevelopment of the new process for omeprazole on a war footing. Not only was the redevelopment completed in weeks, but we also commercialized it with dispatch. We were out there with the product much before Parthasaradhi's new company Hetero Drugs set up their plant.

Omeprazole is still one of our biggest products. Hetero Drugs is doing well. Parthasaradhi is a fine chemist and he had led the process development of many new products in our initial years. Overall, he made significant contributions to the growth of Dr. Reddy's and I wish him well. M.S.N. Reddy also left and we offered him some support initially. I believe he is doing well too. Come to think of it, many who have left Dr. Reddy's have been successful. And that is the way I want it to be. I never looked at industry as a zero-sum game, even when competition was at its stiffest. The more trees in the woods, the richer the forest.

Many people have marvelled at how Satish, my son, accepts Prasad, my son-in-law, as the senior man in the company. For a decade or so after they joined my business, their spheres of activity were different—Prasad was running Cheminor and Satish was in Dr. Reddy's. The question of their working together really came up when we decided to merge the two companies in 2000. I talked to them about the future. I told them I would like Prasad to be the vice chairman and chief executive officer (CEO) of the merged entity and Satish, the managing director and chief operating officer. I explained my reasoning—Prasad was the older of the two and had joined the business earlier. He was a mature leader who had managed Cheminor independently and led it out of a crisis to growth. Satish readily agreed and has never had any regret. As for me, both men are equally strong pillars, each bringing different skills to the enterprise.

Satish and Prasad have been running Dr. Reddy's for over a decade after the merger, making deals, expanding the product offering, entering

My two pillars: *My son-in-law, Prasad (left), and my son, Satish (right)*

new markets and retaining our deep strength in bulk drugs and generics. Because they get along so well, Dr. Reddy's has avoided the debilitating family feuds that some companies in India have suffered. They have been able to build a strong and deeply committed organization and have scaled up systems to keep it running efficiently. They have been instrumental in attracting powerful minds to our board of directors and have benefited from their sagacity.

I have been fortunate. More importantly, perhaps, Dr. Reddy's and its investors are in safe hands.

7 1 DOLLAR = 1 RUPEE

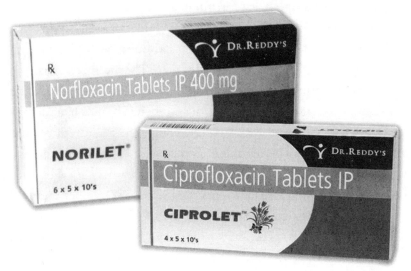

The game-changing quinolone duo: *Norilet and Ciprolet ushered in the era of affordable medicine in the early 1990s*

The expansion funded by the public issue cleared the decks for Dr. Reddy's to set a scorching pace of growth. The trigger was norfloxacin, the first of a new class of anti-bacterial compounds called fluoroquinolones. More significantly, perhaps, the launch of the drug by Dr. Reddy's was the first demonstration that new medicines could be both affordable for consumers and a profitable business in India.

Norfloxacin was discovered by scientists at Kyorin in Japan and licensed to Merck. It worked by disrupting the replication of bacterial DNA and quickly destroyed certain kinds of infection. Our foray into fluoroquinolones, beginning with norfloxacin, was similarly disruptive of the established business model at that time and I was accused by some in the industry of destroying its profitability. On the contrary, I think it energized drug companies to price new drugs affordably and reap the benefits of explosive growth. In the process, Dr. Reddy's firmly established itself as a player of consequence in the industry.

Dr. Reddy's started its formulations operations in 1987. We contracted out the manufacture of our formulations and some of our early ones, particularly the painkillers, did quite well. However, Dr. Reddy's was a small player in a crowded field. The multinationals apart, the big Indian companies were Ranbaxy and Cipla followed by Unichem and a host of smaller companies with entrenched brands like Alembic, well known for Glycodin Terp Vasaka, a cough syrup it introduced soon after Independence when prohibition put paid to its alcohol business. I was familiar with the formulation end of the pharmaceutical business, having built it earlier both in Uniloids and Standard Organics, and knew it was more consistent and profitable than the bulk drug business. I was naturally keen to grow our formulations business rapidly but also needed to find the right formula to compete with entrenched players. After all, why should doctors switch their prescriptions for products from established companies when we were small and relatively unknown?

Cipla and Ranbaxy were growing very fast by launching new drugs and Cipla did it particularly well. The new Patents Act of 1970 abolished patents for medicinal products, though processes to make them were still patentable. It came into effect in 1972, the year Yusuf Hamied took over the reins in Cipla after his father passed away. Yusuf was quick to seize the opportunity. He kept track of all the new products getting into the market in the USA and Europe—there were always issues of *Drugs of Today*, *Drugs of the Future* and *Scrip* on his table. He would spot a new drug, figure out its chemistry and decide to launch it. Getting a licence to import the bulk drug or the advanced intermediate was quite a task in those days, but Yusuf's stature and connections were such that when he wanted a licence he got one. And soon, there was yet another new drug in the market from Cipla. Yusuf was undoubtedly a guru in this game. I learnt the ropes of this approach from him, but was hesitant to embark on it till about 1987. By then, however, I had established our initial bulk drug business of methyldopa and the public issue gave me some financial leeway to think on a bigger scale.

Around this time, I started reading *Scrip* seriously and the first new class of drugs that intrigued me was the fluoroquinolones. Norfloxacin, the first drug in this new class, had been approved in the USA in late 1986. Was this the opportunity I could seize? All the bulk drugs I had earlier developed had a ready demand in India as the formulations were in the market. Norfloxacin was a riskier proposition—it had not yet been introduced in India and there was no established demand. However, it was an opportunity to be among the first in the market with the formulation. I was sure of a sizeable cost advantage as I would also be manufacturing the bulk drug. The idea grew on me because the fascinating history of antibiotics suggested that there would be a real need for a new one like norfloxacin.

I knew that resistance develops every ten years or so as organisms involved in the infection develop ways to fight the antibiotic and render it ineffective. The history of antibiotics is replete with examples, but penicillin is perhaps the most telling one. In 1928, Sir Alexander Fleming, a bacteriologist at St Mary's hospital in London, demonstrated that a mould—*Pencillium notatum*—killed many disease-causing bacteria and named the substance it secreted penicillin. About a decade later, Oxford scientists Lord Howard Florey and Sir Ernst Chain isolated the active ingredient. The three were jointly awarded the Nobel Prize in Medicine in 1945 for the discovery of penicillin and its anti-infective properties. They were, however, unable to produce it in quantity. The Second World War broke out and there was great urgency to produce large quantities of penicillin to treat infections from wounds. Florey was sent off with a small quantity of penicillin to the Peoria Labs at Illinois in the USA where a great deal of work on fermentation processes was going on. Florey teamed up with Andrew Moyer, an expert on the nutrition of moulds, and they succeeded in developing a process for producing commercial quantities of penicillin. All that could be manufactured was earmarked for the war effort and there were no civilian supplies, with the result that the drug was commonly known as 'military penicillin'. It was only after the war that the drug became widely available and was so effective that it was considered a miracle drug.

Though resistance to penicillin was reported within a few years of its use, its significance was not recognized. The 1950s and '60s were the golden years of antibiotics. With so many new drugs coming into the market, there was little concern about resistance to antibiotics.

On hearing the news that scientists at Oxford had succeeded in isolating penicillin, Selman Waksman, an emigrant from tsarist Russia who had already achieved international renown as a soil microbiologist at Rutgers University, focused on finding new antibiotic strains from the soil. One of the most extraordinary finds was by Albert Schatz, the brilliant son of a Russian Jew and an Englishwoman, who was Waksman's doctoral student. Schatz was one of the few scientists who could put a date and time to their discovery. He recalled later that he realized he had a new antibiotic on 'October 19, 1943, at about 2:00 in the afternoon'. He sealed it in a test tube, gave it to his mother, and named it streptomycin. Waksman took the credit for the discovery on the ground that he had directed the research and Schatz's contribution was small. This invited a lawsuit from Schatz which was later settled out of court. In 1952, Waksman received the Nobel Prize, not for the discovery of streptomycin as was first announced but for 'ingenious, systematic and successful studies of the soil microbes that led to the discovery of streptomycin'.

Spurred by the success of penicillin, Merck secured exclusive rights for streptomycin and invested in its development. However, the grant of exclusive rights to Merck of such an important drug generated controversy. There were apprehensions that Merck alone would not be able to satisfy the demand for the drug. Merck defused the situation by deciding to alter its licence from Rutgers to a non-exclusive one. Controversies apart, the world got the first antibiotic effective against tuberculosis, a magnificent scientific achievement that saved innumerable human lives.

The 1950s also saw the discovery and development of several other important antibiotics, including chloramphenicol, tetracycline and vancomycin. The 1960s brought metronidazole, sulphamethoxazole and trimethoprim, all three of which I was very familiar with. The physicians now had at their disposal a whole range of powerful tools to fight infectious diseases and the consequences were dramatic. There were some estimates that antibiotics alone had added eight years to the average life expectancy in the USA. There was so much of confidence in the efficacy of antibiotics that the US surgeon general William H. Stewart reported to the Congress in 1969 that it was time to 'close the book on infectious diseases'.

Even as the US surgeon general was brimming with optimism, resistance was developing to many of these antibiotics. Within a decade, it was clear that new antibiotics would be needed. The fluoroquinolones seemed to have arrived just in time.

In April 1987, I went on a business trip to Manila. Ofloxacin, a quinolone discovered by Daiichi about a year after norfloxacin, was popular there. Daiichi was a leader in sulpha drugs and they had progressed into quinolone research in collaboration with Gunma University's School of Medicine in Japan. Daiichi had licensed the drug to Glaxo in Italy and Roussel in France. *Newsweek* labelled it the 'Almighty Antibiotic', but it had not yet been approved in the USA— that happened only in late 1990. I then went to South Korea. In Seoul, I met some bright and enterprising young people in the pharmaceutical industry. They talked animatedly about how the anti-bacterial scene was changing with norfloxacin.

I then decided to visit Japan and Kyorin. Curiously enough, Kyorin had also collaborated with Gunma University's School of Medicine. They had a modest office and I marvelled at the ability of a small company to make as important a discovery as norfloxacin. I thought to myself that perhaps, one day, Dr. Reddy's would also discover new drugs.

The fact that Kyorin had licensed the drug to Merck in the USA and it had been approved by the Food and Drug Administration (FDA) tipped the scales in favour of norfloxacin. I came back to Hyderabad and decided to make it. But by the time we developed the process and commenced manufacture of the bulk drug in 1988, Cipla and Ranbaxy were already in the market with the formulation under the brand names of Norflox and Norbactin. They had followed their practice of importing either the bulk drug or the advanced intermediate to make the formulation. They were fast, but their costs must have been high.

Norflox and Norbactin were priced at 8 rupees per tablet, an unheard-of price at the time. Doctors were writing prescriptions for the drugs, but I was told they were hesitant to write more, as only the well-to-do could afford them. I made my calculations and met with our marketing people. I told them that this pricing was wrong. Doctors wanted to prescribe this drug, but middle-class people could not afford 80 rupees for a course of ten tablets. If the price was halved, the market would grow manifold. I asked them what market share they would get with the price halved. T.R. Bhoopathy, our marketing head, was enthusiastic. He said, 'We will take over the market and become number one.' However, he was apprehensive that we would lose money at this startlingly low price. I reassured him that it would be profitable, as, unlike Cipla and Ranbaxy, we were producing our own bulk drug and could contain costs with process efficiencies and large volumes. I asked him to go ahead.

I branded the product Norilet and Bhoopathy launched it, not at 40 rupees as I had suggested but at 38 rupees for a strip of ten tablets. There were shock waves in the industry, but the doctors were pleasantly surprised. Ranbaxy representatives told the doctors that our 'cheap' product may not be good! However, many physicians who knew we were exporting bulk drugs did not believe that. They asked how a company exporting drugs to the USA and Europe could make substandard stuff. They said they would prescribe the drug and would discontinue it if they did not see the expected results. Prescriptions of Norilet soared, but those of Norflox and Norbactin fell so much that within three months their stocks were being returned from the market.

Cipla and Ranbaxy were compelled to cut their price to match mine. The doctors saw this and the impression grew that we were a straightforward company that priced products reasonably. All of a sudden, Dr. Reddy's, which had launched its formulations just three or four years earlier, was being talked about and established competitors were forced to respond to our presence in the market. But they were bigger companies with a bigger field force. Cipla remained number one in the market with Norflox, though Ranbaxy lagged behind us.

Cipla and Ranbaxy were quite annoyed. I did not know Parvinder Singh of Ranbaxy at the time, but my relationship with Yusuf Hamied soured. He was very angry for several years and then gradually cooled down. I needed him as I was making several bulk drugs so I continued to go to him. I told him, 'Yusuf, you can't make everything. Bulk drugs are not your business. So, buy them from me.' We sold some new bulk drugs to Cipla and re-established our relationship.

Norfloxacin was a turning point for Dr. Reddy's. But it was not long before Ranbaxy turned the tables on us. Ciprofloxacin, a Bayer product which went on to become the gold standard of quinolones, was approved a year after norfloxacin. Smarting at being beaten by Cipla in the race to the market with ofloxacin, Ranbaxy rushed to develop ciprofloxacin. They branded their product Cifran and launched it in May 1989 at 180 rupees for a strip of ten tablets. It seemed a challenge thrown at us—'let's see what you can do'! Cadila was caught in a trap. They had imported the bulk drug and if they priced their formulation at 180 rupees a strip, they would have lost money from the first consignment onward. We produced ciprofloxacin and priced it so that the formulators who sourced the bulk drug from us could sell the finished dosage at 180 rupees a strip and make a profit. Dr. Reddy's was considered a saviour by about ten formulators, who would otherwise have not been able to compete with Ranbaxy.

Dr. Reddy's was the first and only indigenous supplier of ciprofloxacin bulk drug, and it remained so till the first quarter of 1993.

We also launched our own brand of ciprofloxacin with the brand name Ciprolet. Predictably enough, the prices came down. The benefit to consumers is obvious enough, but how did we benefit?

For most of the new drugs that we produced, such as norfloxacin or ciprofloxacin, our costs were a fraction of the price of the imported drug. I did not succumb to the temptation of pricing the new bulk drugs that we developed on par with the imported price. I felt this would be a short-sighted approach as high prices for the bulk drug would result in high prices of the formulation, and this would limit the demand for both the formulation and the bulk drug. I knew from experience that demand exploded when prices were reasonable.

I had another problem to solve. I intended to manufacture the finished dosage and compete with my customers of the bulk drug who would also be making it. I could not upset them by pricing the bulk drug so high that they could not compete with us.

My pricing formula was therefore simple. If the bulk drug cost me 200 rupees to produce, I would price it at 400 rupees for the market. This was invariably much lower than the landed cost of the imported bulk drug. My customers were happy and the additional advantage was that I had enough leeway to reduce prices when competition came in and prices came down. I would then add 200–400 rupees to take care of the formulation and marketing costs and arrive at the price of my formulation. This kind of pricing of the bulk drug and formulation allowed others to compete though they bought the bulk drug from us. My simple formula worked because the alternative of imports was usually more expensive and I had virtual monopoly of a new drug for some time before competition set in, efficiencies improved and bulk drug prices eroded.

The pricing paradigm for new drugs changed and they became affordable. Availability improved because the bulk drug was manufactured indigenously at cheaper prices. And, of course, I made money in both—the bulk drug and the formulation.

By 1994, Dr. Reddy's was the market leader in quinolones and 70 per cent of revenues were accruing from this class. Soon enough, competition forced the prices down. I had foreseen this situation and knew we had to build our formulation business to safeguard ourselves from sudden crashes in the prices of bulk drugs. I had therefore built a portfolio of formulations, including enalapril, an antihypertensive (Enam, 1989), omeprazole, an anti-ulcer drug (Omez, 1991), ketorolac, a painkiller (Ketorol, 1992) and cetirizine, an anti-histamine (Cetrine, 1993). T.R. Bhoopathy worked tirelessly to launch these brands. In 1995, he left the company. S. Chandrasekhar, who had joined Cheminor Drugs earlier, took charge as senior vice president of formulations marketing. He brought a vitality that galvanized the sales force and sales galloped. As we manufactured the bulk drugs for all these products we could be profitable despite the drugs being priced competitively. These drugs are sold globally and continue to be money spinners for Dr. Reddy's even after two decades.

I followed the same principle in pricing these formulations as for norfloxacin and ciprofloxacin. I had an additional thumb rule when it came to pricing chronic medications. I knew that unlike short-term medications, patients would be very sensitive to the price of chronic medications that they needed to buy month after month. For example, Enam, an antihypertensive, was priced at 1.20 dollars in the USA. I thought an antihypertensive at this price would increase the blood pressure of patients rather than reduce it. Without the benefit of expertise in economic theory, I thought a dollar in America should be like a rupee in India. Enam was therefore initially priced at 1.20 rupees a tablet. Sales took off like a rocket!

The financials of Dr. Reddy's reflect the profitability of the strategy of providing reasonably priced medicine. In December 1991, Dr. Reddy's declared a bonus of one share for every two shares. Just over a year later, in January 1993, it was a bonus of one share for every one share. In May 1994, the bonus was two shares for one share. So, one share in 1991 had become nine shares in 1994—and the company was declaring a dividend of 30 per cent. I knew I had to make nine times the profit of 1991 in 1994 just to maintain the dividend.

Around this time I got to know Parvinder Singh of Ranbaxy. I met him first in the lounge of the Delhi airport. He asked me outright, 'How do you keep announcing these wonderful results?' Like Yusuf Hamied, Parvinder was a technocrat and had inherited a well-established business. His father, Bhai Mohan Singh, was a moneylender who came from Pakistan. He lent money to a small drug-manufacturing operation which had been started by some Punjabis; since they could not pay it back, he took over their company. That is how he came into the business. Ranbaxy built its fortune on diazepam, a tranquillizer. It had been discovered by Roche. However, using its influence with the government, Ranbaxy prevented Roche from launching the product in India. It imported the bulk drug from Italy and launched the product it called Calmpose. It became a blockbuster and Ranbaxy earned tons of money. Bhai Mohan Singh sent Parvinder to Michigan, just as I had sent Satish to Purdue. Parvinder completed his PhD in pharmacy from Michigan and joined Ranbaxy. His horizons were broader than those of his conservative father and he battled with him to bring in new products. It was Parvinder who was responsible for ampicillin, amoxicillin and several other new products being launched by Ranbaxy. Eventually, Parvinder had to part ways with his father.

Parvinder was very good at his work and made a major contribution to the pharmaceutical industry. When I first met him, Dr. Reddy's was launching one new product after another. Having been affected by the price crash brought about by our launch of norfloxacin, he was anxious to make sure that I did not repeat it. I was the president of the Indian Pharmaceutical Congress Association at one time and Parvinder had been the president five years before me. He had tremendous connections in Delhi. I regarded him as my senior, and we became good friends. I was deeply grieved when he was afflicted with cancer and passed away in 1999. I was struck by the irony of the chief of such a large pharmaceutical enterprise being helpless in the face of this remorseless disease. Parvinder had always been appreciative of our discovery research programme and had acknowledged that we were ahead of Ranbaxy in this. I thought it would be a wonderful tribute to the memory of Parvinder if our cancer research programme, which was then under way, succeeded.

About a decade after we slashed the price of norfloxacin and ushered in the era of affordable medicines in India, Yusuf Hamied made affordable Indian medicine available in Africa. He faxed a dramatic offer to sell Triomune, a triple-combination medicine for AIDS patients, to Médecins Sans Frontières for their programme of free distribution in Africa. Triomune was a cocktail of three medicines, stavudine, lamivudine and nevirapine, each patented by a different multinational company in the developed world. Instead of multiple pills a day, patients needed only two doses of Triomune, once at sunrise and the other at sunset—a simple regimen, ideal for Africa. The most stunning part, however, was the price—350 dollars per patient per year as against 10,000–15,000 dollars in Western countries. The *New York Times* published the story on the front page the day after the fax, on 7th February 2001. It created an unprecedented stir. Yusuf's father, Khwaja Abdul Hamied, would have been proud had he lived to see the day. He was a DSc from Berlin University and established Cipla in 1937 with a great vision. It was he who prepared a blueprint for industrial research in the country, which ultimately led to the setting up of the Council of Scientific and Industrial Research (CSIR). Above all, he was a great nationalist. Mahatma Gandhi had visited his factory on 4th July 1939, coincidentally American Independence Day, and wrote that he was 'delighted to visit this Indian enterprise'.

Indian enterprises have since proved their mettle by making available affordable generic medicines to India and the world. So much so, India is now regarded as the 'pharmacy to the world'. I have toiled for forty-five years in the industry and reaped the rewards. But nothing can give me more satisfaction than to see such recognition of Indian enterprise and to know that Dr. Reddy's has played its part.

8 LUXEMBOURG TO NEW YORK

A landmark year: *RDY was NYSE's*
best-performing new stock in 2001

Fuelled by the heady beginnings of economic reform and liberalization initiated by the then finance minister Manmohan Singh, the Sensex, the BSE Sensitive Index, trebled between 1991 and 1994. During the same period, Dr. Reddy's stock grew an astounding 360 times in value, if one accounted for the three bonus issues between December 1991 and May 1994.

The price appreciation in Dr. Reddy's stock reflected the striking growth in the company's revenues and profits. Dr. Reddy's crossed 1 billion rupees in annual revenue in 1991–92. Two years later, in 1993–94, annual revenues were nearly 1.8 billion. Profits had grown two and a half times during the same period, from 103 million rupees to 253 million. The increase in the share price was sustained by the belief among investors that Dr. Reddy's would maintain its heady pace of growth by introducing new medicines and expanding its presence in lucrative export markets.

New products and markets, however, require sufficient funding. It may have been possible to leverage the earnings of Dr. Reddy's by taking large loans to fund the expansion, but cash flows would have been very tight. Besides, I needed to have some flexibility to ensure that my fledgling discovery programme could continue without affecting the cash requirements of the bulk drug and formulation business.

Fortunately, a new avenue of raising equity in international markets had opened up around that time. One of the measures Manmohan Singh announced in his 1992 budget speech was that Indian companies would be permitted to raise equity in international financial markets by issuing depositary receipts. Depositary receipts had underlying equity shares in Indian companies, and holders were entitled to dividends and voting rights just like equity holders. The depositary receipts could be listed in international stock exchanges and traded, but only by foreign entities or non-resident Indians. The scheme came into effect from April 1992.

Reliance Industries was the first to take advantage of this new opportunity. In May 1992, less than two months after the scheme became operational, Reliance Industries made an issue of global depositary receipts (GDRs) and listed them on the Luxembourg Stock Exchange. A few other companies, including a couple from the Birla group, followed. While the possibility was intriguing, I was cautious.

By the next year, however, GDRs became an established avenue for equity financing among Indian companies. In early 1994, Tata Electric issued GDRs and listed them on the Luxembourg Stock Exchange and so did Wockhardt, a pharmaceutical company. I heard that Ranbaxy, too, was in the process of issuing GDRs.

Around this time, the Hinduja Group, a diversified business house with international operations, established a financial advisory company in India and they pitched a GDR issue to Dr. Reddy's on the strength of their relationship with Baring Brothers, a globally known investment banker.

In early 1994, I was confident that Dr. Reddy's would cross the milestone of 50 million dollars in that financial year. Manufacturing capacity was strained and Chary was insistent on expanding capacity quickly. I thought it would be very useful to raise 50 million dollars in GDRs and sounded out Satish and Prasad on the matter. They were confident of the future and believed that Dr. Reddy's had matured as an organization with systems in place to deliver on growth. Vasudevan, our chief financial officer, was enthusiastic about making the GDR issue. I asked him to go ahead.

I had a crucial meeting with Baring in London. I was told that the lady who headed the division that would be responsible for our GDR issue was a 'tough' investment banker. She came to the point very soon. She said our performance was great and so was our cash flow. Her question was, 'Why do you need to make an issue?' I did not beat around the bush. I told her that while our existing business could grow with internal accruals and debt, I needed a cushion as I had embarked on drug discovery. Though returns could be enormous if we succeeded, it was a risky business at best. There was no way I could hire the best talent I could get and then let them down if there were temporary upheavals in our main business. I told her I needed some head room. My straightforward answer convinced her.

An international issue has to be marketed to international institutional investors. The preparation was intense and after the issue was announced, the company had to make presentations to hard-nosed investors across the globe. These promotional tours, or 'roadshows' as they are called, were orchestrated by Baring, the managers of the issue. Chary, Venugopal (who had been instrumental in setting up our Russian business), Vasudevan and I set off on a whirlwind tour.

Dr. Reddy's made a successful issue of 48 million dollars in July 1994 and the GDRs were listed on the stock exchange at Luxembourg. I remember somebody telling me that we were the youngest company in India to have issued GDRs. The Luxembourg listing made a difference to the company's profile. Equity analysts from the financial capitals of the world started to take note of Dr. Reddy's and so did the financial press. Most importantly, my drug discovery programme was now well funded.

For a couple of years after the GDR issue, everything went well. Dr. Reddy's continued to expand its bulk drug offering, introduced new formulations into the market and pressed ahead with its discovery programme. By 1995–96, our turnover had crossed 2.3 billion rupees and our profit exceeded the half-million mark for the first time. There was money in the bank.

What followed was perhaps the problem of plenty. We expanded our Russian business aggressively and relaxed credit norms as we had the money to fund it. We also invested our surplus cash in the stock market, hoping to earn more than what the banks offered as interest. In 1996–97, both the Russian economy and the stock market in India crashed. We had to write off 160 million rupees of bad debts in Russia and 140 million rupees in share market losses. Our profit was down 40 per cent over the previous year despite our revenues exceeding 2.5 billion rupees. It was a particularly bad year for Cheminor, too, as Hoechst Celanese prematurely terminated a contract and there were production disruptions when the manufacture of some bulk drugs was shifted to the new plant in Visakhapatnam.

When the time came to take stock of the annual results for 1996–97, I spent some time introspecting. I harked back to the time I had started out as an entrepreneur to set up Uniloids when the country was starved of affordable medicines. I had then written out a goal for myself that I had preserved over the years. I felt I had strayed from my central purpose and decided to make a public commitment to it, lest I stray again from it in a moment of weakness. For the first time, our annual report carried a statement of my vision for the company.

I was simple and direct:

Twenty-one years ago when I entered the Indian pharmaceutical industry as a technocrat-entrepreneur, I nursed a dream. I observed that drugs launched in the developed West were prohibitively expensive. . . . So I wrote out the mission of my life: to bring new molecules into the country at a price the common man could afford.

Thirteen years later, in 1989, I had launched Norilet at half the market price and a number of drugs thereafter. A new business model based on affordable pricing took root in the Indian pharmaceutical industry. My first dream had been achieved substantially. It was time to announce my second and I did so in my vision statement:

In seven years from now, we might emerge as the first company from the Third World to put a patented drug on the marketplace. There used to be a time when I would dream with my eyes open, when I said I would innovate for the benefit of the poor in India.

I am dreaming again. Dr. Reddy's Laboratories will innovate again. Not just for India. For mankind.

It was no doubt a dream, but not a wild one. By the time I was writing out my statement of vision in our annual report for 1996–97, our discovery efforts were paying off. We had licensed our first molecule to Novo Nordisk for development and had entered into an arrangement with Debiopharm, a Swiss company specializing in oncology to take our cancer discoveries forward.

I was brimming with optimism. By 1997, Dr. Reddy's and Cheminor had built up a sizeable export market and my sights were firmly set on the developed-country markets, particularly the USA which was difficult to penetrate but very profitable. Prasad had made significant strides in developing bulk drugs for the USA in Cheminor since it had first exported ibuprofen some ten years earlier. He had also built up world-class manufacturing facilities to meet the exacting regulatory standards of the FDA. Cheminor had filed its first application for approval of a generic drug in the USA for ranitidine and had entered into a strategic alliance with Schein to develop the generic business. Medicines with about 40 billion dollars of annual revenue were going off patent in the next ten years. I wanted a piece of the action and I was confident we would get it.

My optimism was well founded. We regained our growth momentum and crossed the half-million-rupee mark in profits again in 1998–99. We then made a big move. In 1999, we acquired the shareholding of the promoters of the Chennai-based American Remedies and merged it with Dr. Reddy's. With the merger, Dr. Reddy's emerged as the third largest pharmaceutical company in the country.

In 2000, we made another big decision. We decided to merge Cheminor and Dr. Reddy's. Their combined revenues in 1999–2000 were nearly 8 billion rupees. Dr. Reddy's' financial position was very comfortable, but Cheminor's was not. On the other hand, the future was bright for Cheminor as it had invested heavily in developing products for the long-gestation but very profitable US market. Further, many economies in costs could be achieved since there was an overlap in their business.

The time seemed to be right for thinking aggressively about moving to the next stage of growth by investing in the development of the US market, growing globally through acquisitions and stepping up our drug discovery effort. Obviously, all these ambitious plans needed money. Once again, we thought of an international issue of capital as it would not only bring in the money but also further increase the visibility of our business.

If a drug company wanted its discovery efforts taken seriously, it needed to be listed in either New York or London. A London- or New-York-listed company talking of discovery efforts was entirely different from a company based in southern India talking of the same thing. If a company is in London or New York, analysts not only track the company's shares but also keep an eye on its science.

London was the early favourite in listing destinations in India and was certainly an option. However, our most profitable market with the greatest potential for growth was the USA. The New York Stock Exchange (NYSE) was the largest and most fabled exchange in the country. I discussed the matter with Prasad and Satish as well as our board of directors and decided on an issue of American depositary receipts (ADRs) in late 2000, with a listing on the NYSE. Vasudevan assured me that our accounting standards satisfied US requirements and there would be no problem in compliance. The next big decision was to pick an investment banker. The scramble that investment bankers put on to get a share of our business was fascinating. Several famous companies pitched for our business and we picked Merrill Lynch because they offered the best deal. I had also known Hemendra Kothari, the boss of the Indian arm of Merrill (formally known as DSP Merrill Lynch) for some time. He had brought the American Remedies deal to us and I was comfortable with him.

Very soon, we were hosting a huge team from Merrill that had come to perform due diligence on the company. There was a mountain of paperwork and a number of legal hoops to jump through. After all this was done, it was time to go on the roadshow. We prepared meticulously and had answers ready for likely questions. We practised our speeches, checked our suits and ties and shined our shoes. It was time now to beat a path to the analysts and fund managers in whose hands lay the millions that entrepreneurs like me needed to build our businesses.

The roadshow was to be a three-week affair. We split into two teams that would eventually converge in New York City. I led one team with Vasudevan and Cameron Reid, head of our North America operations who had contributed greatly to building our business. Prasad, Satish and Swaminathan Subramaniam, the articulate vice president of Clinical Research, made up the second team.

Roadshows should really be called roller coasters. Our roadshow for the GDR issue seven years earlier had prepared us for this one. We were hopping on to flights, scampering from city to city, rushing from one appointment to the other, pumping hands, making presentations. From breakfast to late evening, it was a complete whirl. Merrill had assigned a deal captain to our teams and he was always on the mobile phone, calling ahead, smoothening our way, ensuring that cars were at the door and coordinating our entry into corporate boardrooms. Merrill was alarmed that each one of us seemed to have a different opinion or expressed things differently on occasion. So we went through rehearsals to ensure we spoke with one voice. Fortunately, since we all knew each other, it took us less than an hour to coordinate our positions. Some of the bigger fund managers were wise to all this. More than one requested that Merrill people stay out of the room during our presentations, clearly aiming to test our responses without taking cues from our tutors.

Our first stop was Mumbai, India's financial capital. Prasad and Satish then travelled west to Europe, while my team headed east to Singapore. My favourite hotel in the Lion City is the Grand Hyatt because of its proximity to the Orchard Road shopping area and the Borders bookstore across the road. But this was a roadshow. The Merrill team, led by the deal captain who accompanied us on the tour, booked us into Singapore's Ritz Carlton no less. On the other side, Prasad and Satish were staying at the Savoy in London and the Ritz in Paris. Daimler limousines waited for them at airports and at their hotels when they emerged for meetings. Lunch was invariably in a fancy restaurant, dinner in a fancier one. The talk was about vintage and the quality of the cut glass, and whether the wines had proper 'legs'. Starters and entrées were ordered, with great deliberation. By the end of the trip, Prasad and Satish had developed a taste for gourmet food and expensive red wine!

Every money manager of significance was contacted. Prasad and Satish even went to Edinburgh in Scotland to call on the investment managers who handled the money for Scottish Widows, which had started business nearly two centuries earlier to provide for widows, and had a reputation for investing wisely. At each session, an Eton-educated man, Bhuvanesh Lamba, introduced them in a sing-song voice. Merrill certainly knew how to create an act! Even so, when I saw the stretch limo outside my hotel on the final day as we left for the NYSE, I put my foot down. I was not going to ride that car.

During my swing through Singapore, Hong Kong, San Francisco and finally New York, I spoke passionately about our molecules and the deal with Novo Nordisk. I also told investors about the patent challenges we were mounting in the USA and the confidence that we would win some of these challenges. A tiny incident in Hong Kong gave me the assurance that our share sale would go well. An analyst at an office we visited looked at my visiting card and told me he was going to preserve it as a souvenir. That affected me deeply. Clearly, the world outside India had begun to hear about our work and my commitment to discovery research. Not all of it was smooth sailing though. In Boston, Punita Kumar-Sinha, daughter-in-law of former Indian finance minister Yashwant Sinha, and manager of the NYSE-listed India Fund, was one of the sceptics. She declined to put money in Dr. Reddy's. I don't hold anything against her for that. Dr. Reddy's stock performance that year, however, proved our worst doubters wrong.

Yet, as we approached our 11th April listing, we got the jitters. Since 26th March 2001, when we had formally announced our ADR issue, the share price on the BSE had been hammered down by over 20 per cent. The Dow Jones Industrial Average, the world's benchmark index, had begun to fall. Then, just before the share sale, an analyst put out a report panning the whole ADR issue as a bad idea for Dr. Reddy's. The reference price for the sale in New York was based on the closing price of the stock the previous evening in Mumbai. We were to learn that odd things can happen when big money is involved. For no apparent reason, our stock was battered in the closing hour of trading in the BSE, shedding almost 4 per cent. The net effect of this was that our stock dilution would become greater if we were to raise the amount of cash we had set out to. On top of that, we were being advised to offer the ADRs at a discount to the value of the underlying share in India. We were in a quandary: do we proceed, or step back and wait for better times? There was a lot of tension in the air. Having come so far, it didn't make sense to withdraw. We decided to go ahead. That decision was taken at midnight. We finally issued the ADR at 10.04 dollars at a steep discount to even the hammered-down price of the share on the BSE. To this day, we are not aware who fixed the stock price to our disadvantage.

Finally, the big morning came. We put on our suits and ties and drove to Broad Street in Lower Manhattan. When we arrived at the stock exchange building with its Corinthian marble facade, we glanced up proudly to see the Indian tricolour fluttering alongside the stars and stripes. It was a special moment for all of us at Dr. Reddy's, indeed for all of India. Ours was the first pharmaceutical company in the Asia-Pacific region, outside of Japan, to be listed on the NYSE. Besides, it was a huge milestone for me personally. New York is a long way from Tadepalli.

When Dr. Reddy's listed on the exchange, NYSE was headed by the charismatic Richard Grasso. The opening ceremony at 9.30 a.m. was a brilliantly choreographed exercise. Once we arrived at the 208-year-old

RDY trades commence at NYSE: *(From left) Vasudevan, Cameron, Satish, Grasso, me, Prasad; Uday is on the extreme right*

building, we were led to the huge boardroom where Grasso started off with a warm welcome. Breakfast was served. Then he took us on a guided tour of the exchange. Everything was timed to perfection.

A minute before opening time, Grasso led us on to the floor of the exchange. And suddenly it hit us—the open outcry, the sense of frenzy. This was the pulse of capitalism. As Grasso kept up a running commentary, we were led to the balcony, handed the hammer and asked to strike the gong. There was applause as Dr. Reddy's became an NYSE-listed share.

It was an occasion for celebration. We moved from the exchange to lunch at Tse Yang, a Chinese restaurant on 51st Street fabled for its Szechuan cuisine. The Reddy team was there and so were the Merrill people. The issue size was eventually 132.8 million dollars and 30 million dollars were earmarked for discovery research. Merrill walked away with fees of 8 million dollars. Not surprisingly, the price of Dr. Reddy's shares on the BSE began to rise once the NYSE listing was over.

Dr. Reddy's was the last ADR listing that year on the NYSE and the best-performing new stock. Five months later, terrorists linked to the al-Qaeda would fly planes into the twin towers of the World Trade Center, striking at the heart of the free market. Heroically, Grasso managed to get the exchange up and running a mere six days later, although his building was just a few blocks away from the World Trade Center.

Sadly, Grasso was fired two years later because of a furore over 140 million dollars of deferred compensation that lay hidden in the exchange's books. In his farewell message, Grasso spoke of the honour and privilege of serving the world's greatest equities market for thirty-six years. Without the advantages that society bestows on those with a college education, Grasso, a boy who was raised in Queens, had clawed and climbed his way to the top of his game. Grasso used to come to work in an armoured car. He would have been horrified had he come to know I had declined a stretch limousine.

9 'PILL FACTORY TO THE WORLD'

The *Forbes* cover says it all: *Exports were 65 per cent of revenues in 2001–02*

In December 2001, *Forbes* magazine carried a cover story on Dr. Reddy's with the headline 'Pill factory to the world'. The story was about our discovery efforts, but it also talked about our supplies of bulk drugs to some of the largest generic players in the world as well as the progress we had made in exporting our formulations. 'The company symbolizes enormous national potential,' said the article. As a matter of fact, the 'enormous national potential' of India as the supplier of affordable medicines to the world had been in the making for more than two decades.

I was clear from the very beginning when I set up Dr. Reddy's and Cheminor in the early 1980s that the export markets were an opportunity waiting to be grabbed. Of all the markets, the USA was the most attractive and my sights were firmly set on it. However, the regulatory requirements were onerous and the feasibility of marketing generic products for an Indian company had yet to be established. No Indian company was exporting generic finished dosages to the USA, but I was confident that it was only a matter of time before that market opened up to Indian enterprise. In the meanwhile, other markets of the world beckoned.

Indian pharmaceutical companies followed multiple approaches to penetrate global markets. Most companies started with exporting finished dosages through local agents in various countries and struck deeper marketing alliances in important markets. The second approach was to establish joint ventures with the local partner bringing in substantial knowledge of the market and local presence. The third option was to establish a direct presence in a foreign market through representative offices, subsidiary companies or acquisitions.

Not surprisingly, given its long history, Cipla was an early entrant in the export business. Rather than establish joint ventures or a direct presence, Yusuf Hamied chose to concentrate on forging marketing alliances with local partners in a number of countries. He built large manufacturing facilities in India for a wide variety of drugs and dosage forms to supply the global markets. By the late 1990s, Cipla was making generic versions of 400 of the 500 largest-selling brands in the world and exporting a substantial number of them. Yusuf's childhood friend was Zubin Mehta, the renowned conductor of classical Western music, and like him Yusuf orchestrated all of Cipla's manufacturing and logistical complexities with aplomb. Cipla's products are currently sold in about 170 countries, perhaps the largest number for any Indian company.

Ranbaxy, too, commenced exports of bulk drugs and finished dosages quite early. It was the pioneer among Indian pharmaceutical companies in setting up joint ventures. Ranbaxy's patriarch, Bhai Mohan Singh, set up the first one in Nigeria in the late 1970s when I was still with Uniloids. Though this eventually fell apart, it gave Ranbaxy a foothold in Africa where it subsequently expanded. Two more joint ventures followed in the 1980s in Malaysia and Thailand. In 1989, Bhai Mohan Singh made a division of his properties and business among his sons and Parvinder Singh got control of Ranbaxy, though his formal accession to leadership had to wait till February 1993. That was when he emerged successful, after a bitter family struggle in the boardroom, to become the unquestioned leader of the company that was to become India's largest pharmaceutical enterprise the following year. In the decade he was in control, he laid the foundation for the transformation of Ranbaxy from a traditional family business to a company with global ambitions, aided in no small measure by Davinder Singh Brar who succeeded him to the helm of affairs. Parvinder's son, Malvinder Singh, became the CEO of Ranbaxy in 2006. Sadly, the FDA raised serious issues relating to the quality of its products and the integrity of its data. In an astute move, Malvinder sold the family's stake in Ranbaxy to Daiichi Sankyo in 2008. The going has not been good for Ranbaxy in recent years and it will be a challenge for Daiichi to turn around its acquisition.

Dr. Reddy's and Cheminor were new entrants into the business in the mid-1980s. Not surprisingly, our initial route to global markets was through bulk drugs, our main strength at that time. Dr. Reddy's commenced exports of methyldopa in 1986, about a year after starting production, and won the ICMA award for export performance that year. An unfortunate explosion in the methyldopa plant of Merck in Puerto Rico in June 1986 resulted in a temporary short supply and helped Dr. Reddy's accelerate its penetration of global markets for the product. But it was ultimately the cost and quality that sustained exports. In the following year, the methyldopa plant went through a successful inspection by the FDA. Exports commenced to the USA as well as to West Germany (the Berlin Wall was yet to fall), the USSR (the Union of Soviet Socialist Republics was yet to be dissolved),

Japan and several other countries. The key factor that accelerated the exports of bulk drugs and attracted a great deal of interest in the pharmaceutical world was, however, the development of norfloxacin and ciprofloxacin. Though these were relatively new drugs, we had commenced export of these bulk drugs to several countries in the Far East and Europe as early as 1989–90.

Initially, Cheminor was manufacturing only bulk drugs and its major focus was on exports. By 1989, it was the largest producer of ibuprofen in Asia and the third largest in the world. Buoyed by the demand, Cheminor embarked on setting up the largest bulk drug manufacturing facility in India near Visakhapatnam to cater to the production of the new bulk drugs it was developing. Several of these were developed for the first time in India—domperidone (1993), dextromethorphan (1994) and naproxen (1996)—strengthening the impression among customers that Cheminor was consistently able to offer new drugs. The new plant started operating in 1991 and by the mid-1990s, Cheminor was exporting 70 per cent of its production to a number of developed countries in Europe, including Spain and Italy, as well as to Japan and Korea. Most notably, more than half of its production was exported to the USA.

In those days, Spain and Italy were the acknowledged leaders in bulk drug production. I was particularly pleased that we were able to export both old drugs such as methyldopa and ibuprofen and new drugs like norfloxacin and ciprofloxacin to these countries.

The export of finished dosages followed in the wake of the export of bulk drugs. In 1991–92, Ciprolet, Dr. Reddy's brand of ciprofloxacin, helped to accelerate the growth of formulation exports. Dr. Reddy's doubled exports in that year and never looked back. By the mid-1990s, Dr. Reddy's was exporting more finished dosages than bulk drugs. The early 1990s were years when India was running short of foreign exchange. It gave me quite some satisfaction when Dr. Reddy's turned a net foreign exchange earner in 1993–94, Cheminor having achieved this milestone several years earlier.

During the 1980s and 1990s, we chased every opportunity we could. The marketing team pursued every lead it came across and clinched deals, big and small. I travelled extensively, made contacts, and decided in which country we needed to have a substantial presence, either directly or through joint ventures, based on gut feel as much as on data.

I considered Russia a very important market and was keen on entering it even when it was part of the erstwhile USSR. Our Russian odyssey began in 1992 and it is an interesting story, replete with chance encounters, booms and busts.

The Russian market is basically a branded generic business. As in India, brands are promoted in Russia even for generic drugs, though at that time the government also made large purchases through tenders, with payments being made in Indian rupees. This was a mechanism designed to plug the trade deficit that India had run up with the USSR, primarily because of large defence purchases. Sometime before the collapse of the USSR, I went to Russia to visit a pharmaceutical trade fair. On the seat next to me was Rita Singh, the wife of an air force officer who seemed to be involved in some sort of trade in Russia. Some years later, she floated a clutch of high-profile steel, pharmaceutical and helicopter charter companies, all called Mesco. She raised large amounts of money through issues of equity in these companies. She was in the news for her lavish lifestyle, including the permanent suite she had in the Maurya Sheraton in Delhi and her blue Rolls Royce parked in the portico of the hotel. Somewhere along the way, though, she landed in deep financial difficulty.

I struck up a conversation with Rita Singh; she clearly knew a lot about the Russian market. I wondered if there was any way in which we could work with her to enter the Russian market, but it was fortunately only a passing thought. Another person I ran into during that trip was P.V. Venugopal. He was a mechanical engineering graduate from the Indian Institute of Science (IISc) in Bangalore (now Bengaluru) who had retired from the navy as commander. He was a live wire and said he was working with some traders from Calcutta. I told him I was planning to set up operations in Moscow and asked him if he would be interested in leading that effort. He said that he was happy where he was and I left it at that.

Sometime later, I was staying at the Taj Mansingh in Delhi and got a call from the lobby. The person asked if I was Dr Reddy. When I said yes, he identified himself as Venugopal and asked if he could come up. I was puzzled that he wanted to meet me, particularly without any prior intimation, but I was free and asked him to come up. Venugopal came to the room and was nonplussed when he saw me. It turned out that he had come to see Dr Prathap Reddy of Apollo Hospitals who was apparently toying with the idea of setting up operations in Russia! Anyway, he came in and I offered him a cup of coffee. I returned to my theme, and this time I succeeded in persuading him to join us. He came on board in 1992 and set up a representative office of Dr. Reddy's in Russia.

We registered our leading brands, including Omez, Ketorol, Nise and Ciprolet in Russia and all of them became the number one brands. Overall, we were among the top three in a dozen molecules.

Medicines to Moscow: *P.V. Venugopal (right), T.R. Bhoopathy, M.V. Ramana (first and second from left) and I saw off the first chartered flight in 1994*

Logistics were not easy, so we chartered Ilushin IL-76 cargo flights from Uzbekistan Airlines to airlift material from Hyderabad to Moscow. The first flight left in February 1994 with 18 tonnes of medicines and the event was considered important enough to be covered in the national news on television. The cargo flights continued once every six weeks throughout 1994. The Chechnya war was on at that time and we once chartered an Antonov AN-124, the largest cargo plane in the world, to rush supplies to the war zone.

Wanting to deepen our presence in Russia, we entered into a joint venture agreement with Biomed, a leading pharmaceutical manufacturing outfit which had been privatized following the reforms of 1992. The joint venture was inaugurated in October 1995 by P. Chidambaram, our commerce minister at that time, in the presence of Russian health minister E.A. Nachaev. It became operational in November 1996 though the formal function to mark the event took place in March 1997 during the visit of H.D. Deve Gowda who was then our prime minister. In the meanwhile, we had commenced exports to other countries of the erstwhile USSR and had set up representative offices in Tashkent, the capital of Uzbekistan, in 1994 and later in Kazakhstan in 1997.

In the quest for aggressive growth, we were liberal with our credit terms in Russia. This was a mistake, and we were saddled with substantial bad debts in 1996–97. We survived the crisis and seemed to be all set for steady growth on prudent credit terms when another crisis struck. In 1998, the Russian currency suddenly crashed to less than a third of its

Russia, 1997: *Prime Minister H.D. Deve Gowda at our joint venture*

value—from 6 roubles a dollar in August to 21 roubles a dollar a month later. Russia declared a ninety-day moratorium on certain external debt obligations and restructured its internal debt to avoid a complete collapse of its banking and financial system. Food prices doubled and inflation that year was over 80 per cent. In Moscow, about 100,000 people took to the streets in protest, fearing loss of their life's savings deposited in banks. Naturally, Dr. Reddy's lost money as well.

Serious questions were raised about our Russian operations. I was in a quandary. Was it really worth continuing in Russia, in the face of risks and an uncertain future? On the other hand, I was unwilling to believe that Russia was a basket case. Here was a country that had at one time beaten the USA in the space race and had put Sputnik into space in October 1957. I was optimistic that they would bounce back on the strength of their technology. Since 1965 India had been very dependent on Russia for military hardware as well as on its natural resources, including oil. Most importantly, Russia had provided IDPL with the technology and training to manufacture bulk drugs in the mid-1960s, as indeed other industries critical for the country's development. No other developed nation had done so much for India.

I passed on the problem to Satish. I did not want to exit Russia, but did not tell him that. I wanted him to make his own decision as commercial considerations were involved. Satish made a trip to Russia and evaluated the situation carefully. He came back and told me that we should not leave the country. Russia became Satish's baby and he did a splendid job of rebuilding our Russian business, revamping the organization and pumping up our sales force.

In 2000, less than two years after the rouble crisis, our sales in Russia and the CIS (Commonwealth of Independent States) countries had stabilized and crossed 12 million dollars. It more than trebled in the next four years. In 2012, revenues crossed 250 million dollars, which was particularly gratifying as the year marked two decades of our presence in Russia. M.V. Ramana became head of our Russian business some years after Venugopal left and was instrumental in consolidating our presence in the country despite the decision to exit from the joint venture in late 2004. He is now head of our emerging markets business, including Russia and China. Ramana is confident that the Russian business will grow and surpass India as the second largest market for Dr. Reddy's after the USA.

China was another market that we explored, starting with the export of relatively small quantities of formulations. In 1995, we set up a wholly owned subsidiary in Hong Kong to facilitate trade with mainland China and set about understanding the market and expanding our presence. We struck a deal with Mark Lu, a Canadian of Chinese origin based in Taiwan. He had a pharmaceutical business in Canada and had established another, the Kunshan Rotam Pharmaceutical Company, at Kunshan, about forty kilometres from Shanghai. We formed a joint venture, Kunshan Rotam Reddy Pharmaceutical Company Limited, for the manufacture of bulk drugs and finished dosages in 2000.

Foreign companies have been operating in China for a long time. Merck opened an office there over 100 years ago and so did Wellcome and Glaxo. Despite this, joint ventures between foreign and Chinese companies were slow to be established, though the pace has picked up significantly in recent years, particularly in biotechnology and research. One of the first joint ventures to be established was Xian Janssen Pharmaceutical Company in 1985. It is an interesting story. Paul Janssen, the legendary founder of Janssen Pharmaceutica, was deeply interested in the health situation in China and visited the country several times. On one of his visits in 1976—the year that Mao Zedong died—Janssen met George Hatem at a hospital in Beijing. Hatem was a medical doctor of Lebanese origin who had been brought up in the USA. He studied medicine in Beirut and Geneva and travelled to China, where he settled down. He took the Chinese name of Ma Haide and was the first foreigner to be granted Chinese citizenship. He was quite well known in China where he worked alongside Mao, and some said he had been Mao's personal physician.

Hatem was deeply committed to improving health care in China. He and Janssen were drawn to each other by their common conviction. Janssen was keenly interested in helping eliminate parasitic diseases in developing countries and was told that China had already done so. He asked Hatem how this had been achieved and Hatem had no qualms in telling Janssen that this was not the case. Janssen and Hatem decided to work together on tackling this problem and agreed that a pharmaceutical factory to make Western medicine available would help. After years of patient negotiations, Janssen succeeded in entering into a complex agreement with the authorities, whereby he would provide the technology and management while the Chinese would finance the project and be the owners. The product to be manufactured was mebendazole, a Janssen product to treat parasitic intestinal worm infections. This was a case of heart over head, as all the effort could not have been justified by the financial outcomes. The factory commenced operations in 1984, the year Dr. Reddy's was established. The following year, Janssen clinched a deal to establish Xian Janssen, which started production five years later and proved very profitable. Years later, I was in China and happened to visit Xian, famed for the terracotta soldier sculptures dating back to the third century BC. I made a detour just to go past the Janssen factory. I stopped and took some pictures from the outside and felt I was at the site of pharmaceutical history.

The size of China's pharmaceutical market is dazzling. China overtook Germany to become the world's third largest economy in 2007. It was expected to overtake Germany in 2013 or so to become the world's third largest prescription market after the USA and Japan. The generic market alone exceeds 40 billion dollars and its growth has been fuelled in recent years by the health-care reforms initiated in 2009. These reforms were sparked off by the wide disparities in health care—the rural areas were distressingly underserved—and the high costs that were said to be the consequences of privatization. A Chinese saying, 'Once an ambulance siren wails, a pig must be taken to market', reflected the concern over unaffordable health care. The major component of the reform was to provide universal insurance to cover basic medical needs and this triggered an increasing demand for generic drugs. However, accessing this large market profitably is an even larger problem. The regulatory process for approval of drugs is complicated and the industry is fragmented by intense competition among the 5000 or so local companies, the majority of which are small- and medium-sized enterprises. Distribution is complex with thousands of companies operating, though there has been some consolidation in recent years as a result of prodding by the government. Hospitals are the major buyers of generic drugs and retail off-take is relatively small. State-funded hospitals are largely restricted to a list of essential medicines and getting a product on the list is complicated. A vigorous system of price control is in place and frequent price cuts are the norm. State-funded hospitals are also switching over to tender-based procurement, adding to price pressures. Kunshan Rotam Reddy achieved break-even in 2007 and is persevering, but progress is slow.

Satish clinched another interesting joint venture in South Africa. Dilip Shah, the director general of the Indian Pharmaceutical Alliance since its formation, introduced us to the J&J Group in South Africa. This group has nothing to do with Johnson & Johnson, but is named after its founders, Jay Naidoo and Jayendra Naidoo. They are not blood brothers, but brothers-in-arms. Both started out in the trade union movement and have spent a large part of their lives striving to build a just and equitable democracy in South Africa. Jayendra was in the thick of action, negotiating the peace process in the 1990s before he

Brothers-in-arms: *Jay Naidoo (left) and Jayendra Naidoo*

co-founded the J&J Group with Jay in 2000. Jay was the general secretary of the South African Trade Unions and a noted political activist.

The last prison that Nelson Mandela was confined to was Victor Verster, near the town of Paarl in the Cape area. It was in Victor Verster that Jay first met Mandela who received him and a few others with a warm embrace on the momentous morning of 11th February 1990. It was Jay who went to the airport to receive Winnie Mandela and escorted her to the prison. A little while later, Nelson Mandela walked out to freedom, hand-in-hand with Winnie, after twenty-seven years of incarceration.

No man who walked the long road out of prison with Mandela could be anything but extraordinary. One of the most remarkable things about Jay Naidoo is that he wears his achievements lightly and is without a trace of bitterness despite his travails in the struggle against apartheid. He went on to become a minister in Mandela's cabinet, with the portfolio of reconstruction and development and later posts, telecommunications and broadcasting. He then went into business and co-founded J&J with his long-time friend Jayendra Naidoo. Jay is also the chairman of the

Jay Naidoo with Nelson Mandela

Global Alliance for Improved Nutrition, a UN-sponsored and Gates-funded alliance to tackle malnutrition among children. He invited me to join its board, which I did for a while.

Jay's last name is a giveaway of his Indian origins. He traces his roots to Gollapalli in the Chendragiri district of North Arcot in the state of Tamil Nadu, from where his maternal great-grandmother, Angamma, left for distant Africa in 1852. Jay visited Gollapalli in 1999—the same year that he reaffirmed his wedding vows to Lucie, his French-Canadian wife of many years, in the Lakshminarasimhaswamy temple in Malleswaram, Bangalore, tying an Andhra-style *mangalsutra* and exchanging garlands in a typical south Indian Naidu wedding. However, all this nostalgia never clouds Jay's identity. He is first and always a black South African.

We set up Reddy's Laboratories (Proprietary) Limited, South Africa, in 2003 as a joint venture with the J&J Group. Jay accepted our invitation to be the first chairman of the company, with Vikash Salig as the CEO. Vikash had earlier worked in Aspen, a leading pharmaceutical company there, and coincidentally was another South African of Indian origin.

I knew Jay's heart was not in business. Sure enough, he went back to his relentless pursuit of social justice, while Jayendra continues with the business of the J&J Group. We bought out J&J in 2010–11 by mutual agreement. Vikash moved to the USA for personal reasons after doing a splendid job during his tenure as CEO. Dr. Reddy's in South Africa is now a wholly owned subsidiary. I hope it will serve the needs of the South African people as its first chairman, Jay Naidoo, would have wished.

We also set up joint ventures in New Zealand and Australia, not with established businesses but with individuals. After the operations commenced, the joint-venture partners opted to leave and Dr. Reddy's bought out their stakes.

Joint ventures often help in facilitating entry and reduce risks, particularly when market knowledge is limited. But in order to be long-lived, both partners need to bring in value continuously, be aligned to the same goals and be prepared for the long haul.

By 2005, Dr. Reddy's products were being sold in over sixty countries and accounted for over 65 per cent of our total revenues. The complexities of packing medicines for so many countries and making a large number of small deliveries—in addition to the demands on management time these entailed—were not commensurate with the earnings from the markets where we had only a marginal presence. Prasad and Satish therefore set about rationalizing our international business, and from 2008 onward explored options to restructure our presence in our marginal markets. As a consequence, they negotiated a strategic alliance with GlaxoSmithKline in June 2009 to develop and market generic products manufactured by Dr. Reddy's to many countries across the world.

For the most important markets, however, my approach from the beginning has been to go it alone, even if we had to start with alliances. The most important market to me was the USA. Europe, too, appeared to be a significant opportunity. We first had a limited alliance in the USA and then built our own presence there, brick-by-brick. In contrast, we tried to buy our way into Europe with a dramatic move—and sobering consequences.

10 EUROPEAN FORAYS

First European generic foray, Romania, 1996: (R–L) Me, Cristina
Garlasu, P.V. Venugopal and Cristina's husband

No Indian pharmaceutical company had its own office in Europe till we
set one up in France in 1993. It was an unusual move for that time, but
we went ahead as we thought we could better serve customers of our
growing European bulk drug business. Ranbaxy set up their regional
office in London in 1994 and then acquired Rima Laboratories in Ireland
in 1996 for manufacturing generics.

Cameron Reid, head of our US business, introduced Prasad to
Luc Lamirault, a French national who was in charge of the bulk drug
business of Roussel Uclaf, the second largest French pharmaceutical

company before it was acquired by Hoechst in 1997. Prasad asked Luc if he would be interested in setting up our subsidiary in Europe and invited him to Hyderabad. Luc was probably sceptical about Indian companies. He spent a day at our plants and was quite surprised—our facilities seemed bigger than those at Roussel. I met him after his visit and outlined our discovery research programme to him. Luc was astonished that a company in India had embarked on discovery research. He decided to join us. Reddy Cheminor SA was incorporated in France and Luc set up our first office in his house at Saint-Denis-D'Authou—a quaint habitation of 500 people about 120 km from Paris—as it was the quickest way and he wanted to waste neither money nor time. The business grew—as did Luc's family—so Reddy Cheminor moved to a proper office in the city of Chartres, about forty kilometres away. Luc was with us for a decade and contributed substantially to building our bulk drug business in Europe. He now not only runs his own regulatory consulting company but is also the first vice president of the General Council of Eure-et-Loir and the councillor of the canton of Thiron-Gardais.

Romania was the first of our significant forays into the generic business in Europe. The communist regime of Nicolae Ceauşescu was displaced in the Romanian revolution of 1989 and the country began a transition to democracy and a capitalist market economy. In mid-1993, Romania applied for membership to the European Union. Around that time, Dr Nelu Ionescu, the Romanian ambassador to India and Sri Lanka, visited Hyderabad seeking to increase bilateral trade between Romania and India. P.V. Venugopal was instrumental in following up this lead and contacted the Romanian Chamber of Commerce and Industry for further information. Coincidentally, the person at the India desk was Cristina Garlasu, the daughter of the ambassador who had visited us, and she provided clear answers to many of Venugopal's questions.

The situation in Romania was interesting. First, pharmaceutical majors were not as entrenched in Romania as they were in Western

Europe. Second, Romania had gone through a period of political upheaval and economic isolation. I intuitively felt that the country would overcome its distress and that the economic liberalization then under way would lead to growth and increased demand for medicines. Most importantly, the drug regulatory system in Romania did not require us to undertake expensive and time-consuming redevelopment of the products that we sold in India and Russia, so we could make a quick and low-risk entry. I asked Venugopal to go ahead and set up a Romanian operation.

Venugopal was impressed with Cristina and offered her the job of country manager though she had no experience in pharmaceuticals. Cristina accepted our offer and chose a villa for her office. Romania is a beautiful country and our office was a delight. I visited it in the spring of 1996 when the magnolia trees were in spectacular bloom. The Indo-Romanian Chamber of Commerce held a function at the Elisabeta Palace in Bucharest to mark the start of our operations in the country. The palace had been the residence of King Michael of Romania till he was forced to abdicate by the Communists in late 1947 and exiled from the country. Interestingly, King Michael is the great-great-grandson of Queen Victoria, who was crowned the Empress of India in 1876.

Many things have changed in Romania since then. The Elisabeta Palace was restored to Michael though the monarchy had been long abolished. The economy has grown rapidly, particularly after the turn of the millennium and we have benefited from it. The country finally joined the European Union in 2007 and the drug regulatory system changed vastly to conform to the requirements of the European Union. Our office in Romania has grown to ninety people and our brands are now well known in the country. One thing that has not changed, however, is that Cristina continues to be our country head.

Our first notable foray into Western Europe for the generics business was with an acquisition in March 2002. After our ADR issue in 2001, we had the money to expand and Europe was a large market. We therefore looked for a toehold in Western Europe. The UK seemed to be an ideal location as it was English-speaking. Cameron Reid, the head of our generics business in the USA, and Luc Lamirault zeroed in on BMS Laboratories, a relatively small pharmaceutical business with annual revenues of around 10 million pounds (about 14.2 million dollars). We acquired it along with its wholly owned subsidiary, Meridian Healthcare, for 9 million pounds (about 12.8 million dollars). The company had a portfolio of about 100 products, though a number of them were small-volume and yielded low revenue. The acquisition came with a packaging facility in Beverly and a formulations manufacturing unit in London which also did some contract manufacturing. We shut down the latter as it was quite rudimentary, but the packaging facility at Beverly continues to be operational. Business has grown in the decade since we made the acquisition, but very slowly.

Our big move was when we acquired betapharm, Germany's fourth largest generic company, in February 2006, for 480 million euros (about 570 million dollars or 25 billion rupees at the then prevailing exchange rates). It was an audacious move as Dr. Reddy's total revenues for the previous year were only 370 million dollars (16 billion rupees). The biggest cross-border deal till then was Tata Tea's acquisition of UK's Tetley for about 420 million dollars in 1999. betapharm was the largest overseas acquisition by an Indian company at that time outside of the oil and gas sector.

betapharm had attracted a great deal of interest from a number of companies. Ranbaxy was one of them and in the end it was a bidding war with them that we won. betapharm seemed to be an attractive proposition for a number of reasons. It had a share of about 3.5 per cent of the generic market in Germany with a portfolio of about 150 products and a healthy pipeline. It had a 250-strong sales force and had clocked consistent growth. It did not have a manufacturing facility, but had contract manufacturing arrangements, which suited us perfectly as we thought we could gradually shift to lower-cost manufacturing in India. Above all, we did not have a presence in Germany and it made sense to buy into Europe's largest generic market.

betapharm is headquartered in Augsburg in southern Bavaria. The city has a hoary history. It was founded in 15 BC and is Germany's third oldest city. I was fascinated by its antiquity and the wonderful way in which its historical sites were preserved. Though its main railway station was built in the 1840s, the first for a major city in Germany, it still functions. I was invited to tea by the mayor when I visited Augsburg and he told me about some of the city's famous inhabitants. Augsburg had been home to Bertolt Brecht in his childhood as well as to Mozart's father, whose house is now a tourist attraction. Rudolph Diesel, the inventor of the engine that bears his name, was sent to stay with his uncle in Augsburg when he was twelve and studied at the Industrial School there. I glanced at the local newspaper the next day in my hotel room and the picture of the mayor with me caught my eye. There was also a news story below the picture and I was about to telephone the reception to request a translation when I remembered that I had obtained a certificate of competence in translation from German when I was doing my doctorate. I thought I should have a go at reading it and was quite pleased to find that I remembered enough German to get the gist of the news item.

Augsburg is also home to Anita Bose Pfaff, the daughter of Netaji Subhas Chandra Bose. As is well known in India, Netaji's health was shattered by long incarceration in British prisons. Released from detention on the condition that he would leave the country, Netaji went to Vienna for medical treatment in 1933. He also completed his monumental book, *The Indian Struggle 1920–1934*, while in Vienna with secretarial help from Emilie Schenkl, the daughter of an Austrian veterinarian, whom he married in 1937. He came back to India to become president of the Congress party in 1938 and to lead protests. He was arrested again. In 1941, Netaji escaped from detention disguised as a Pathan and reached Peshawar. He went on to Kabul from where he crossed over to Russia. He then travelled to Moscow masquerading as an Italian count. From there he reached Germany to garner support from the Nazis for the struggle in India. He stayed in Berlin for about two years and met Adolf Hitler in 1942. Anita, Netaji's only child, was born in Vienna the same year.

Anita lives in Augsburg with her husband, a former member of Germany's parliament. Both were professors of economics at the University of Augsburg and Anita was particularly interested in social and health policy. She invited me to dinner and I have memories of a very pleasant evening. Anita bears a striking resemblance to her father whose face is familiar to every Indian.

Anita was on the advisory board of beta Institut, a non-profit organization in the betapharm group. She was closely associated in an advisory role with two of its programmes: one providing support to women with breast cancer and the other researching the rehabilitation of critically sick children.

The tranquil environs of Augsburg gave no hint of the torrid times that were to follow our acquisition of betapharm. A few months after the acquisition, we had problems with Salutas, where a large number of betapharm's products were contract manufactured. In 2005, Salutas had become a subsidiary of Sandoz, the generics arm of Novartis, which had a significant generic business in Germany and was our competitor. It took till early 2007 to sort out our problems with them. In the meanwhile, sales suffered and we also had to accelerate the transfer of production to Hyderabad.

Then came a bombshell.

Under the system that prevailed in Germany, generic products were branded with the company's name and promoted to doctors and chemists. In 2007, the German government pressed ahead with amendments to laws to contain rising health-care costs. It allowed insurance companies to call for tenders for the supply of drugs to chemists for filling prescriptions of those insured by them. In effect, doctors no longer chose the manufacturer of generic products but insurance companies did. The sales force, which was betapharm's strength, no longer mattered. The first tenders for sixty-four products were called by Allgemeine Ortskrankenkasse (AOK), the largest state insurer covering over twenty-four million people—about a third of the population—and finalized in November 2008. betapharm quoted, but was hobbled by the uncertainty of supply from Salutas and the complexities of the ongoing transfer of production to Hyderabad. Generic companies quoted steep discounts to remain in business. Prices of generics plummeted and with them the profitability of the generics business in Germany.

The 25 billion rupees we had paid for betapharm was largely for the value of its ongoing business and not for its physical assets. It was therefore accounted for as intangible assets and goodwill. With the core of its business collapsing, we needed to account for the impairment. We wrote off 14 billion rupees in 2008–09. Because of the write-off, for the first time in our history, we reported a net loss of over 5 billion rupees, a dark shadow over our silver jubilee year. We wrote off another 8.5 billion rupees in the following year, erasing the value of the acquisition from the balance sheet of Dr. Reddy's and moved on.

Our other acquisitions in Europe and elsewhere did not fare as badly. We made an interesting acquisition of Chirotech Technology Limited in the UK in 2008 for 32 million dollars (about 1.3 billion rupees). Chirotech was a subsidiary of Dowpharma, a unit of Dow Chemical Company headquartered in the USA. Chirotech has a technology development centre at Cambridge engaged in developing chemical processes for complex bulk drugs and intermediates for customers in the pharmaceutical industry. It also has a production facility at Mirfield in West Yorkshire, which can scale up laboratory processes and manufacture products on a limited scale.

I loved the idea of acquiring Chirotech when I got a glimpse of their technology platforms. As I had suspected when I had first heard their name, they have considerable expertise in chiral chemistry, particularly chemical and enzymatic catalytic methods, based on which they offer an impressively wide range of chiral compounds for the pharmaceutical industry. This technology platform would potentially be useful in the development of more efficient processes for certain kinds of bulk drugs at Dr. Reddy's.

Chirotech has deep expertise in the synthesis of prostaglandins which are fascinatingly complex chiral molecules. Just a few milligrams of prostaglandins are produced in the human body in a day, but when used as a drug they have a wide range of pharmacological effects, including inducing childbirth as well as abortion, treating glaucoma, peptic ulcers, pulmonary hypertension and even for growing longer eyelashes!

Though the human body produces prostaglandins without any fuss, their chemical synthesis in a laboratory is a different story altogether. Prostaglandins are a group of unsaturated carboxylic acids with twenty carbon atoms, and were first isolated in the 1930s by Ulf von Euler of Sweden from human semen. Believing them to be a secretion of the prostate gland, he named them prostaglandins, but they were later shown to be secreted by many other tissues in the body. Structural elucidation had to wait for more than twenty years. Amazingly, the first chemical synthesis of the major prostaglandins was achieved by Harvard's Prof. E.J. Corey in 1967, after just about two years of effort. By 1969, Corey developed a unique synthetic scheme where all the prostaglandins could be synthesized from one intermediate compound which has come to be called Corey's lactone. Corey won the Japan Prize in 1989 for this pioneering contribution to the synthesis of prostaglandins. Just a year later, Corey won the Nobel Prize in Chemistry for his contribution to organic synthesis as his mind-boggling achievements spanned the entire spectrum of organic chemistry. The son of Lebanese immigrants to the USA, whose mother struggled to bring him up after the early death of his father, Corey is probably the greatest living chemist. Most accomplished chemists dream of developing one reaction that bears their name; Corey has at least half a dozen reactions named after him and used in laboratories all over the world. His work, particularly the development of the theory of retrosynthetic analysis, revolutionized the teaching of chemistry at Harvard University where he is professor emeritus, actively enjoying what he calls the 'intrinsic beauty' of organic chemistry.

Chirotech moved into more spacious premises in Cambridge Science Park in 2011 which now houses the Chirotech Technology Centre. I

Chirotech moves to Cambridge Science Park, 2011: *Yusuf Hamied (centre)*
inaugurates Chirotech's new premises

made it a point to attend the formal opening of the centre by my old
friend Yusuf Hamied. I was amazed when I received a letter from David
Cameron, the prime minister of the UK, appreciating the investment
and wishing us success. I was very touched by the gesture and felt
that Dr. Reddy's was welcome in the UK. I could not help wondering
if India is as hospitable and welcoming to foreign investors. It could
make a big difference.

Chirotech not only excels in chiral chemistry but also makes activated
methyl ether polyethylene glycols (mPEGs), which are used for the
conjugation of proteins, antibody fragments and peptides, to improve
the stability and delivery of biological drugs. Interestingly, Dr. Reddy's
sourced activated mPEG from Chirotech even before the acquisition for
manufacturing pegylated filgrastim, an important biological product.
A new manufacturing facility was set up in 2010 at our Cuernavaca site
in Mexico with a multi-tonne annual capacity for pharmaceutical-grade
mPEG alcohols; part of the output will be supplied to Chirotech for
producing activated mPEGs at the Mirfield facility. These products are

sold under the PEGtech brand and I am optimistic that we will be a global leader for this product group.

Our Cuernavaca plant in Mexico manufacturing bulk drugs and intermediates was acquired from Roche in 2005 for 61 million dollars. The company was called Industrias Químicas Falcon de México and manufactured eighteen bulk drugs and intermediates. It was the first overseas bulk drug plant that we acquired. It had a very good steroid manufacturing facility. Dr. Reddy's did not manufacture steroids in India. The principal bulk drug manufactured in Cuernavaca was naproxen, which was an old product for us. Many were surprised that we made this acquisition 10,000 miles away from India for a company whose major products we were capable of manufacturing in Hyderabad. That it was so far from India was part of its advantage—it was so much closer to the USA, which is our principal bulk drug market. The process chemistry for the major products was familiar, but we had acquired not just the plant but the business. Most importantly, we had acquired a new set of customers.

We also acquired a real live falcon with our acquisition of Industrias Químicas Falcon de México. I was invited to view it when I visited the plant sometime after its acquisition. The falcon is a fearsome bird of prey and some species apparently dive at speeds of over 300 kilometres per hour, which must make them the fastest animals on the planet. Around the time that we acquired the Cuernavaca plant, a scholarly study was published on the IQ of birds based on their feeding habits, and the falcon topped the charts. I did not know for sure, however, what the feeding habit of our falcon was and what it would make of an alien despite its intelligence, so I kept a safe distance. The falcon, however, seemed to be quite comfortable with its Indian visitors.

More importantly, the people at the Cuernavaca plant were comfortable with their Indian ownership. Cuernavaca has a tradition of not being unnerved by foreign presence. Located eighty-five kilometres from Mexico City, Cuernavaca was where American psychologist Timothy Leary of Harvard University experimented with eating psilocybin mushrooms in the 1960s. For the first time he experienced the psychedelic effects of psilocybin, a tryptamine compound structurally similar to the antidepressant serotonin, which naturally occurs in this group of mushrooms. Leary was an advocate of psychedelic treatment and went on to conduct major experiments on their use. This eventually got him fired from Harvard. The Hotel Camino Real Sumiya where I stayed in Cuernavaca was once the home of Barbara Hutton, the granddaughter of Frank Woolworth, who founded the Woolworth chain of department stores in the USA. She inherited a fortune and ran through seven husbands in her rather tragic life; one of them was the famously debonair Cary Grant, who ruled Hollywood for three decades. The hotel still has an authentic Kabuki theatre built by Japanese craftsmen who were brought to Cuernavaca.

We were far less quirky than these earlier residents of Cuernavaca; though English is a foreign language there we spoke the language of chemistry which was comfortingly familiar. Among the major issues that confronts a global organization is to make sure that employees in far-flung outposts have a sense of belonging to the parent organization. I am glad that Cuernavaca is now fully integrated into Dr. Reddy's.

When I visited the Cuernavaca plant, the first thing that struck me was its sophistication. It is nothing like an Indian bulk drug manufacturing facility. The design philosophy is vastly different from frugality, which is the hallmark of Indian plants, and there is a lot of automation. There is much that we can learn from them.

The most recent acquisition we have made is also in Europe and it is yet another technology acquisition. Late in 2012, we acquired the entire shareholding of OctoPlus N.V. in Leiden, Netherlands, for 27 million euros. OctoPlus has a specialized drug delivery platform which enables the safe formulation of long-acting injectables. The principal advantage of this technology is that it avoids bursts of drug release in some injectables where the drug release is designed to occur over an extended period of time. OctoPlus is currently making losses, but hopes to break even soon. It has about forty customers and the technology will be valuable for several generic long-acting injectables that will be manufactured by Dr. Reddy's.

I am particularly pleased by the technology acquisitions we made in Europe. Germany, France and Britain were at the forefront of advances in medicine and chemistry in the nineteenth century and the first half of the twentieth century. The grievous devastation of the Second World War was a setback for humanity, but more so for Europe. All of this has been written up and is well known, but sometimes the enormity of a distant tragedy sinks in fully with a personal encounter. I was once travelling to Oslo to meet people in Borregaard, a pulp and paper company in Norway, which also made lignin-based vanillin, a key raw material for the manufacture of methyldopa that was in short supply soon after we started its manufacture in Dr. Reddy's. I noticed that the person seated next to me seemed to have a problem walking, perhaps from some old injury. I struck up a conversation and my curiosity was aroused when he said he was a Norwegian chemical engineer. I asked him about himself, which was perhaps an impolite thing to do, and was taken aback when he said he was interned in a Nazi concentration camp and was lucky to be alive. He told me a little about what happened there. When I pressed him like a journalist with more questions, he asked me to stop. He told me he woke up with nightmares even after four decades and did not want to dwell on the past.

The Norwegian survivor was travelling to a family get-together in Oslo. He told me they were a large family and, after the war, made it a point to meet once a year. It seemed to me that they valued their togetherness so much more because it was nearly lost. I was deeply moved.

The British and the Europeans have rebuilt their lives, their science and their economies with great courage and resilience after they were shattered by the Second World War. They are investing in science with a sense of purpose and I hope the notable outcomes will be for the benefit of humanity. Our facilities in Cambridge and Leiden are small indicators of the potential of British and European science and scientists and the difference that they can make.

11 POT OF GOLD

The US team, around 2002: *(L–R) Seshu Srinivas, Andrew Miller, Cameron Reid, Prasad and Satish. (Rear row) Adam Levitt, Mark Hartman and Tim Crew*

For most people around the world, America is the land of boundless opportunity where hard work leads to prosperity and happiness, regardless of social hierarchies. This is the essence of the 'American dream'. It is rooted in the values enshrined in the Declaration of Independence. Over the years, far from being tarnished, it has been burnished to become a glowing beacon of hope for hundreds of millions of people yearning for freedom, dignity and success. Millions of people from distant lands have flocked to America in pursuit of the American dream.

The prospect of getting rich quickly has added to the lure of America. In 1848, gold was discovered in the settlement of Coloma, on the banks of the American river in California. News spread remarkably rapidly, and the gold rush started. In the year that followed, 90,000 people streamed into California chasing their dreams, confident that with perseverance, hard work and luck, they could find their pot of gold. They were largely Americans, but over a third of them were foreigners from every continent in the world, including Chinese gold merchants and miners from Asia.

This was in 1849. Jumble the figures of the year a little and you will come up with 1984, the year in which the generic gold rush began to the largest market in the world by value, and the most profitable one. Dr. Reddy's was established the same year. Though the opportunity was open to pharmaceutical companies all over the world, the regulatory requirements of the FDA were so demanding that only technologically evolved companies could realistically hope to chase the American dream. American companies were, of course, the first to take advantage of the legislative changes. Teva, the Israeli generic company, made a significant early impact and emerged a generic behemoth on the back of a series of aggressive acquisitions in the 1990s, even as Indian companies were taking their first steps.

An understanding of the regulatory history of the USA is necessary for appreciating the enormous opportunity that opened up for generic companies in 1984. This was the year Republican Senator Orrin Hatch and Democratic Congressman Henry Waxman pushed through the bipartisan Drug Price Competition and Patent Term Restoration Act. Commonly known as the Hatch Waxman Act, it paved the regulatory pathway for the introduction of generic medicines into the USA. Prior to 1962, the FDA approved medicines if they were shown to be safe. Thereafter, new licensing regulations permitted approval of drugs only if they also demonstrated efficacy. One consequence was that generic versions of patented drugs also needed to furnish evidence of efficacy, at least from published scientific literature. The problem was that adequate published literature was not often available and few generic companies were willing to go through the trouble and expense of putting together a package that would meet with FDA's approval. Thus, though patents had expired for a number of drugs, there were no generic versions available to bring down the prices of patent-expired drugs.

For the first time, the Hatch Waxman Act laid out an abbreviated procedure for the approval of generic drugs if they were identical to the branded drug without the need to prove safety and efficacy again. The clear and relatively inexpensive regulatory pathway spurred the quick introduction of generic drugs after their patents expired. Obviously, the companies that held the patents and sold the branded product lobbied hard against the Hatch Waxman Act. The legislation, however, finally went through as these companies were also given several benefits, including the extension of patent terms to compensate for the regulatory review period. It was a tough balancing act and the compromise was hard fought but, to their credit, Hatch and Waxman pulled it off, saving billions of dollars in health-care costs in the USA. Orrin Hatch is now serving his seventh consecutive term as Senator and Henry Waxman, his twentieth as Congressman.

Apart from clarity in the regulatory pathway, the USA has laws that mandate or permit generic substitution of branded drugs unless prohibited by the prescribing doctor. These are state laws and are therefore not uniformly applicable throughout the country. As of 2011, fifteen states in the USA compelled substitution, while thirty-five permitted pharmacies to substitute generics. Forty states required generic substitution if the patient was prescribed drugs under Medicare, the federally funded insurance programme, which covered about forty-nine million people at a huge cost of about 550 billion dollars. Because of these laws, generic companies are saved the expense of promoting a generic product to doctors but they have to ensure that the product is stocked in the pharmacy. Generic products are therefore marketed directly to large retail chains like Walmart and distributors who, in turn, sell to pharmacies as well as to hospitals and other institutions that buy in large quantities. The competition to get on to the shelves of the retailer is intense among generic manufacturers, and unless a generic company is cost-efficient it will be out of the market.

The Hatch Waxman Act also provided an incentive for generic manufacturers to challenge the validity of patents that were wrongly granted, or develop a formulation that did not infringe the patent. This was to encourage the earliest possible entry of an affordable generic. Patent challenges invariably invite expensive litigation and, as an incentive, the first generic manufacturer to challenge the patent is granted the exclusive right to market the generic for 180 days, provided the challenge is successful. If a company succeeds in launching a generic drug with 180 days of exclusivity, it hits the jackpot. Generic prices during the 180-day exclusivity are very high—as much as 50 per cent to 80 per cent of the price of the branded drug. After the exclusivity, prices crash to as little as 3 per cent to10 per cent of the branded price, depending on the intensity of competition.

When the Hatch Waxman Act was passed in 1984, less than one in five prescriptions was filled in the USA by generic drugs. By 2000, one of two prescriptions was filled by generics, reflecting the explosive growth in the generic market, particularly in the 1990s. I wanted a piece of the action and so did Prasad. Naturally, I watched the moves of other Indian companies closely.

Ranbaxy's foray into the USA, with its dramatic ups and downs, attracted a lot of attention. Ranbaxy started off quietly exporting bulk drugs in the late 1980s to the USA. Parvinder was, however, convinced that it was necessary to make a dent in the lucrative market for generic drugs and it was cefaclor, a second-generation cephalosporin,which provided the opportunity. It was marketed by Eli Lilly under the brand name Ceclor from 1979 onward and became the world's top-selling antibiotic. Eli Lilly's patents for the product expired in 1992, though it continued to be protected by process patents. This meant that any company that could develop a process different from the patented one could enter the market.

Ranbaxy developed a different process to manufacture cefaclor by the end of 1991 and made huge investments in putting up a manufacturing plant. It was quite a risk as the plan to break into the market was still unclear. Fortunately for Ranbaxy, Eli Lilly recognized the possible threat from Ranbaxy entering the global markets with a much cheaper cefaclor and struck a deal to pick up their entire production of the penultimate intermediate of the bulk drug at 2000 dollars per tonne. Ranbaxy's costs would not have been more than a fourth of this. The huge margin ensured that the potentially damaging early investment in building production facilities paid off handsomely. A year later, the two companies formed a joint venture, Eli Lilly Ranbaxy, to market Eli Lilly's products in India. But the crowning moment was in January 1995 when the two companies signed an agreement to market Ranbaxy's generic products in the USA and other countries. This was followed by an agreement to set up two more joint ventures, one in India for developing generic products and the other in the USA for developing new products. Ranbaxy then acquired Ohm Laboratories,

The Ranbaxy–Eli Lilly Alliance, 1995: *Parvinder Singh (left) and D.S. Brar (centre) forged a landmark but short-lived alliance*

a pharmaceutical company in the USA, in 1995. It was poised to stride into success when disaster struck.

Ranbaxy submitted its application for approval of cefaclor to the FDA in late 1995 and Parvinder went to meet Eli Lilly's management at Raleigh in 1996 brimming with optimism. He was in for a rude shock. He was summarily told that Eli Lilly was calling off the joint venture for marketing generics in the USA, which effectively put paid to all their joint ventures. This was a huge setback for Ranbaxy. Though Parvinder did not know about it then, Eli Lilly had clinched a sweet deal with Mylan, a generic company in the USA, to distribute cefaclor for a fee rather than for a revenue or profit share. Ranbaxy coped with the situation as best as it could and decided to go on its own into the American market. It made a deal with Eli Lilly to buy their cefaclor and sold it through Teva at a loss, so that it would have a ready market when its own product was approved. Ranbaxy also obtained a licence for some old Lilly products to have a basket of products to market so that its own operations would have a chance of achieving viability quickly. Ranbaxy's cefaclor was approved in 1997. By 2001, Ranbaxy recovered lost ground and crossed the 100 million–dollar mark for revenues from the USA.

Sun Pharma, founded by Dilip Shangvi, followed a different path. Beneath the soft-spoken, unassuming and unflappable exterior lurks the shrewdest brain in the business. Dilip Shangvi started off at the distribution end of the business as a stockist in Calcutta for Torrent and Tamil Nadu Dadha Pharmaceuticals. He set up Sun Pharmaceutical Industries with a few psychiatry products in 1983 and a small manufacturing unit for formulations in Gujarat. He focused on high-margin neuropsychiatry and cardiovascular products, so that he could concentrate his field force in the big cities, where specialists in these diseases practised, and marketed his products effectively. He acquired companies and brands in a series of carefully calculated moves in the 1990s. Several companies that he acquired were not doing well and he turned them around, a pattern that he continued in later years. Though Dilip Shangvi is a commerce graduate, he is scientifically oriented. He invested in setting up a process research laboratory in the early 1990s.

In 1997, Dilip Shangvi made two interesting decisions. He acquired Tamil Nadu Dadha Pharmaceuticals, the company for which he was the stockist some twenty years before, and established a presence in oncology and women's health. He also invested in Caraco, a loss-making company in Detroit, signalling his serious intentions to compete in the American market. He gradually built up his stake in Caraco as well as a portfolio of generic products for the USA. Though there were hiccups, Dilip Shangvi navigated the complextites with his trademark astuteness and Sun Pharma emerged as an important generic company in the USA.

My first foray into the US market was, unsurprisingly, with bulk drugs. Cheminor went through a successful inspection by the FDA for its ibuprofen in 1987 and exports commenced. Just when everything seemed to be going well, Ethyl Corporation in the USA lodged a complaint in July 1991 seeking imposition of anti-dumping and countervailing duties on imports of ibuprofen from Cheminor. Ethyl Corporation was a large manufacturer of chemicals for the petroleum, plastics and chemical industries. Its subsidiary, Whitby Pharmaceuticals, was also a leading producer of ibuprofen in the country. In September 1991, the US International Trade Commission held that the domestic market was hurt by Cheminor's receipt of 'subsidies' from the Indian government and dumping of bulk ibuprofen into the American market at less than fair value. I was quite surprised as the only benefits we had from the Indian government were advance licences to import raw material for exports, exemption from customs duties for import of raw material and from excise duties for export production, a concessional rate of interest to finance exports and exemption from income tax on export profits. Barring the income tax exemption, manufacturers in the USA had pretty much the same advantages, if not more. Despite this, the US Department of Commerce imposed a countervailing duty of 44 per cent and a dumping margin of 116 per cent on Cheminor's ibuprofen. A legal wrangle followed and I had my first taste of litigation in the USA.

In a tactical move, we withdrew ibuprofen for a short while from the US market and Ethyl Corporation withdrew its complaint as they were unable to show that our entry had harmed the sales of their ibuprofen. The direct consequence of the dispute was that our sole distributor, Flavine International, cancelled its orders for ibuprofen. This was a blessing in disguise as we decided to have a direct presence in the USA. The person who joined us to lead the effort was Cameron Reid. Prasad first met Cameron when he was working as the executive vice president of Roussel Corporation, a division of Roussel Uclaf. Cameron was interested in sourcing bulk drugs from Cheminor. They got along well and Prasad asked Cameron if he would be interested in joining us. Cameron was hesitant as he had entrepreneurial ambitions, so we offered him a 25 per cent stake in the US business. The stake was not the only thing that Cameron found attractive. Years later, somebody asked Cameron why he had left a big corporation like Roussel to join us. Cameron's response was typically laconic. He said, 'Because they are quick and flexible.'

Cameron joined us in late 1992 and set up Reddy Cheminor Inc. in New Jersey, the heartland of the pharmaceutical industry in the USA. Without wasting any time, Cameron started work from his basement while he scouted around for an office. He found a house that seemed suitable and we bought it for about 400,000 dollars. Strangely, this seemed to be a pattern for starting our operations. I had rented a house in Hyderabad for an office and laboratory when Dr. Reddy's was set up; later, our operations in France and Romania too began in houses. The decision to set up our own office proved a crucial factor in accelerating our growth in the USA.

Cheminor did well to develop a number of bulk drugs for the USA. While ibuprofen was an old drug, some of the subsequent bulk drugs developed by Cheminor for the USA were new drugs in anticipation of patent expiry. Generic manufacturers are always in a rush to develop their formulation and be among the first to launch the drug after patent expiry, so they are normally willing to pay a higher price initially for assured supplies that do not infringe any process patent. The prices of course decline as more competition sets in. Cheminor, therefore, switched its attention to such bulk drugs—ranitidine was the first of the new drugs that it developed.

While bulk drugs were good business, I was keen to move up the value chain in the USA and market finished dosages that were more profitable. So was Prasad, who worked tirelessly with his team to build a formulation facility to FDA standards on the outskirts of Hyderabad. The plant was commissioned in 1996–97 and an application was filed with the FDA for generic ranitidine in December 1997—the first application for FDA approval from Cheminor for a generic product.

A successful patent challenge would, of course, be the icing on the cake. The problem was that we knew little about the minefields in patent litigation. It seemed sensible to partner with a generics company that knew the ropes and would give us access to the market.

Cheminor entered into not one but two alliances. As subsequent events proved, it was prudent to have two strings to the bow. First, there was an agreement with Par Pharmaceutical to market fourteen generic products in 1995. Par Pharmaceutical had been founded in 1978 and had a growing generic business. In 1997, Prasad and Cameron forged a further alliance for Cheminor with Schein Pharmaceutical, a leading generics company in the USA. Schein also picked up a 12.8 per cent stake in the equity of Cheminor for 10 million dollars and a position on the board of directors. We anticipated that we would benefit from their knowledge of the generics business. At that time, Schein had about 160 generic products in the market and one of the largest sales forces for a generic company. However, the alliance was terminated when Schein was acquired in mid-2000 by Watson Pharmaceuticals, another generic company in the USA. But we still had access to the market for our initial products because of our agreement with Par

Pharmaceutical. We launched ranitidine in 2000 through them, our first product in the US market.

Prasad and Cameron charted an aggressive course for our generics business in the USA and September 1998 saw a landmark event. Cheminor filed its first patent challenge for Eli Lilly's fluoxetine, a drug to treat depression. Eli Lilly had initially obtained approval for the 20 mg strength of fluoxetine in December 1987 and marketed it under the brand name Prozac. Subsequently, it introduced the 10 mg strength in 1992 and the 40 mg strength in 1997. The brand sold more than a billion dollars. Though other companies had challenged the patents by filing for regulatory approvals for the lower strengths, we were the first to file for the 40 mg strength and Eli Lilly promptly sued us. If we succeeded, we would hit the jackpot with 180 days of marketing exclusivity for this strength.

In February 1999, we challenged the patents of Astra Zeneca's Prilosec and in the following month, Bayer's Cipro. These were our stellar drugs in India—omeprazole and ciprofloxacin. In 2001, we were locked in combat with Eli Lilly again when we challenged the patents for Zyprexa, the generic name of which is olanzapine. This was followed by a filing with the FDA in December 2001 for approval of an alternative to Pfizer's widely used antihypertensive, Norvasc. This was not the usual patent challenge by a generic company, but had a twist to it, which again was a landmark event.

The active ingredient in Norvasc is amlodipine. Pfizer had developed two salts, amlodipine besylate and amlodipine maleate, and submitted clinical data obtained from the trials of both the salts to the FDA. They, however, chose to obtain approval for marketing amlodipine besylate as it was easier to make into tablets. The term of the patent covering amlodipine was set to expire in February 2003, but it was granted an extension till July 2006 to compensate for the time taken for regulatory review as provided for in the Hatch Waxman Act. We thought the patent term extension ought to apply only to amlodipine besylate, the product on the market. We therefore developed amlodipine maleate and filed for approval to get an early entry. We did not use the normal route of an abbreviated new drug application for approval of a generic product based on bioequivalence with the innovator product, but as amlodipine maleate was previously unapproved, we filed a full application for new drug approval, mainly based on published literature, to establish safety and efficacy—a 'paper NDA' (New Drug Application), in the parlance of the US drug industry. Pfizer promptly sued us.

The paper NDA was the first for an Indian company. Pfizer was marketing Norvasc from 1992 and it had grown to be the company's second largest brand after Lipitor with US sales of 2 billion dollars in 2002. When we filed for approval of amlodipine maleate in December 2001, there was no other challenger and the prospect—if we succeeded—of an extended period of exclusivity till the patent term extension expired in 2006 was enticing, to say the least. Our *total* revenues in 2001–02 were 16.5 billion rupees, about 270 million dollars. The revenues from just this one product, even assuming a modest share of the Norvasc market at a steep discount to Pfizer's price, could well have exceeded our total revenues at that time. It is easy to see why we were excited. Pfizer was to receive another jolt about a year later. Ranbaxy challenged the Lipitor patents in early 2003. Lipitor was the number one product of Pfizer and the world's largest selling drug, clocking revenues of over 7 billion dollars in 2002 in the USA alone. Pfizer had reason to be more than a little annoyed with Indian generic companies.

In just about three years, we had entered into litigation to be the first to the market with some of the world's bestselling drugs sold by some of the world's biggest companies—Eli Lilly, Bayer, Astra Zeneca and Pfizer. The annual sales in the USA of just two molecules—omeprazole and fluoxetine—were 7 billion dollars, about twice the size of the *entire* market for all formulations in India at that time! Of course, once generics are introduced after patent expiry of the molecule, the prices fall to a small fraction of the price of the branded drug and the competition gets intense for market share. Even so, it is easy to see why the US market is so lucrative.

More challenges were to follow. These involved not only the ability to develop products quickly and win the race to be the first to file for regulatory approval, but also legal capabilities to identify the ones with weak patents and then conduct the expensive and complex litigation. Prasad and Cameron retained Budd Larner, a legal firm in New Jersey, to handle the litigation. Andrew Miller, a shareholder in Budd Larner, was our primary contact. He later joined us for a while to be general counsel to handle the increasing litigation, before he went back to the firm.

In July 2001, the District Court of Indianapolis ruled against Eli Lilly in the fluoxetine case. This was the first time any Indian company had successfully challenged a patent and obtained 180-day exclusivity in the USA. We launched the product on 3rd August 2001, a landmark event for the Indian pharmaceutical industry, and this was reflected in our financial performance. Profit in 2001–02 more than trebled over the previous year to 4.6 billion rupees.

We did not succeed in invalidating the patent of olanzapine—Eli Lilly's Zyprexa—but there were other patents for the product that were also challenged, so we retained the right to launch the product with 180-day exclusivity after the expiry of certain patents. We failed in the challenges to Bayer's Cipro and Astra Zeneca's Prilosec. Our greatest disappointment was, however, in the amlodipine litigation with Pfizer. We succeeded in the first instance before the District Court of New Jersey in December 2002, but Pfizer appealed and the judgement of the district court was reversed in February 2004.

In the meanwhile, we continued to file applications for other generic drugs whose patents were expiring and further patent challenges built up a good portfolio of products. In 2003, we decided to enter the generic over-the-counter (OTC) market. As the name implies, OTC drugs are those which can be sold 'over the counter' without a prescription. Prasad and Cameron struck a fifteen-year deal with Leiner Health Products in 2003 to distribute Dr. Reddy's OTC products, and Prasad joined their board of directors. Leiner launched four of our products and the OTC business was off to a good start.

Cameron left us after an eventful tenure in March 2004, having made an enormous contribution in building not only our bulk drug and generic business in the USA, but also in shaping the licensing agreements for new drug discoveries. Before he left, he helped to set up our sales and marketing team in the USA. We now market all our products ourselves. It was fortunate that we built the team, as our tie-up with Leiner ended abruptly. In the first quarter of 2007, the FDA inspected Leiner's manufacturing facilities in the USA and noticed instances of non-compliance with Good Manufacturing Practices regulations. Leiner was forced to suspend operations. As a result, there was a vacuum in the market and we were compelled to consider our future course of action. We decided to go ahead on our own. Perrigo is the market leader in the OTC segment and far ahead of us, but we are steadily building the business.

In 2009, we broke into the Top Ten in the generics business in the USA and currently earn 45 per cent of our generic revenues from the country. It is our most important and valuable generic market.

Prasad and Satish not only continue to build the generics business but are also creating new opportunities. In 2008, we made our first acquisition of a manufacturing facility in the USA when we took over BASF's pharmaceutical contract manufacturing business and the manufacturing facility in Shreveport, Louisiana, for 40 million dollars. This opened the possibility of tendering for government supplies in the USA, which is restricted to manufacturers based in the country. In late 2010, we acquired the manufacturing site of GSK's oral penicillin facility in Bristol, Tennessee, as well as the rights for their well-known Augmentin and Amoxil brands which had lost patent protection. This gave us an entry into the penicillin segment where we had no presence. Another significant event in 2008 was the setting up of a subsidiary, Promius Pharma, to enter the speciality business with in-licensed products, initially in the dermatology segment.

Generics were a step up from the bulk drug business. Dr. Reddy's and other Indian companies have an established presence in the American generic market now, but it is becoming increasingly competitive and margins for run-of-the-mill generic products are getting squeezed. The quest in the generic business is now for products where the competition, at least initially, is limited and margins are expected to be better for a reasonable period of time. Such products are usually difficult to make. Perhaps the most difficult are the biological drugs where patent expiries have commenced, but there are no established generic players. The regulatory requirements for approval of generic biological drugs in the USA are evolving, but are likely to remain onerous, adding to the difficulty.

We have come a long way from the days we exported methyldopa and ibuprofen in the late 1980s. Few would have thought that Indian companies would become significant players in the generic business in the USA. Few now will think that Indian companies will scale the next peak of launching generic biological drugs in the USA. I am optimistic, however, that Dr. Reddy's will find a way in the course of time. As a matter of fact, Dr. Reddy's has made significant progress in this direction.

12 BIOTECHNOLOGY'S NEW DAWN

Herbert Boyer, Genentech: *The pioneer of recombinant DNA*

Biological drugs, sometimes called biologics, are marvellous outcomes of the 'new biotechnology' that can make a dramatic difference to people suffering from grievous illnesses. Sadly, biologics under patent are prohibitively priced even by the standards of the developed world, so they are quite out of reach of people in developing countries like India where medicines are largely an out-of-pocket expenditure. Patients in most developing countries, including India, can hope to have access to these drugs only when generic versions, known in the USA as biosimilars, become available.

Biotechnology is a term that has been used for many decades to mean a biological process for the manufacture of any product; for example, the making of cheese, the brewing of beer or the making of fermentation products such as lovastatin, the first of the cholesterol-reducing statins. The biological process uses living organisms to make products, improve plants or develop micro-organisms for specific uses.

Biotechnology is now so familiar a term that one tends to forget that its widespread usage is of fairly recent origin. It was only in 1984 that the US Office of Technology Assessment, taking note of the enormous progress in the second half of the twentieth century, tentatively labelled these developments 'new biotechnology'. In 1994, it officially defined new biotechnology as 'the industrial use of DNA, cells and bioprocessing techniques'. The therapeutic potential of the new biotechnology excited both scientists and venture capitalists. Within the decade, Dr. Reddy's too ventured into it.

Two scientists, Stanley Cohen of Stanford University and Herbert Boyer of the University of California in San Francisco, were responsible for a spectacular breakthrough that was the dawn of the era of the new biotechnology. The two met at a conference at Hawaii in 1972 and got talking over 'hot pastrami and corned beef sandwiches' in a local delicatessen. Luckily, it was not in a boardroom with lawyers around so they decided to collaborate by the time the conversation ended. The results were quick. Within months, they demonstrated that 'foreign' DNA could be 'cloned' or replicated in a bacterial host, which acted as a natural biological factory. DNA thus replicated in a living cell is recombinant DNA or rDNA. Interestingly, the duo of Cohen and Boyer, whose names are now inseparably linked for this achievement, did not get a joint Nobel Prize. Cohen was, however, awarded the Nobel Prize in 1986 for a different achievement—the discovery of growth factors.

Boyer went on to earn much more than the prize money of a Nobel. Robert Swanson, a twenty-eight-year-old biochemist turned venture capitalist, sought him out with a business proposition soon after the Cohen–Boyer experiments were completed. After a four-hour meeting, this time at a local bar, Boyer decided to borrow 500 dollars and start a company called Genentech with Swanson. The rest is history. Genentech's first target was to make recombinant insulin. Till that time, the only insulin available was derived from animal sources and it had some therapeutic limitations. There were also apprehensions that demand would not be met as the population of diabetics was increasing rapidly. The commercial case for producing pure recombinant insulin, identical to human insulin, was compelling.

The path to preparing synthetic insulin was paved by Frederick Sanger, the great British biochemist, who had sequenced insulin in the early 1950s after a decade of effort which earned him the first of his two Nobel Prizes in Chemistry. Only three others have received two Nobels since the prizes were first awarded in 1901. Sanger's work laid out the precise sequence of the amino acids of the two chains that make up insulin, twenty-one of them in the A chain and thirty in the B chain. The challenge of producing synthetic insulin was soon picked up by academic groups and two of them independently succeeded almost simultaneously in the early 1960s, one at the University of Pittsburgh and the other at the RWTH Aachen University in Germany. It was, however, terribly cumbersome; the Pittsburgh process, for example, had about 200 steps and it was uncertain if it could be adequately purified. The notion of producing recombinant human insulin, free of the limitations of animal insulin and the complications of chemical synthesis, was indeed an alluring one. Could the Cohen–Boyer method be the answer?

Boyer wanted to do a test run on a tiny gene before attempting to produce recombinant insulin. He chose somatostatin, a gene made up of fourteen amino acids, for his test run. He inserted the somatostatin gene into living bacteria and, for the first time ever, produced somatostatin outside of a human being on 30th August 1977. The hour of recombinant DNA had finally arrived.

Just about a year later, Genentech announced that it had succeeded in preparing recombinant insulin, identical to the human one. The date was 24th August 1978 and I like to think of it as the day on which the biotechnology industry came of age. Genentech was feted with enthusiasm in the stock market and Boyer made it to the cover of *Time* magazine in 1981, a rare distinction for a scientist though several of his academic contemporaries were dismayed by what they thought was his indulgence in crass commercialism.

Genentech's insulin was the first ever recombinant DNA product for human use and it was approved in the USA and Europe in 1982. In the meanwhile, the product had been licensed to Eli Lilly. Commercial production began in 1983, exactly sixty years after Eli Lilly had started commercial production of bovine insulin discovered by Banting and Best. For the first time, diabetic patients on insulin had no apprehension of the side effects of the earlier insulin of bovine or porcine origin.

The pace of further approvals was relatively slow in the 1980s. Hoffmann-La Roche and Schering-Plough obtained approvals for their interferons to treat hairy-cell leukaemia in 1986 and Merck obtained the approval for the first recombinant hepatitis B vaccine in the same year. Genentech obtained approval for two more relatively smaller products in the decade, which ended in a flourish as Amgen debuted with recombinant erythropoietin.

By the time I decided to seize the biotechnology opportunity in the late 1990s, the pace of development of new biological drugs was showing signs of acceleration. Amgen had obtained approval for Neupogen in early 1991 for the treatment of chemotherapy-induced neutropenia, a condition where the count of neutrophils, which make up 60–70 per cent of the white blood cells, is reduced to dangerous levels by chemotherapy. Neutrophils destroy bacteria in blood and are a fundamental defence mechanism of the body against infections. Neupogen, whose generic name is filgrastim, is an essential adjuvant treatment with chemotherapy as it increases the neutrophil count. It seemed to be a good product to start off with as opposed to the older products approved in the 1980s. It also helped that Amgen had forgotten to patent the product in India.

In the 1990s, only a few companies had ventured into biotechnology in India and Hyderabad was home to several of them. Shanta Biotechnics, a company founded by K.I. Varaprasad Reddy—surprisingly, an electronics engineer by training—succeeded in developing the first indigenous recombinant hepatitis B vaccine with help from the Osmania University and the Centre for Cellular and Molecular Biology (CCMB) at Hyderabad. It subsequently expanded its product portfolio. A French group then acquired the majority stake in Shanta in 2006. It has since been acquired by Sanofi. Another Hyderabad-based company is Bharat Biotech, set up in 1996 by Dr Krishna Ella and his wife, Suchitra. They started with the hepatitis B vaccine and have since developed several other products.

When we set out to make filgrastim, the only recombinant products which were indigenously manufactured were vaccines to prevent disease. But no recombinant therapeutic drug to treat a disease was made in India. In 2001, Wockhardt introduced erythropoietin, a drug to treat anaemia caused by chronic kidney disease. It was the first indigenously manufactured recombinant therapeutic drug. A few months later, Dr. Reddy's introduced the generic version of Amgen's Neupogen, perhaps the first therapeutic protein developed from the clone stage in the country, and it kicked up a storm.

Amgen had licensed the product to Hoffmann-La Roche for India. Roche was headquartered in Switzerland and the product was marketed in India by Nicholas Piramal. The company was previously Nicholas Laboratories and the diversified business group of Ajay Piramal acquired the company in 1988 in its first foray into pharmaceuticals. This was followed by the acquisition of the Hoffmann-La Roche subsidiary in India in 1993 along with the exclusive right to market a number of Roche products. This was how Neupogen came to be marketed by Nicholas Piramal.

We branded our product Grastim. We received approval of the Drugs Controller General (India) in June 2001 and introduced our product into the market at half the price of Neupogen. I was told that the doctors using the product were happy with their experience and even happier with the price at which it was being sold. The adviser to the ministry of science and technology in the Department of Biotechnology lauded the launch as 'an important milestone'.

Then came the bombshell.

All medicinal products are required to have an insert along with the medication that provides details of the medicine, the indications for which it can be used, the summary of the evidence from clinical trials, the dosage, adverse effects and so on. Nicholas Piramal filed a complaint in September 2001 against Dr. Reddy's before the Monopolies and Restrictive Trade Practices Commission (MRTPC), alleging that the statements in the Grastim insert were false, misleading and tantamount to unfair trade practice. Their main grievance was that the insert would lead people to believe that Grastim had undergone various clinical trials that demonstrated efficacy, whereas it was Neupogen that was used in clinical trials. It is normal practice for generics to have an insert that replicates the one of the innovator, except for the brand name of the innovator. It was never our intention to create an impression that Grastim was used in the clinical trials whose results had been reported, so we promptly made an offer to make the situation clear by making changes in the insert. Nicholas Piramal also objected to certain other information contained in the insert. We agreed to make all the changes demanded and obtained clearance for the new insert from the Drugs Controller. MRTPC dismissed the complaint. The matter should have rested there, but it did not.

There was intensive media coverage of the dispute. Many of the reports were factual, but some were quite surprising in content. These reports said the amino acid sequence of Grastim was not the same as Neupogen. I was aghast and asked for the facts. It turned out that in our sales brochure, the sequence of the 175 amino acids of filgrastim was printed as a design element and there were errors in a few of them. It also turned out that the Neupogen monograph had two printing errors in the sequence and the comparison therefore revealed some differences.

I heaved a sigh of relief that Nicholas Piramal's case was based on printer's devils and not actual analysis. We had irrefutable evidence that our sequence was right, not only based on our own analysis but also that of CCMB and IISc.

Fresh salvos followed. Newspapers reported that Nicholas Piramal had analysed samples of Grastim procured from the market and found 'either an impurity or a drug aggregate'. A news report stated that Nicholas Piramal had alerted all the leading haematology and oncology associations in the country about its findings. Another publication quoted an unnamed molecular biologist as saying that bacteria could escape during the purification process and this would be a potential hazard: that impurities could affect immunogenicity or bioavailability, thereby increasing the potential of toxicity. Dr Swati Piramal, director and chief scientific officer of Nicholas Piramal, clarified the position of the company. She was quoted as saying, 'It's not about patents or trademarks. Not about MNCs versus Indian companies. But it's a battle for safe and effective drugs for the patients—to ensure that doctors are not misled and get correct information from pharma companies. And we feel it's our duty to fight to the finish.'

The 'fight' was taken to the Drugs Controller, the ministry of health and even some members of Parliament. Every 'development' somehow found its way to the newspapers. Nicholas Piramal asked that Grastim be withdrawn and an expert from Roche was also said to have met the Drugs Controller.

An expert group was formed by the Drugs Controller. It was headed by Prof. N.K. Ganguly, director general of the Indian Council of Medical Research, with Dr Nitya Anand, the legendary former director of the Central Drug Research Institute, and Dr Amit Ghosh, the serving director of the Institute of Microbial Technology. They obtained samples of Grastim and Neupogen from the market and analysed it. The drama finally ended in January 2003. There was complete transparency as the expert group presented its findings to the Drugs Controller in a meeting where both Dr. Reddy's and Nicholas Piramal were present. Contrary to all the news that had been published, the expert group found that there was no difference between Neupogen and Grastim. Nicholas Piramal asked for, and obtained, a copy of the test reports, but apparently had nothing further to say. Nicholas Piramal had indeed fought the 'fight' to its logical conclusion.

The expert group recommended that we change our brand name to something else as it was not desirable to have a brand name that corresponded so closely to the generic name. We pointed out that it was the practice in India as there were so many brands and a brand name that incorporated part of the generic name made it easy for the doctors to remember it. There was no legal compulsion for us to change the name, but we did so nevertheless. Dr. Reddy's filgrastim was rebranded Grafeel.

Dr. Reddy's filgrastim had overtaken Neupogen in volume soon after its launch in 2001. Volumes, however, dropped in the next two years as doctors hesitated to prescribe the product. A doctor in Mumbai's Tata Memorial Centre told a newspaper he did not know whether Grastim was as good as Neupogen or not but would not risk prescribing Grastim. If I were in his place, I would have done the same. No wonder Dr. Reddy's sales suffered. By 2005, however, we regained our lead and have been ahead of Neupogen ever since, though the price of the latter has dropped to match ours in the last three years.

Cartikeya Reddy, who was earlier with Genentech and Bayer, joined us in early 2004 to head the biotechnology division. He has done a marvellous job of developing a portfolio of 'firsts'. The first product developed and launched under his stewardship was the biosimilar of Genentech's MabThera, a remarkable drug initially launched to treat some lymphomas and later found useful in other conditions, including rheumatoid arthritis. MabThera was marketed by Roche in India and its generic name is rituximab. Conscious of the issues faced in the launch of filgrastim, Cartikeya was very careful when our rituximab was launched under the brand name Reditux. We published a book at the launch with all the details of the characterization and purity of Reditux. There was not a whisper of criticism and sales took off. Our price was 40 per cent of Roche's price, which was still very expensive. I was very pleased when Prasad and the marketing team headed by Ritha Chandrachud—she is now with Merck & Co. in Singapore—devised a simple patient-access programme for those who could not afford it. It is called Sparsh, which means 'touch' in Hindi. All that doctors have to do is to requisition Reditux through the website and it is delivered free of cost at the requested time. There are no checks or quotas for doctors. Sparsh accounts for about a quarter of the total usage of Dr. Reddy's rituximab in India. Some people find it amazing that there is no misuse of the programme. I do not see anything surprising in this. If one can trust a doctor with one's life, surely one can do so with a few vials of Reditux.

Reditux was the world's first biosimilar monoclonal antibody when it was launched, and it remains the only one so far. Dr. Reddy's has followed it up with the launch of darbopoetin, the biosimilar to Amgen's Aranesp. It is a heavily glycosylated protein and our biotechnology division has done well to develop it. We have branded it Cresp and it is the first—and only—biosimilar for Aranesp in the world.

Dr. Reddy's has struck a deal with Merck Serono, a company in the E. Merck Group of Germany for biosimilars. In a reversal of the usual tale, the German company will manufacture and market biosimilars based on the technology developed in India and be a source of supply of affordable medicines to the Western world.

I am particularly pleased with this alliance. E. Merck is no ordinary company. A bit of its long and complex history, as well as its Indian connection, may be of some interest. It had modest beginnings in 1668 when Friedrich Jacob Merck purchased a pharmacy called Engel-Apotheke—German for Angel Pharmacy—in Darmstadt, Germany. The pharmacy continues to be run by the Merck family even today. Merck's manufacturing operations were started in 1827 by Heinrich Emanuel, the sixth-generation Merck to inherit the pharmacy. The holding company of the German Merck is known as E. Merck, after Heinrich Emanuel. Merck in Germany is perhaps the oldest pharmaceutical enterprise in the world.

Its connection with India dates back to the late 1880s when Willy Merck visited India and got a first-hand impression of its potential as a market as well as a source of raw materials on account of its rich plant life. The first Indian office of E. Merck opened in 1912 and its India connection since then has been sustained by both business and culture. Not surprisingly, the German Merck's business suffered during the war years and it was not until 1957 that Sarabhai Merck, a joint venture with Vikram Sarabhai, commenced production of ascorbic acid at Baroda, marking the re-establishment of the E. Merck business in India. Later, in 1967, E. Merck (India) Private Limited, the first Asian subsidiary, was established in Bombay and was the first company in the E. Merck Group to go public in 1981. It is now known as Merck Limited.

Jon Baumhauer is an eleventh-generation descendant of Friedrich Jacob Merck and is the present chairman of the executive board of E. Merck KG, the principal shareholder of Merck KGaA as well as the chairman of the family board. He came to India several times and in media interviews spoke about the visit of Rabindranath Tagore to his grandparents' home in Munich and the Tagore Week celebrated in Darmstadt, the ancestral home of Merck. I was astonished to learn that Baumhauer's grandmother, Elisabeth Wolff-Merck, had translated Tagore's play *Chitra* into German and her husband's firm published it in 1914, a year after Tagore received the Nobel Prize in Literature. Over the next eleven years, twenty volumes of Tagore's works were published, cumulatively selling over a million copies. The E. Merck companies continue to support Tagore festivals even today and have instituted the Merck–Tagore Award for honouring notable cultural exchanges between Germany and India.

The deal with the German Merck for manufacturing and marketing biosimilars to the Western world is not only a milestone for the biotechnology industry, but also has a personal significance. One of my first attempts at making a career in the pharmaceutical industry involved the Indian subsidiary of the American Merck. It's been a long and eventful journey from one Merck to another.

13 MERCK TO MERCK

The Gift of Sight: *Merck & Co. is on the verge of eradicating river blindness without ever selling a tablet to treat it*

As I look back at my life in the pharmaceutical industry, good science, affordable medicine and profitable business emerge as the three dominant themes that have energized and sustained me. These themes can sometimes be at odds with each other. But I had the advantage of a great example in Merck & Co. in the USA, the company that inspired me the most.

Merck & Co. was set up as the American subsidiary of the German parent and commenced operations in 1891. The 80 per cent shareholding of the German parent was confiscated during the First World War by the US government, but they could not expropriate the 20 per cent shareholding of George Merck, the grandson of Heinrich Emanuel Merck, as he was an American citizen. George Merck, however, bought his company back in 1919, when the US government put the confiscated shares of the company on sale and Merck & Co. was reborn as an independent American company.

Merck & Co. merged with Sharp & Dohme in 1953. The combined entity continued with the same name, Merck & Co., in the USA, but international operations outside North America went under the name of Merck Sharp & Dohme. In 1958, Merck Sharp & Dohme was established as a joint venture in India, with the American company holding 60 per cent of the equity and the Tatas being the principal Indian shareholder.

My first encounter with Merck & Co. was in 1963, the year that it gave the world its first measles vaccine. Armed with a BSc (Tech) degree and a letter of introduction from Prof. Kamath to a Dr Mitra, I took a bus to attend an interview at the Merck Sharp & Dohme factory in Bombay. It had begun to drizzle as I got off the bus, but I set off in a hurry to be on time for the interview. The drizzle turned into a downpour and I reached my destination drenched. I took one look at myself dripping water and wheeled around to head back. There was no way I could present myself for an interview wet and bedraggled.

The name of Merck Sharp & Dohme ceased to exist in India in 1984, with the company being renamed Merind that year. In the early 1990s, Merck & Co. exited the joint venture and the Tatas acquired their shareholding. Incidentally, within the decade, the Tatas sold out to Wockhardt, a pharmaceutical company established in the early 1960s by Habil Khorakiwala in Bombay. It was only in 2004 that Merck & Co. re-established itself in India as MSD Pharmaceuticals Private Limited.

At the time of Merck & Co.'s exit from India in the early 1990s, there was great disquiet in the pharmaceutical industry with talk of patents for medicines being reintroduced in the country. The general perception was that this would be a serious blow to the Indian pharmaceutical industry which made only generic drugs. I for one had profited from making generic versions of Merck & Co.'s products. Methyldopa, the first bulk drug I manufactured at Dr. Reddy's, was a Merck & Co. product, approved way back in 1962 for the treatment of hypertension. I missed out on lovastatin, but in 1989 Dr. Reddy's had reverse-engineered enalapril, another drug to treat hypertension and the first billion-dollar blockbuster in Merck & Co.'s history.

The exit of Merck & Co. from India was also significant as there was a widespread belief that patents were being reintroduced in the country under pressure from the developed world and the multinational pharmaceutical industry. I heard the Tatas did everything possible to keep the partnership with Merck & Co. going. J.R.D. Tata himself met P. Roy Vagelos, the chairman and CEO of Merck & Co. The story that did the rounds was that Vagelos was terribly annoyed over India's stance on patents and said India would be a 'pariah' country if it did not respect patents. JRD, apparently, was furious and that was the end of the joint venture.

I could understand Vagelos's dismay. Innovation was critical for the future of medicine and needed good science. For good science to be nurtured and investments in research to be profitable, patents were essential. However, prices of medicines under patents would be prohibitively expensive and few people in need of the medicines would be able to afford them. I also needed to consider the impact of patents on the business I was in. Few people were clear on all the implications and what the future held. As I thought about these issues, one thing became clear. Merck seemed to have struck a profitable balance between good science and a good conscience. How they did so is an inspiring story and it had a profound impact on me.

George Merck's son, George Wilhelm, joined Merck & Co. soon after the First World War began. In a career that spanned more than four decades, the younger Merck laid the foundations for the company to become the legend that has inspired generations of people the world over. Less than a decade after taking over the reins of the company in 1925, George W. Merck made the path-breaking decision to get into serious research and set up the Merck Institute of Therapeutic Research. It was revolutionary for the USA at that time; unlike in Germany, serious research was generally conducted by scientists in university laboratories, not by pharmaceutical companies. Merck & Co. worked on the frontiers of science and the results were spectacular. Five Nobel Prize–winners were in some way associated with the medicines that Merck & Co. developed in the 1940s and '50s, and the number has probably grown to a dozen now. Merck has also been home to outstanding scientists who have not won the Nobel but have nevertheless made enormous contributions to science. Maurice Hillemann is perhaps the greatest of them and is acknowledged to be the scientist who has saved more lives than any other in the twentieth century. Hillemann joined Merck & Co. in 1957 from E.R. Squibb, now Bristol-Myers Squibb, as head of the newly created virus and cell biology department. It was at Merck & Co. that he discovered the majority of the forty or so vaccines with which he was associated, the largest number for any scientist in the world. One well-known story about him, reflecting his dedication, goes thus: when his daughter fell ill with mumps, he took a throat swab and cultured the virus, now named Jeryl Lynn after her, to produce a mumps vaccine. Eventually, he also produced the MMR vaccine—for measles, mumps and rubella. It was the oldest vaccine using multiple live strains of virus that is in use even today and it includes the Jeryl Lynn strain.

George W. Merck set the scientific tempo that was to last a long time. Even after his death in 1957, Merck & Co. scientists continued to produce breakthrough drugs for an astonishing number of diseases. Many of these were during the tenure of P. Roy Vagelos, the extraordinary head of research at Merck & Co. for a decade from the mid-1970s, before he went on to become president and then chairman for another decade. It was during his time, and because of his commitment, that the world's first cholesterol-lowering drug—lovastatin—made it to the market under the brand name Mevacor. Merck & Co. was not the first to discover a statin—the distinction belongs to Sankyo but that drug did not make it to the market because of serious adverse effects. As a matter of fact,

Sankyo's setback prompted Vagelos to suspend the trials of Mevacor for a while, but it eventually went back to the clinic and was approved in 1987. In the meanwhile, Merck & Co. developed another statin as a backup in case Mevacor ran into problems. This was none other than simvastatin that turned out to be even better and went on to become another blockbuster drug with the brand name Zocor. Statins are one of those giant leaps in science that have contributed to increased longevity by reducing the risk of cardiovascular mortality. Merck & Co. will stand out as a pioneer in the development of this class for all times to come.

Simvastatin turned out be a great business opportunity for Dr. Reddy's too. In 2006, we clinched a deal to market simvastatin and another drug with the generic name of finasteride in the USA, as the authorized generics of Merck & Co.'s Zocor and Proscar. This was the first time any Indian company had launched an authorized generic in the USA.

More than the business with Merck & Co. and the admiration for their science, it was the philosophy of Merck & Co. that medicines are for people, not for profits that provided me with lasting inspiration. In 2006, Dr. Reddy's crossed a billion dollars in revenue for the first time, aided by the revenues from Merck & Co.'s authorized generics. It had taken us twenty-two years, but it was the shortest time for any Indian company to achieve a billion dollars of annual revenues. It was a momentous occasion for us and I pondered on what to say to my colleagues in my message to them. I recalled the speech of George W. Merck at the College of Medicine in Virginia in 1950, more than half a century earlier. This is the message that I mailed to every employee in Dr. Reddy's on 4th December 2006:

Dear Colleague:

Last Friday, we crossed 1 billion dollars of turnover in a financial year for the first time. This was a historic moment for the company and every one of you made it happen.

I share with every one of you a quiet pride at achieving this milestone. But more than that, I am also very grateful for the part every one of you has played in achieving it. It would not have happened if you had not put your mind to it; equally, it would not have happened if you had not put your heart into it.

It is interesting that last Friday happened to be the 1st. As I look back over the last two decades of our existence, there have been a number of 'firsts'. We were the first Indian pharmaceutical company to be listed on the NYSE, to license a NCE to a multinational, to receive 180-day exclusivity for a generic in the US and to market an authorized generic in the US.

There will be many more milestones to mark our journey into the future. I am confident that our scientists at Discovery Research will make another happen, that of being the first Indian company to put a NCE into the market, firmly establishing us as the leading pharmaceutical company from India.

We have cause to celebrate, reason to look forward to the future with optimism. It is also an occasion to be reflective. Our roots may be in India, but we have grown to be a global company. We have operations in over 30 countries and revenues from over 60. Our employees, shareholders and customers are from across the globe. And as I reflect on what could effectively bind us and collectively energize us, it appears to me that it must be from grasping an opportunity that comes from the business we are in.

Life. Research. Hope. This sums it up. Nothing has perhaps inspired me more than the plaque I read many years ago at the entrance to Merck Global Headquarters, immortalizing the words of George W Merck:

'We try never to forget that medicine is for the people. It is not for the profits. The profits follow, and if we have remembered that, they have never failed to appear. The better we have remembered it, the larger they have been.'

If we can remember the credo of George Merck, and remember it well, there will undoubtedly come a time when our milestones and our 'firsts' come not in relation to India, but the world, ethically, responsibly and profitably.

With best wishes,
Dr Anji Reddy

The 'opportunity that comes from the business we are in' I was referring to was the opportunity for the pharmaceutical industry to provide medication, relief and hope to every person in need, at an affordable price. This was the philosophy that moved me to launch norfloxacin at half the prevailing market price and enalapril at 1.20 rupees a tablet in the late 1980s. I had also demonstrated that reasonable prices made eminent commercial sense. For the record, Dr. Reddy's crossed the 2 billion–dollar mark in annual revenues for the first time just four years later—again in the shortest time for an Indian pharmaceutical company.

Crossing revenue milestones in record time was, however, the farthest thing on my mind when I visited Merck & Co.'s headquarters at Whitehouse Station in New Jersey and read George W. Merck's inspiring motto. I had reached early for my meeting and had time to spare. I looked around the reception area and spotted a seven-foot sculpture of an African boy leading a blind man at the other end of a stick—a sight that is not uncommon even in India. I walked across to have a closer look at what appeared to be a marvellous piece of art even from a distance. The sculpture was called *The Gift of Sight*. I read the inscription below the sculpture and it took a few moments for the extraordinary implications to sink in. And when they did, it was electrifying. One company had given the gift of sight to millions in Africa.

Perhaps it ought not to have had that effect on me, as I knew the story behind the sculpture, even if I had not known about the sculpture itself. Indeed, most people in the pharmaceutical industry would have been aware of the story. But seeing the sculpture unexpectedly was like sighting the words of George W. Merck being poured into bronze and the magnificent bronze breathing life and meaning into his words. How electrifying it was to recognize how much of a difference the science of just one company and just one of its products could make to humanity!

The one company was of course Merck & Co. and the one product was ivermectin, which Merck & Co. had named Mectizan.

The story began on a golf course in Japan from where Merck & Co. scientists obtained soil samples in the mid-1970s. One of the 40,000 they screened yielded a surprisingly effective agent against parasites. From this starting point, Dr William Campbell, a scientist in Merck & Co.'s animal health division, derived ivermectin that was lethal to parasites in livestock and it became the largest-selling veterinary drug in history. Ivermectin was also effective against a parasite that was closely related to *Onchocerca volvulus*, which caused onchocerciasis, river blindness, in human beings. The disease is transmitted by the bite of common black flies carrying the parasite and is endemic in Africa and some countries in South America. The World Health Organization (WHO) estimates that more than 125 million people are at risk of river blindness. It is one of the most horrifying diseases imaginable.

Once the parasites are transmitted into a human being, they grow into adults and produce millions of offspring annually for about twelve years. There can be up to 200 million of these parasites in one human being. Adult worms grow up to two feet in length and cause lumps under the skin. Immature microscopic *O. volvulus* crawl under the skin constantly and cause unbearable itching. Eventually, they reach the eye and cause blindness. The disease and the parasite were identified as early as 1915 in Guatemala, but a cure evaded science till ivermectin came along. The only previous programme to combat river blindness, launched by Robert McNamara when he was president of the World Bank fifteen years before ivermectin, was to spray the banks of fast-flowing rivers, the breeding ground of black flies and destroy their larvae. The programme was targeted at the carrier, not the parasite.

When Campbell obtained enough data to demonstrate safety and potential effectiveness of ivermectin against *O. volvulus* in human beings, the programme was turned over to Dr Mohammed Aziz, an infectious disease specialist of Bangladeshi origin, in Merck & Co.'s clinical research group. Convinced of the need of this drug and the demand for it, Campbell and Aziz discussed its clinical development with Roy Vagelos, head of research at Merck & Co. at that time. Vagelos was convinced of the demand. He was also sure that the people most in need of the drug could not pay for it. Nevertheless, he cleared the proposal for one of the most complicated clinical trials possible, and a very expensive one at that, in collaboration with WHO.

Ivermectin was approved for human use in France in 1987. Merck & Co. did not go to the FDA as there was no river blindness in the USA, but France had a North African population with incidence of the disease. The dose was a magical one tablet *once a year* that would provide immediate relief from the symptoms by killing the immature parasite. Continued for the fertile lifecycle of the adult for about twelve years or so, the drug could eliminate the parasite from human beings. Since human beings are the only host—there is no animal host for the parasite—the disease could be eradicated like smallpox if all infected human beings could be treated for the entire cycle.

Vagelos held a press conference in October 1987 to announce the approval of ivermectin for human beings. By this time, he was chairman and CEO of Merck & Co. He knew he would need to announce the price of the drug. He did not make any complex calculations of the costs to justify pricing. There was no time for him to consult his board of directors. However, he remembered, and remembered well, George W. Merck's credo that medicines are for people, not for profits, and made a very simple, understated announcement. Merck & Co. would 'give the drug free to any person endangered by river blindness anywhere in the world for as long as it was needed'.

The board of directors approved the decision, the employees cheered, and the world applauded. Merck & Co. topped *Fortune*'s list of 'most admired companies'—not just the most admired *pharmaceutical* companies—for an amazing seven successive years from 1987 to 1993. An international consortium of dozens of non-governmental and government agencies managed the delivery of the drug to those who needed it, whose silent gratitude was perhaps the most valuable accolade Merck & Co. could have ever received. In 2011, Colombia became the first country to apply for WHO certification that river blindness had been eliminated. In October 2012, Merck & Co., after twenty-five years of running the Mectizan donation programme and distributing more than a billion treatments, reaffirmed its commitment to continue with its donation 'for as long as it was needed'.

Merck & Co. grasped the opportunity of the business they were in with their hands and with their hearts. They are on the verge of eliminating one disease, potentially affecting the lives and livelihoods of more than 125 million people.

Critics point out that Merck & Co.'s copybook has been blotted by the issues surrounding the withdrawal in 2004 of the painkiller rofecoxib, which Merck & Co. sold under the brand name of Vioxx, and the allegations of illegal promotional activity of Vioxx that led to criminal fines and civil settlements amounting to nearly a billion dollars in 2012. This is true and I am not unmindful of it. But I am also mindful of the good that has come out of the science of Merck & Co., ethically and profitably. That is what inspires and energizes me even today.

Vagelos was often uncomfortable about the pricing policies of multinational companies. Risking the disapproval of his peers, he charted his own course in some ways, to moderate the pricing of Merck & Co.'s products in the USA. He was more open about his discomfort after he retired from Merck & Co. and what he said in an interview with *Knowledge@Wharton* in 2006 is revealing:

[India was] important in introduction of modern HIV drugs in Africa when the multinational large pharmaceuticals were putting their head in the sand and saying that they could not possibly provide drugs to Africans, because the prices would have to have been too low to allow them to even recover their costs. Well, when the Indians started putting in generic drugs and making a profit, that was very embarrassing, as it should have been to the multinationals. And each one then, somehow out of magic, was able to introduce a program picking their own country, where they did a magnificent job at introducing HIV drugs, which they could have done before without getting a black eye. But the whole industry took a terrific bashing, which was well deserved.

I do not know if the multinational pharmaceutical industry has learnt from the 'terrific bashing' that it received from the AIDS drugs episode, but it does appear that they are again 'putting their head in the sand' with respect to the pricing of biologics. Worse, some innovators try to delay the entry of affordable generic versions even after patent expiry. As recently as February 2013, the FDA commissioner while addressing the Generic Pharmaceutical Association Meeting in Florida is reported to have said that attempts to undermine trust in biosimilars are 'worrisome and represent a disservice to patients who could benefit from these lower-cost treatments'. I am hopeful that our deal with Merck Serono to manufacture and market biosimilars in the Western world with our technology augurs well for Dr. Reddy's continuing to provide the world with affordable medicine.

Decades have passed from the time I applied for a job with Merck Sharp & Dohme to when Dr. Reddy's signed a deal with Merck Serono. In the meanwhile, Dr. Reddy's and the Indian pharmaceutical industry have scripted a success story in bringing affordable generic medicines to the world and are on the verge of adding another splendid chapter to it with generic biological drugs. What is missing from the narrative so far, however, is the discovery of new drugs in India. To tell the truth, I had been toying with the idea since the early 1990s when I was pondering over the implications of the possible change in patent law for affordable medicine and the Indian pharmaceutical industry.

14 'PATENTLY ABSURD'

The discovery research facility: *We embarked on the quest for new drugs in 1993—the first Indian company to do so*

For twenty years after the Patents Act in India abolished patents on medicines in 1972, the pharmaceutical industry in India witnessed an unprecedented wave of growth as domestic companies raced to the market with new medicines soon after their approval in the USA or in Europe. Dr. Reddy's was riding the crest of this wave.

Storm clouds were, however, gathering on the horizon. The Uruguay Round of negotiations to replace the General Agreement on Trade and Tariffs had commenced in 1986 and was progressing in fits and starts. The most contentious aspect of the negotiations was the agreement on

Trade-Related Aspects of Intellectual Property Rights (TRIPS). While TRIPS covered all kinds of intellectual property, including copyright, trademarks, designs, geographical names used to identify products and the layouts of integrated circuits, some of the most acrimonious debates between the developed and developing nations were about patents, particularly patents for medicines, which would delay the availability of affordable new medicines. The developed countries led by the USA were bent on ensuring that patents were granted for a uniform term by all countries in all fields of technology, which obviously meant that India and the developing world could no longer deny patents for medicinal products. The Indian pharmaceutical industry was appalled by the prospect and feared this would stunt its growth as it could launch new drugs only after patent expiry. Many politicians were vociferous in their opposition as they thought it would inevitably end the era of affordable medicines, and newspapers added to the noise. There was so much opposition in India and many other developing countries that it was by no means clear what the final outcome of the Uruguay Round would be. It was politically incorrect in many circles, including in the domestic pharmaceutical industry, to be supportive of India becoming a signatory to TRIPS.

I was elected president of the Indian Pharmaceutical Congress Association in 1992 in the middle of this raging debate and delivered the customary presidential address in January 1993. Instead of skirting the issue, I pointed out that a new global order was in the making and most nations had accepted the new patent regime. I bluntly asserted that 'the issue before us is not whether to accept the patent regime but a question of when it will be accepted'. I maintained that if the patent regime were to be accepted even ten years later, the time had already come to adopt the Japanese model of advancing into basic research, discovering new molecules and then forging alliances with multinational companies based in Europe and the USA to codevelop and market the new molecules. I went further out on a limb and said, 'Basic research in this direction is an arduous task and is said to be expensive. Drug discovery and development in these countries is estimated to cost between 100–200 million dollars. It is my considered opinion that in the Indian context such an endeavour may be accomplished with an expenditure of 100 million rupees per year. An expenditure of this magnitude is within the reach of some companies in India.'

Disbelief was writ large on the faces of some in the audience. There were also some who thought these views were patently absurd. They were proved wrong.

The Uruguay Round was concluded and the agreement to set up the World Trade Organization was signed on 15th April 1994 at Marrakesh, Morocco. TRIPS was an annexure to this agreement and India was required to issue patents for medicinal products from 1st January 2005. Quite gratifyingly, by the end of 1994 itself, Dr. Reddy's Research Foundation had made substantial progress and there was a distinct possibility of filing three patent applications internationally for novel anti-cancer molecules in the year that followed.

As a matter of fact, I had decided to embark upon drug discovery a few years earlier, well before any domestic company had even started thinking about it. Even as I was speaking in Bangalore, my research centre was under construction at Miyapur, on the outskirts of Hyderabad. Years before I started Dr. Reddy's, I had bought a grape garden from a friend and built a farmhouse on it. It was in this farmhouse one morning in late 1990 that I harked back to my student days and then my career as an entrepreneur—I do not know what triggered this train of thought. I had started off as a researcher and had published my first paper in 1967 on 'Estimation of Liquid Diffusivity'. Since then, I had done some work in process development but most of my time had gone into setting up companies and managing them. They had been challenging times and I felt a sense of achievement, but the lure of research was strong.

I recalled the story of Paul Janssen, who had been a legend in his lifetime. His father was from a farming family and had been a medical doctor before he went on to establish a pharmaceutical business. In the first instance, the elder Janssen marketed the drugs of Richter, a Hungarian firm, in Belgium, Netherlands and the Belgian Congo. Subsequently, the firm progressed to manufacturing galenicals and firmly established itself as a pharmaceutical business by the time Janssen enrolled in the university at the ancient city of Namur in southern Belgium to study physics, chemistry and biology. Later, he graduated *magna cum laude* in medicine at the University of Ghent.

Janssen's exposure to both chemistry and medicine convinced him of the relationship between the structure of compounds and their pharmacological effect. He decided to get into drug research and started out in 1953 on the third floor of his father's factory. He had four assistants to help him—they had not been to university but were eager to work.

Incredible as it may seem, he discovered his first novel compound the same year. Ambucetamide, for menstrual pain, was launched as a drug in 1955 and continues to be marketed in some parts of the world. He went on to establish the business that was eventually named Janssen Pharmaceutica. Initially, the business was conceived of as an independent research company—he intended to develop new drugs and license them to established pharmaceutical companies. His only revenues would be the income from his research activity. This was unprecedented.

Also unprecedented was Janssen's productivity. Drug after drug came out of the Janssen laboratories at an astonishing pace. Janssen and his scientists discovered more than seventy drugs that made it into the market in fifty years, most of them for human beings. One of these was Lomotil, an anti-diarrhoeal licensed to G.D. Searle, which made it to the moon in the medical kits of the astronauts of the Apollo space mission. I chuckled to myself as I thought about the story of how Searle decided to license Lomotil. Janssen had met somebody in the senior management of Searle and made a pitch with lots of data to license Lomotil. He was told that diarrhoea was unknown in the USA and politely shown the door. He was disappointed, but left behind some samples of the drug. Sometime later, the daughter of the person he had met at Searle had a bad case of diarrhoea. The father was frantic and remembered the samples of Lomotil on his desk. He administered it to his daughter and the rest is history. Searle licensed the compound and marketed it in many countries around the world, including India.

The story stuck in my mind as I had a curiously similar experience. At one point of time, chloroquine, an anti-malarial, was invariably in short supply and I thought it would be a useful and profitable drug to make. I applied for a licence to manufacture it, but I was given to understand that the government felt there was already enough manufacturing capacity, so I forgot about it. One fine day, the licence landed on my desk and I was quite surprised. I asked our liaison person in Delhi about it and I was told that the daughter of the concerned joint secretary to the government had contracted malaria and he had decided that more capacity for chloroquine was needed as malaria was rampant. Sometimes, one is moved more by personal experience than by data and analysis.

Janssen sold his company to J&J in 1961. But an important term of the deal was that the company would retain its identity and Janssen would remain at the helm. He continued with his outstanding research, obtained more than 100 patents and published over 850 scientific papers. Janssen also expanded the pharmaceutical business globally.

The story of mebendazole, the first Janssen product in China, illustrates his dedication to research for the alleviation of suffering, apparently without much regard for commercial considerations. I had read somewhere that Janssen had heard of the problem of intestinal infestation in the Belgian Congo during a casual conversation with a doctor who had served there. The disease resulted in worms in the stomach and it was thought to be caused by eating raw or undercooked flesh. Few pharmaceutical companies would have bothered about a disease in Congo. I did not know if the disease was prevalent elsewhere, but I instinctively felt that it would have made no difference to Janssen's decision to find a cure. He zeroed in on a class of anthelmintic compounds known as benzimidazole carbamates, which were used as veterinary medicines and developed mebendazole, the first molecule in this class for human beings. Mebendazole was approved for use in 1972. It not only continues to be in use, but is also on the WHO's list of essential medicines. As a matter of fact, four of Janssen's products appear on this list. Nothing more needs to be said of his commitment to human health. Many years later, I read that Janssen bemoaned the fact that so many promising treatments remained undeveloped 'especially for people with a serious illness not common enough to make it cost-effective for the pharmaceutical industry to invest in finding a cure'. Even after his retirement from the company in 1991, Janssen's zeal continued unabated and he pursued cures for multi-drug-resistant tuberculosis and affordable medicines for HIV/AIDS till he died in 2003. Every one of Janssen's twenty-two honorary doctorates and eighty-plus honours for medicine and science was richly deserved.

Sitting in my farmhouse one morning, I wondered if there was anything more joyous than discovery or more rewarding than finding a cure for disease. Janssen had started out with 1000 dollars, 100 mice and a hot plate. It occurred to me that I was relatively better placed. My mind also wandered to my childhood and my first brush with medicines, which strangely enough was to treat menstrual pain, the indication for ambucetamide, Janssen's first drug. My father had developed a herbal remedy to relieve menstrual pain, which he gave out free. It must have provided some relief as people in the village came to him for his proprietary medicine often enough.

I also recalled a lecture in my student days at NCL in Pune. It was by a scientist of Indian origin working in the USA. He was on a committee that funded research and he told us the story of a high-school student who had applied for a grant. The committee was intrigued enough to interview him. The student presented his research proposal for 50,000 dollars and said it had a 99.99 per cent chance of failure but if it succeeded it would revolutionize the electronic industry. The chairman of the committee asked him to 'take 75,000 dollars and fail gloriously'. This anecdote made quite an impression on me. Committees tend to play safe and I thought it was gutsy of the committee to take the decision to fund a risky research proposition generously. The chairman had probably made the difference to this committee. There seemed to be a lesson for me in this story.

All research is risky, but not mortally dangerous if it is frugal. I was aware that bringing a drug into the market consisted of two broad stages—the first, to discover a compound and determine its activity and toxicity; the second, to prove its safety and efficacy in human clinical trials. The second stage of 'clinical development' was by far the more expensive part and would necessarily require a partnership with a big company that had the expertise and could afford to take the risk. The first stage of synthesizing the compound was not beyond our reach. We could afford to 'fail gloriously' if the molecule did not make it to the second stage.

I asked myself, 'With twenty years of experience of synthesizing a plethora of drugs that involve two to twenty steps, can I not get into drug discovery on the strength of our chemistry?' Many new drugs were analogues of previously discovered drugs. Making analogues involved spotting promising molecules in development and improving them by modifying the chemical structure. This was a risky venture, but not a gamble.

I had pondered over these issues on and off in the past, but what was different that day in the farmhouse was that I moved instinctively and without conscious effort to a conclusion. I found a ladder to climb to the top of my farmhouse and looked around. The grape garden looked very nice. I thought it was the ideal place for research and the grape garden would look even nicer with a research laboratory for drug discovery next to it. A lazy morning in my farmhouse was transformed into a momentous one.

I commissioned Subash Narayan, an architect in Hyderabad, to design the facility for Dr. Reddy's Research Foundation. I was clear I did not want a drab building that looked like a government institution but something like a research facility in a university. Subash Narayan had studied in the USA and understood what I wanted. He came up with concepts and designs that I quite liked.

I was also clear that I needed to build a certain kind of culture in Dr. Reddy's Research Foundation, far different from that which prevailed in government research laboratories. Quite by chance, I had visited the Institute of Advanced Study at Princeton. We were selling ibuprofen in the USA and I went there on a business trip. Our representative met me after I landed in New York and told me that a Prof. Bhattacharya had called from the institute and asked for a meeting. I was quite excited as I had read about the institute in an issue of *Time* magazine in 1962 when I was a student in Bombay University. Every Indian will remember 1962 as the year India went to war with China. I remembered the cover of one issue that year—it had V.K. Krishna Menon, then our defence minister, with a cobra hovering behind his shoulder. Later that year, India lost the war with China and Krishna Menon lost his job. A few issues later, there was a cover story on John Glenn's space mission which talked about the Institute of Advanced Study at Princeton—that was the first time I heard of it. I discovered it was a unique institution and one of the world's leading centres of knowledge. Science and intellectual curiosity seemed to permeate the air in the institute that had been home to some of the best minds of all time. Albert Einstein had worked there and so had von Neumann and Robert Oppenheimer. One did not apply for a job at the Institute of Advanced Study—one had to be invited. I grabbed the chance to visit Princeton.

It turned out that Prof. Bhattacharya was working on the HIV virus and had read about me in a story in *The Economist*. He thought I was a wealthy industrialist who might fund his research! He must have been disappointed; nevertheless, he took me to lunch in the cafeteria. He introduced me to Marvin Goldberger, the director of the institute and a distinguished theoretical physicist. He was standing in line with everybody else to pick up his food and said he was a good friend of S. Chandrasekhar's, the famed astrophysicist who had won the Nobel Prize in Physics. Incidentally, Chandrasekhar was the nephew of Sir C.V. Raman, the only Indian scientist to have won the Nobel Prize—both Chandrasekhar and Har Gobind Khorana were American citizens when they won their Nobels, the latter for medicine. Harish-Chandra, who began as a theoretical physicist and worked with Homi Bhabha at the IISc and later switched to mathematics, had been the IBM von Neumann Professor of Mathematics at the institute for a long time. My head was swimming at the thought of being in the same place as all these great men of science. After lunch, my host showed me around some of the buildings and we wandered through the library. We stopped at the chair that Einstein had used. He persuaded me to sit on it. I was electrified. I heard more from Prof. Bhattacharya about the work culture at the institute, where everybody had the freedom to pursue their interests, spurred by the quest for excellence. Nobody told the faculty what to do; it was for them to decide what to pursue. I knew this was the culture that I needed to encourage in my research foundation.

My first task was to find a suitable person to lead it. Excellent scientific minds in pharmaceutical research were working abroad, but they would hardly be inclined to come to India. There would be no point in advertising in the newspapers for the position. I was wrestling with this seemingly insurmountable problem and asked Dr G.S.R. Subba Rao of the IISc for advice. Dr Subba Rao was himself a distinguished chemist and had obtained his DSc from the Andhra University at Waltair in my home state of Andhra Pradesh before he went on to obtain his second doctorate from Manchester. He suggested I consider Dr A. Venkateswarlu, an excellent chemist who had done his PhD at the University of Pennsylvania and postdoctoral research at Harvard under Prof. E.J. Corey. Venkat had worked for over a decade as head of discovery research at SmithKline Beecham in India and then moved on to CIBA Atul.

I thought it a promising lead. I also thought there was a good chance that Venkat would be interested in the position as I instinctively felt that a good chemist who had worked in drug discovery would be bored working on basic chemicals and dyestuffs at CIBA Atul. I requested Dr Subba Rao to fix a meeting with him and we had lunch at the Taj in

Bangalore. I was impressed with Venkat and decided he was the right man to lead the research foundation. I told him about my ideas and the kind of research culture I wished to build. I also told him that I knew it was chancy and difficult to come up with a new drug, but that we needed to make a beginning, even if it took the next twenty years to succeed. If nothing else, we would get some publications in good journals. I reassured him that I was not looking for quick returns and that he ought not to have any concerns about the security of his job or that of his colleagues, should he join me. Venkat was initially hesitant, but I was persuasive and he eventually joined us in October 1991.

I discussed the work programme with him and told him he should feel free to work in the areas of his interest. One of Janssen's tenets was to build programmes around his people and not the other way around. Venkat said he was interested in natural product chemistry and thought that camptothecin analogues had a lot of potential. Coincidentally, just a while earlier, a friend and consultant, Arvind Desai, had introduced me to Monroe Wall and Mansukh Wani who had done pioneering work on the extraction of camptothecin from the bark of *Camptotheca acuminata*, a plant known to have anti-cancer properties, at the Research Triangle Institute in the USA. Later, Wall and Mansukh Wani isolated Taxol, one of the most celebrated anti-cancer drugs, from *Taxus brevifolia*. Mansukh Wani was an organic chemist from Bombay. We had a fascinating discussion on natural product chemistry and Taxol over dinner at the Bombay Brasserie in Washington DC, so I had more than an inkling of the potential in this field. I asked Venkat to go ahead.

Arvind Desai was an analyst with Mehta and Isaly and he came periodically to Hyderabad as his sister-in-law lived here. He met me when he was studying the balance sheet of Dr. Reddy's and wanted to know more about our business. I found him to be enormously knowledgeable as he had worked for two decades or so in Pfizer and knew a number of people in the industry. He had seen the story of the pharmaceutical industry unfolding before him. He lived and breathed pharmaceuticals. He told me about his firm—it had been set up by Viren Mehta and Samuel Isaly, who had both worked as vice presidents at Warburg and had left to set up their own firm a few years earlier to provide investment banking and research services to investors. I knew nothing about licensing molecules to multinational companies at that time and needed help. I retained Mehta and Isaly as strategic advisers. I thought that with my vision and their experience we could shape the future of Dr. Reddy's.

Venkat got down to work and built his multidisciplinary team even as the construction of the facility was going on. In November 1993, Dr. Reddy's Research Foundation became operational next to the grape garden. I deliberately did not have any wall or fencing between the garden and the research facility—I thought the scientists might enjoy walking through it when they felt like it. The scientists were free to work in the hours of their choosing and pursue their own scientific interests. I made sure they never had to worry about food or transport. I think people quite liked the environment. A few camptothecin analogues were synthesized that showed some activity. The first patents of the research foundation were filed for them in June 1995.

Even as our camptothecin programme was gathering momentum, an analogue of camptothecin was very much in the news. A Japanese company making yoghurt, Yakult Honsha—*yakult* is the Japanese word for yoghurt—discovered irinotecan and the product was developed by Daiichi Pharmaceutical Company, now Daiichi Sankyo. It was licensed to Pharmacia & Upjohn (subsequently bought over by Pfizer) for the USA and some other parts of the world, while Rhône-Poulenc (now Sanofi) had the rights for Europe, Asia and Africa. The drug was granted priority review by the FDA. Normally, the FDA approves a drug after what are called Phase III trials, where the drug is administered to a sufficiently large population to evaluate its safety and efficacy. However, the tumour response noted in the earlier Phase II trial was so marked that the FDA granted conditional approval for marketing irinotecan in 1996. The drug was evaluated and final approval for the treatment of metastatic colorectal cancer was granted only two years later.

All these exciting developments indicated that we were on to a good thing with our camptothecin programme. We had built a good team at Dr. Reddy's Research Foundation. Dr Reddy's was also doing well and generating adequate cash flows from the generic business. I thought it was time to expand our research activity.

More importantly, I had an idea.

15 INDIA'S FIRST

Welcome Novo: *(L–R) With our consultant Arvind Desai, Satish, Prasad and Bruce Carter of Novo Nordisk*

In early 1994, Sankyo licensed a molecule called troglit8azone to Glaxo for marketing in Europe and to Parke Davis (by then a division of Warner Lambert) for USA. The intended use of troglitazone was the treatment for diabetes. I had been following the news of the progress of Sankyo's troglitazone in early clinical trials for some time. Sankyo's drug was an extraordinary breakthrough, and news of licensing deals reinforced my belief that Sankyo's approach could result in useful new drugs. A programme around glitazones could pole-vault our fledgling discovery effort to the front rank of drug discovery research

154

in diabetes. Just how much of a leap this new science represented is best appreciated with an understanding of the history of advances in diabetes treatment.

The diabetic condition was recognized as an ailment even in ancient times. Sushruta, the famous surgeon of Kashi (now known as Varanasi), is said to have noticed that ants were attracted to the urine of some patients with an emaciating disease. He called it *madhu meha*, honey-like urine. He prescribed *silajatu*, a substance found in nature, which he believed contained traces of six metals, for the treatment of madhu meha as well as obesity. Silajatu is believed to help control blood sugar even to the present day in Ayurveda, the Indian system of medicine. Quite amazingly, Sushruta is believed to have associated madhu meha with a sedentary lifestyle and advised a moderate diet, exercise and the avoidance of stress, such as anger in conduct, for treating it. Nobody knows for sure when Sushruta was born, but it is likely that it was sometime around 1000 BC. Like many Vedic texts in the oral tradition, *Sushruta Samhita* was compiled and transcribed at a later date and was probably added to by various practitioners over time. For more than 2500 years after Sushruta, there was little progress in the understanding of the disease or how to manage it. Death followed diabetes, as inevitably as night follows day.

The twentieth century changed all this. By the early 1900s, it was known that the pancreas was involved in diabetes. Over the next decade or so, it was postulated that islets in the pancreas produced a hormone that regulated blood levels and a French scientist as well as a British physiologist independently came up with the same name for the hormone—insulin—derived from the Latin word for island. But it was still a hypothetical substance and it was Frederick Banting, a Canadian doctor fresh from his basic degree in medicine and a stint in military service in the First World War, who isolated the hormone from the pancreas of dogs, while working with J.J.R. Macleod, the head of the department of physiology at the University of Toronto, and several others. The results were announced to a standing ovation in 1922 at a meeting of the Association of American Physicians. Without being aware that the hormone had been named previously, they—for the third time—called it insulin. Banting and Macleod, who had a stormy relationship, went on to jointly receive the Nobel Prize in 1923 for their discovery.

The joint nomination of Banting and Macleod was made by August Krogh, a professor of physiology at the University of Copenhagen who had won the Nobel Prize in 1920. On a lecture tour in the USA in 1922, Krogh and his wife, Marie, who was also a medical doctor, frequently heard of the discovery of insulin at the University of Toronto. Marie was diabetic herself and this perhaps prompted them to take a detour to Toronto on their way back to Copenhagen. Krogh met both Banting and Macleod and was so impressed by the potential of insulin that he obtained a license to manufacture and market insulin in Scandinavia and set up Nordisk Insulinlaboratorium to do that. The company is now Novo Nordisk, a global leader in diabetes care and extraordinarily focused on it. About three-quarters of Novo Nordisk's revenues come from diabetes care products.

In the meanwhile, Eli Lilly & Co. had also obtained rights for the manufacture of insulin and developed a process that made its production considerably more consistent and efficient. The discovery of insulin was undoubtedly the most dramatic advance in history to tame diabetes. Thanks to its discovery by Banting and his colleagues and its large-scale production—no mean feat for the 1920s—by Eli Lilly and Novo Nordisk, diabetics no longer faced the prospect of imminent death.

The understanding of diabetes increased fairly rapidly thereafter and the complex process of glucose metabolism was unravelled. We learnt that the carbohydrates we consume are broken down into glucose in the digestive system and released into the bloodstream. The increased level of glucose in the blood signals the pancreas to release insulin. Insulin is the hormone essential for glucose to enter the cells in the body to provide them with energy. If there is insufficient or no insulin, blood glucose levels build up and the kidneys work overtime to get rid of the glucose, hence the frequent urination that is a typical symptom of the disease. The frequent urination also causes thirst, another common symptom of diabetes. At the same time, the cells are starved of energy, so they start burning fat, causing weight loss and fatigue that are again typical of diabetes. Once the glucose levels in the blood drop to the right level, the pancreas receives a signal to stop the release of insulin. In healthy individuals, both blood glucose and insulin levels are within a certain range.

As early as 1936, a British clinician, Harry Himsworth, published a paper in the *Lancet* distinguishing between two types of diabetes—one, where people developed diabetes at a young age because the pancreas suddenly stopped production of insulin; the other where diabetes developed later in life because resistance developed to the action of insulin. In the latter case, the body responds by producing more and more insulin to overcome resistance to it, but eventually the production of insulin drops off.

The first major breakthrough after insulin was the discovery of a class of drugs called sulphonylureas, which triggered the production of more insulin to overcome resistance to it. This was yet another drug found by accident when a French researcher stumbled upon the glucose-regulating properties of the drug while researching cures for typhoid. The first of the sulphonylureas came into the market in 1955. It had taken *three decades* after insulin for the next major breakthrough in the treatment of diabetes. Sulphonylureas got better and better as a whole host of them with greater potency and somewhat lower side effects followed. Fundamentally, however, sulphonylureas, while triggering the production of more insulin, did not address the root problem of insulin resistance.

In parallel with the development of sulphonylureas, scientists worked on understanding insulin resistance better and an important advance was made, quite surprisingly, by a nuclear physicist. Soon after the Second World War, Rosalyn Yalow was offered a position by the Veterans Administration (VA) in the USA to work on the use of radioactive substances in the diagnosis and treatment of disease. By

1959, working with a physician colleague at the VA hospital in Bronx, New York, she developed a radioimmunoassay to determine the amount of insulin circulating in the blood of adult diabetics. Yalow received a Nobel Prize in 1977 for her work, the second woman to receive the award for medicine.

Yalow's work led to the confirmation that when insulin resistance develops, the body's first response is to produce more insulin. This prompted a great deal of thinking about drugs to counter insulin resistance and that became the next holy grail of diabetes treatment.

In the late 1970s, Takeda in Japan, while investigating the lipid-lowering effects of fibrate analogues that they had experimentally synthesized, discovered that some of them also had glucose-lowering effects in mice. This eventually led to the discovery of a family of chemical compounds that had marked glucose-lowering effects. Takeda chose a lead compound and gave it a name—Ciglitazone—and licensed it to Upjohn, but it did not go far into development as it had too many side effects. On the other hand, a later discovery of Sankyo that came to be called troglitazone was attracting a lot of attention after its biological activity was published and it progressed in clinical trials.

For the first time, more than forty years after the discovery of insulin resistance, a drug to increase sensitivity to insulin was administered to man and the results were promising. Unlike the sulphonylureas that increased insulin production, Sankyo's troglitazone addressed the root problem of insulin resistance in adult-onset diabetes and therefore did not have the problem of hypoglycaemia or depletion of the insulin-producing cells in the pancreas. It was truly a great breakthrough in drug discovery and of immense significance in the treatment of diabetes.

The competition to make a better glitazone was intense. Takeda, smarting at being overtaken though it had discovered the first glitazone, redoubled its efforts and came up with pioglitazone. By 1990, the world knew that SmithKline Beecham was also in the race as its first patent filed for yet another glitazone—rosiglitazone—was published. More companies, including Pfizer and Aventis, were to follow.

By the time I made up my mind about getting into glitazone research, it was clear that several companies were ahead of us. I was, however, not daunted. I knew that very often in drug discovery, it is not the first-discovered molecule that is the best but later analogues. The best-known example is perhaps in the statin family—lovastatin was the first statin and was followed by pravastatin and simvastatin, which were both better, but atorvastatin and rosuvastatin which followed were even more potent. I knew that more companies would join the race for glitazones, with large budgets.

Sometime in 1994, I discussed the possibility of glitazone research with Venkat, Rajagopalan and a few others. I initiated a glitazone programme and decided to lead it. I knew that if our programme had to succeed, we would have to be superfast and make a better and more potent glitazone than anybody else.

Work proceeded rapidly. The known glitazones were synthesized and assays set up to establish their activity and potency. The chemistry team was strengthened when Braj and Vidya Lohray, a husband-and-wife-team, joined us at the end of 1994. Vidya, a particularly skilled chemist, plunged into the glitazone project and soon succeeded in synthesizing novel compounds. They were two to three times more potent than the known ones, but still not good enough.

We must have synthesized fifty to sixty molecules working around the troglitazone moiety. One day, Vidya said she was getting tired of it and I knew we were running short of time—troglitazone had entered Phase III, the final phase of the clinical trials. Vidya wanted to try something around the rosiglitazone moiety and went ahead in that direction. I thought it was time to get back to the basics and think of a fresh approach. I pondered over the structure of the known glitazones. The pharmacophore—the basic structural feature that provided the activity—was similar in all the glitazones, but the scaffold that held it up and made it a usable drug was where the play was. Though I was not an organic chemist, I knew enough of pharmaceutical chemistry to recognize that the scaffold for troglitazone was nothing but α-tocopherol, one of the active forms of Vitamin E. α-tocopherol had antioxidant properties and I thought we did not need that kind of baggage.

Nature has an infinite variety of scaffolds that computer-aided design scarcely betters and chemists have always drawn upon them to design their novel molecules. I, therefore, started to look up the Merck Index, a bible for all pharmaceutical chemists, for compounds that were extracted from natural products. The goal was to find a natural product scaffold which would be suitable for the glitazones. I had not gone through even a third of the Merck Index when I found what I wanted. The compound was glycosine, a quinazolinone alkaloid with hypnotic–sedative properties that was extracted from *Glycosmis pentaphylla*.

Curiously enough, methaqualone, a derivative in the quinazolinone family, was first synthesized in Hyderabad as early as 1951 by Hussain Zaheer, director of the Regional Research Laboratories, Hyderabad, and I.K. Kacker of the chemistry department of the University of Lucknow. The duo was synthesizing quinazolinone derivatives to investigate their analgesic properties. Unprotected by patents, methaqualone was picked up, first in Europe in the 1960s and later by an American company, William H. Rorer—acquired by Rhône-Poulenc in the 1990s—and marketed as a sedative. The brand name was Quaalude and sales boomed. Parke Davis and another company also jumped into the market with the product. People felt 'happy' when they took the drug and the word spread. The reason for the extraordinary uptick in sales was that it began to be abused as a mood elevator and was eventually withdrawn. Hussain Zaheer never patented the compound and abandoned it, or it could have (happily) been termed India's first new drug discovery! It tickled me no end that in the quest for a more legitimate drug, I was utilizing the same scaffold first used some forty years earlier in Hyderabad.

I cut the side chain of glycosine and attached the thiazolidinedione in its place and I had a novel structure on paper. I was in my city office that day, and a new fax machine had just been installed. My first fax went to Vidya with the novel structure asking if she could synthesize it. Vidya called back in less than half an hour. She said that it could be done, but it would take time. On the other hand, she thought the structure could be simplified by shuffling the position of one of the methyl groups and the synthesis of such a compound could be done in a week. I asked her to go ahead. Sooner than I expected, we had a series of compounds that exhibited very marked glucose-lowering effects and we filed our first patent for them in April 1995. The team insisted that I should be the first named inventor as the basic idea was mine. I was persuaded on that occasion, but it was to be the last patent where my name figured.

My next problem was that I needed to let the world know that we had discovered new glitazones. We had chemists and other scientists working within four walls and doing a lot of good work, but how was the world outside to hear about it? At that time, nobody associated India with discovery research. It would be an uphill task to get people interested. It was in that context that I invited Nair, then secretary general of the Organisation of Pharmaceutical Producers of India, to visit our facility. He was contributing to *Scrip*, a magazine that was read by a wide cross section in the pharmaceutical industry, including drug discovery researchers, in-licensing people and top management. I thought it would be useful if our discovery efforts could be featured in it. Nair visited us and was completely taken by surprise at what he saw. He was genuinely impressed that such a facility existed in India and said he had never seen anything like it before. He then asked, 'Dr Reddy, what can I do for you?' I told him that there was nothing specific, but it would be nice if he talked to our scientists and wrote about his impressions.

Nair went back and wrote a piece on the work we were doing with insulin sensitizers, with a bit of speculation about the possible profile of the compounds we were working on. Soon after the news appeared in *Scrip*, I got a call from the president of Bayer International who asked about our compound. The next person who was interested was Bruce Carter, chief scientific officer of Novo Nordisk. I was not ready to talk, so I referred them to Arvind Desai at Mehta and Isaly, whom we had retained to advise us on this transaction. Arvind stalled for time.

Bruce Carter nevertheless came to Hyderabad and visited our research centre where I met him. He was impressed with our facilities and wanted to learn more about what we were doing in the diabetes area. I invited him to my office and talked to him about the work we were doing on glitazones and drew the structures on a white board. Bruce was possibly a little surprised—he would have expected this kind of discussion with a chemist, not the chairman of a company. I told him frankly that we had not come to a conclusion as yet on the best molecule that could be taken forward for development. I then assured him, 'The best is around the corner. I will call you when it comes.'

I instinctively felt that Novo would be the right company to talk to as they were basically a diabetes company and not too big. When we had identified our lead compound—it did not have a name just then, only a number, DRF 2593, I faxed Bruce the good news. I also talked to Arvind and got him thinking about possible commercial terms.

Novo asked for samples for doing their own testing to confirm our results and commercial negotiations accelerated once that was done. Novo came in with an offer of 2–3 million dollars and Arvind recommended our considering it. I did not agree. Arvind was looking at it from a return on investment perspective for the company. I looked at it instead from the perspective of the opportunity it represented for Novo. The global leader in diabetes had completely missed the bus as far as the most important breakthrough in diabetes treatment in forty years was concerned. There were only two other molecules ahead of us in development, apart from troglitazone. Surely our glitazone, which was clearly more potent than the competition, deserved more. I must have sounded hurt and Arvind may well have conveyed that to Novo. They told Arvind, 'We would not like to hurt Dr Reddy,' and upped their offer. We eventually settled for a total consideration of 15 million dollars, with an upfront payment of 3 million dollars and the remainder on milestones being reached, as well as a royalty of 5 per cent if the product made it to the market. Most importantly, we would be the sole manufacturer for global supplies of the product if it made it to the market and we would be paid 8 per cent on sales towards manufacturing costs.

We signed the deal on 1st March 1997. DRF 2593 was the first new chemical entity discovered in India to have been licensed to a multinational company for development. It was a milestone in the history of the pharmaceutical industry in the country.

Before we signed the deal, we retained KPMG to advise us on the structuring and the tax implications. KPMG told us that there was a 15 per cent withholding tax in Denmark and suggested we incorporate a company in Antilles, which would result in a lower tax incidence of around 4.3 per cent. I was assured that it was perfectly legal and everybody concerned—the Reserve Bank of India, the income tax authorities and our shareholders—would be informed in a fully transparent manner.

Just before we incorporated the company in Antilles, I was travelling and stopped over in Amsterdam on the way back to Hyderabad. I picked up the newspapers and found to my horror that Steffi Graf's father had been convicted for tax evasion and sentenced to prison as he had apparently routed her earnings through a company in Antilles. I was quite alarmed and spoke to KPMG in Amsterdam and went across to meet the concerned person. He sensed I was perturbed and reassured me straightaway. He said that Steffi's father had hidden away his income in Antilles and had evaded tax. On the other hand, we were doing the transaction transparently, declaring the income and paying the tax—not evading it. 'Don't worry, Dr Reddy, it's perfectly legal,' he said and took me, a much relieved client, to lunch.

On 29th January 1997, Warner Lambert received fast-track approval from the FDA for troglitazone and launched the product in March with the brand name Rezulin. It became one of the fastest-selling drugs in history. Glaxo launched troglitazone on 2nd October 1997 in the UK with the brand name Romozin. There was absolutely no doubt it would be a blockbuster.

Within the month, the first reports of liver injury in patients on troglitazone were received both by the FDA and the regulatory authority in Britain. By December 1997, Glaxo had voluntarily withdrawn the drug in the face of increasing evidence of liver damage. Despite mounting evidence of harm, it took the FDA till 21st March 2000 to notify Warner Lambert to withdraw the drug.

The withdrawal of troglitazone did not affect the development programme for DRF 2593. Clinical trials of both SmithKline Beecham's rosiglitazone and Takeda's pioglitazone were proceeding smoothly. The drugs were eventually approved by the FDA within months of each other in 1999.

Novo was responsible for all development of DRF 2593 and they went ahead in earnest. One of the preliminary steps was to name the molecule. WHO had developed a system for giving 'international non-proprietary' or generic names to new molecules. Novo was gracious enough to give us the choice. It would obviously be a glitazone as it belonged to that family, but we could choose the prefix to uniquely identify our molecule. We chose the name balaglitazone after Balaji, one of the names of a deity in the Hindu pantheon, particularly revered

DRF 2593 is licensed to Novo Nordisk: *(L–R) Anuradha Altekar, A. Subba Reddy, A Venkateswarlu, Prasad, me, Satish, Bruce Carter, Arvind Desai, Mrs Carter, Anker Lundemose and P.V. Venugopal*

in Andhra Pradesh. Balaglitazone was first dosed in man in March 1998, the first ever new chemical entity discovered in India to have reached this stage. Clinical trials proceeded uneventfully.

The licensing of balaglitazone and its subsequent progress attracted international attention, in part because of *where* it had been discovered. David Pilling, then the correspondent of *Financial Times* of London covering the global pharmaceutical industry, profiled me in 1999. His piece, headlined 'Doctor in Search of Patents', reflected a common view of the Indian pharmaceutical industry at that time:

> Although India has thousands of local manufacturers—experts in pirating western drugs—they have contributed virtually nothing to original research. But Anji Reddy, founder and chairman of the company that bears his name, wants to change all that. Not only has his company developed drug manufacturing skills to western standards, it has embarked on research aimed at discovering drugs of its own.

Pilling added:

> After only a few years of research, scientists working in his purpose-built foundation in Hyderabad found a novel compound to treat diabetes. So promising is their molecule, one of a new class of anti-diabetics, that it has been snapped up by Novo Nordisk, a Danish pharmaceuticals company and a leader in the field.

Dubbing the company's efforts as 'merely India's first tentative steps on a long, pot-holed road', Pilling commented on my discovery strategy with a hint of disdain:

> [H]e wants to make 'analogues', versions of existing drugs that are chemically different enough to warrant a patent. That may be only one step up from outright piracy, but it is a tactic many western drugs companies have used.

The article was published on 30th August 1999. Pilling did not even take note of the fact that we had discovered ragaglitazar, which was not an analogue but a first-in-class compound that we had licensed to Novo Nordisk a year earlier. I do not hold that against him. It was hard enough for people to believe we had discovered an analogue. It was too much to expect that the news that we had progressed to discovering a first-in-class compound would be readily accepted.

Phase II trials of balaglitazone commenced by August 2000 and were completed satisfactorily with no signs of any safety issue. And then, Novo Nordisk suspended the further development of balaglitazone.

But that is another story.

16 GRAVEYARD OF THE GLITAZARS

Do we, or do we not? *Discovery
research decisions are hard*

Soon after balaglitazone was established as a lead development
candidate, there was a discussion on the future of the glitazone
programme. Should there be a pause, or should it continue? Some
scientists felt there was considerable potential in this area and I agreed
that work should continue.

This decision proved to be a momentous one. It led to Dr. Reddy's
discovering a first-in-class compound, a rare achievement for any
pharmaceutical company. The profile of the molecule at the pre-clinical
stage was so promising that Novo Nordisk decided to suspend the

clinical development of balaglitazone and fast-track the development of the new discovery.

The discovery programme was initially focused on continuing to make analogues around the pharmacophore of the glitazones to find a better drug. The drug could be better, for example, if it resulted in greater control over blood glucose or resulted in lesser side effects. The team led by Braj and Vidya Lohray kept up the pace in synthesizing new compounds and testing them out.

In the meanwhile, researchers in academia and industry were contributing to an increasing understanding of how glitazones worked. It was clear in the 1980s itself that glitazones reduced insulin resistance—or increased insulin sensitivity, which is the same thing—so that the body did not need to produce more insulin to overcome the resistance. This was established through studies that measured insulin levels in the body. What remained a mystery, however, was the mechanism by which glitazones achieved this.

The man who paved the way for greater understanding of the mechanism was none other than K. Janardan Reddy, a medical graduate who did his internship in Osmania Medical College in Hyderabad in 1961 and later taught at the Kakatiya University in Warangal, about 150 kilometres from Hyderabad. Janardan Reddy went on to do his MD at the All India Institute of Medical Sciences, Delhi, and then joined the University of Kansas Hospital. He did stellar work on the biology of peroxisomes, which were identified clearly only in 1967 as a sub-unit in a cell with specialized functions. Janardan Reddy demonstrated that a number of structurally diverse compounds—from plasticizers used in the manufacture of PVC (polyvinyl chloride) to herbicides and lipid-lowering compounds—could increase their number. He gave these compounds a name in 1975—peroxisome proliferators. Janardan Reddy then accepted the position of professor of pathology at Northwestern University and continued his work on the molecular mechanisms of peroxisome proliferators and their activation. He was to join our scientific advisory board some two decades later.

Further advances took place, notably in 1990, when two researchers with Imperial Chemical Industries in the UK identified a receptor that could be activated by a wide range of molecules, including fibrates. Their work suggested that the activation of this receptor resulted in peroxisome proliferation. This receptor was therefore called the peroxisome proliferator-activated receptor—PPAR. It was later designated PPARα to distinguish it from the subsequently discovered isoforms, PPARδ and PPARγ.

The connection between PPARγ and glitazones was still unknown. This happened only in 1995 when Glaxo's researchers identified PPARγ as the target of the glitazones. Thus, the molecular mechanism of the glitazones was known at long last, but the reason for this mechanism resulting in the lowering of glucose was still in the realm of speculation, prompting a flurry of research to understand it further. Ironically, Sankyo's troglitazone, Takeda's pioglitazone, SmithKline Beecham's rosiglitazone and our balaglitazone had all been discovered and their potential for increasing insulin sensitivity and regulating glucose was established without the knowledge of their molecular mechanism.

The new knowledge spurred further interest in glitazones and we forged ahead with experimenting with fresh approaches to designing molecules. Within six months of our licensing balaglitazone to Novo Nordisk, Braj and Vidya came up with some novel molecules. One of them was DRF 4158, a potentially better PPARγ activator than balaglitazone; it was eventually licensed to Novartis in March 2001. But it was another molecule, DRF 2725, that was an extraordinary discovery.

By the mid-1990s, PPARα was known to be the target for fibrates that regulate lipids, triglycerides and cholesterol, and PPARγ the target for glitazones known to lower blood glucose. It was also known that the fibrates did not lower glucose and that glitazones did not lower lipids. Though these mechanisms were known, it was standard procedure to test new compounds in animal models for their effects on both lipids and glucose. In those days, I got the test results by fax as soon as they were available wherever I was.

When the results of DRF 2725 came in, I saw that not only was glucose being lowered as might have been expected, but so were triglycerides. This was quite strange, as no other known PPAR compound seemed to have this property.

We did not have a molecular biology department at that time, but I had got to know Anker Lundemose, head of business development at Novo Nordisk, quite well by then and was aware that he had a PhD in molecular biology. I told him what was happening with DRF 2725 and asked him what he thought of it. He joked that he was no great molecular biologist despite his PhD and said he would talk to Patrick Doyle, the head of pharmacology at Novo Nordisk, who had also visited us several times. Patrick asked for a sample of 100 milligrams and tested it in his laboratory. He could barely restrain his excitement when he called me from Copenhagen. He said, 'Dr Reddy, you have a dual—a compound that is both a PPARα and PPARγ activator. It is a first-in-class compound.'

I could understand why Patrick was excited. Most diabetics have elevated triglycerides and LDL cholesterol, the 'bad' cholesterol. The clinical implications of having a compound that had a beneficial effect on both lipids and glucose were enormous—as also the potential market.

Most new molecules are what are called analogues of a previously discovered molecule. Ciglitazone was the first of the glitazones, a first-in-class compound. The glitazones that followed were analogues. Once the first-in-class is discovered, the quest is to discover the 'best-in-class', which was the strategy we were following, even after the discovery of balaglitazone. Along the way, Braj and Vidya had modified the pharmacophore of the glitazones, and had come up with DRF 2725 that regulated not only glucose by activating PPARγ but also regulated lipids by activating PPARα. It was indeed a first-in-class compound.

The implication of having discovered a first-in-class molecule took a while to sink in completely. As a matter of science, it was a major achievement. A first-in-class compound is one which has a structurally novel pharmacophore, usually accompanied by a novel mechanism of action. The golden age of drug discovery was in the 1990s, when the largest number of new drugs was approved every year. Even in this period, barely five or six new molecules were first-in-class and the number now is lower. Even the biggest pharmaceutical companies with very large budgets for R&D do not churn out first-in-class drugs consistently and it is not uncommon to see years go by before they come up with one. Dr. Reddy's had discovered a first-in-class compound for the first time in the country. And we did it in remarkably quick time—in just about four years after we had launched the glitazone programme.

Novo Nordisk was enthusiastic about developing DRF 2725 and we licensed it to them in August 1998, seventeen months after balaglitazone. The pre-clinical work that needs to be done before the compound is first dosed in man is quite elaborate and includes toxicology studies to estimate the safe dosage in man as well as pharmacokinetic studies in animals to explore the absorption and distribution of the drug in the system, its metabolism and excretion. All this work was done rapidly. The animal data from this compound was so impressive that Novo Nordisk noted in its evaluation, 'If we can reproduce the favourable animal data in humans, it will increase the life expectancy of diabetic patients by 10–12 years.' DRF 2725 was ready to enter clinical trials or 'enter the clinic', as it is termed in drug discovery slang. Novo Nordisk decided to suspend clinical trials on balaglitazone and accelerate the clinical trials of DRF 2725 as the commercial potential was appreciably greater.

It is customary to apply for the international non-proprietary name before the drug enters the clinic. Based on the structure of the pharmacophore, glitazar needed to be part of the name, but we had a choice with respect to the prefix. As before, Novo gave us the choice. We chose 'raga', the acronym for 'Reddy alpha gamma agonist'. Agonist in pharmacology means a molecule that binds to a nuclear receptor and activates it, so the acronym reflected the activity of the compound. I liked the name because raga is also very Indian and, since its origin is in

Sanskrit, it is a common word that is used in many Indian languages to denote melody in music. In Sanskrit, it literally means colour or hue but has also been used as a metaphor for emotions, mainly love, joy or desire.

Ragaglitazar was first dosed in man in November 1999, the same year that pioglitazone and rosiglitazone were approved for marketing. Phase I went off uneventfully and Phase II studies to determine efficacy and safety in a relatively small number of patients commenced in August 2000. Again, everything went smoothly and the final phase of clinical trials began in November 2001. In parallel, long-term toxicology studies were going on. Ragaglitazar had been tested for its toxicity in the short term before clinical trials started and it was clean. However, as it was a chronic medication and could potentially be used for a lifetime, it was also necessary to test its effects in the long term. This is normally done in animals and ragaglitazar was being tested on rats and mice. The lifespan of these rodents is about two years and for about one and a half years, everything was fine. Shortly after the eighteen-month mark, one mouse died. It was dissected to establish the cause of death. The mouse had developed a urinary bladder tumour. Some rats had also developed bladder tumours earlier, but it was not a cause for concern as many drugs caused tumours in rats. It was also not known if the tumour was specific to the rodent species. It was particularly important to ascertain this as the urine of rodents is different in composition from that of human beings and the drug could have caused crystal formation in rodent urine, a possible cause of cancer in them. In such a case, it would have been of no relevance to human beings. However, when the mouse died, it was the second species in which the tumour occurred. As a precautionary measure for patient safety, Novo Nordisk immediately announced the suspension of the clinical trial of ragaglitazar until the cause of the tumour could be determined. The announcement was made on 22nd July 2002, possibly the worst day of my life.

Three days later, a Danish TV channel carried the news with an interview of a participant in the clinical trial. The media in Europe and elsewhere picked up the story. Some of the news reports seemed to have got it all wrong. The headline in a German newspaper was completely off the mark. It said 'Insulin causes cancer'—a misunderstanding probably triggered by the fact that ragaglitazar was an insulin sensitizer.

The mood among the scientists involved in discovery research was sombre after the failure of ragaglitazar. As one of them ruefully remarked, it was like an unseeded player entering the finals of Wimbledon and losing.

The only saving grace was that there was very little chance that patients in the trial would be endangered. The rodents on which ragaglitazar was tested had been exposed to it for at least half their lifetime, some of them for all of it. Since ragaglitazar had been shown to be non-genotoxic even before the human trials had commenced, it was very unlikely that any cancers would have developed in human beings in the six months that patients had been exposed to it in the clinical trial. In any case, even if non-genotoxic drugs are carcinogenic, these effects generally do not manifest themselves once the drug is discontinued.

Lars Rebien Sørensen, the CEO of Novo Nordisk, was on vacation when the trial was stopped. I called him, but he had nothing to add. Lars and I had met many times during the course of negotiations for licensing balaglitazone and ragaglitazar. It was perhaps on the first trip Lars made to Hyderabad that he hesitantly asked me as we were driving out of the research facility, 'What made you get into diabetes research?' I could have spun him a yarn about the burden of disease and the good that it would do to humanity. Instead, I gave him a short answer, 'I am diabetic.' Lars did not say anything more. I wondered if it struck a chord with him, as the founder of his company had pursued Fred Banting for a licence to manufacture insulin prompted by the fact that his wife was diabetic. Whatever be the reason, Lars and I got along well.

I decided to go to Amsterdam and meet Lars personally to get a better understanding of Novo Nordisk's thinking about the future of ragaglitazar. Lars invited me to dinner at a restaurant, a forty-minute drive from Amsterdam. I reached early as I normally do when I am abroad and had about half an hour to kill. The restaurant was attached to a church and I wandered into it. It was empty and remarkably serene—a balm for the soul as I contemplated the conversation I would soon have. Lars and I had dinner and it became clear that ragaglitazar would not be resuscitated. As Lars ruefully said, 'one goddamn mouse' had put paid to years of research. He said, however, that they would restart the balaglitazone programme in early 2003. My hope that a drug discovered by Dr. Reddy's would make it into the market remained alive.

In the meanwhile, questions arose about the risk of bladder cancer from the use of pioglitazone. Prodded by the FDA, Takeda, the originator of pioglitazone, had initiated a ten-year study in 2002 to investigate these questions. Further, it was noticed that the use of glitazones, particularly when co-administered with insulin, appeared to increase the risk of congestive heart failure. The American Diabetes Association came out with a consensus statement in December 2003 that pointed to the advantages of glitazones in lowering blood sugar as well as the concerns over the potentially adverse cardiovascular effects in diabetics with their use, and advised physicians to be cognizant of the risks.

News of these concerns heightened the uncertainty about the risks associated with the use of glitazones. Novartis, which had licensed DRF 4158, a PPARγ activator, returned the molecule in early 2003 itself. There were enough signals that the FDA and the European Medicines Agency would be reluctant to grant approval to new glitazones in the face of such uncertainties. Novo Nordisk, therefore, decided to discontinue the development of balaglitazone in October 2004 and returned the rights.

When Novo Nordisk took this decision, long-term toxicity studies in rodents were still under way with Covance, a contract research organization, and it wished to discontinue them. I asked Covance how much it would cost to complete the studies and was told it would be 1 million dollars. I said I would pay for it and the studies were completed. Balaglitazone came out clean without any toxicity concerns. Half in jest, I told my colleagues that the lord after whom balaglitazone had been named had saved the molecule, but ragaglitazar named after me, a mere mortal, was gone.

Late in 2002, we discovered another unique compound—DRL 11605. It activated all isoforms of PPAR receptors—α, δ and γ. It was soon known as the pan-PPAR activator. However, it was a weak PPARγ activator, which was good news as the adverse effects that had surfaced were all associated with PPARγ activators. Unlike activators of PPARα, which regulated lipids, and PPARγ that regulated blood sugar, PPARδ was the target for obesity-related disorders. It seemed to have potentially beneficial effects of weight loss, reducing insulin resistance, and restricting production of sugar in the liver through a mechanism different from that of PPARγ. When combined with its effects on lipids because of PPARα activation, DRL 11605 seemed to be an exciting new approach to deal with the metabolic syndrome, or syndrome X as it was called, which was a bunch of obesity-related conditions that, if untreated, could progress to diabetes and cardiovascular disease.

Amusingly enough, PPARδ grabbed the headlines—and public imagination—during the Athens Olympics in August 2004. A team of US–South Korean scientists had genetically engineered a mouse strain with enhanced PPARδ activity and it was found that such mice could run twice as long as normal ones. They published a paper on their genetically engineered mice in a scientific journal. The media latched on to the story and promptly dubbed them 'marathon mice'. With the Olympics in the news all the time, the discussion quickly turned from the fat-burning and muscle-enhancing effect of PPARδ activation to its potential for cheating in athletics.

We were at the crossroads with our PPAR programme. On the one hand, there was an unmistakable dropping off of licensing interest in these compounds because of the adverse effects seen in approved compounds and the difficulties in obtaining regulatory approval for new PPAR activators. On the other, Takeda and GSK had a deep conviction that their drugs were useful treatments and had mounted large-scale studies to remove doubts about their safety. We had balaglitazone, which had shown no signs of safety concerns and two other molecules at the pre-clinical stage—DRF 10945, a PPARα activator, and DRL 11605, the pan-PPAR activator. With commercial interest waning in the PPAR activator compounds, it was difficult to out-license them for development, but we could not sit on them and wait indefinitely as patent protection would run out. If it eventually turned out that the concerns around the PPARs were misplaced, we would rue the delay in development.

I decided to go ahead with the development of the new molecules on our own. DRF 10945 was first dosed in man in early 2004 in Canada and Phase I studies were completed smoothly. The next year, a Danish company, Rheoscience, came up with an offer to codevelop balaglitazone. We bluntly told them we would not invest any money in further development. However, they were quite keen and we ultimately struck a deal whereby they would invest all the money for further development in return for rights in Europe and China as well as a milestone payment from us if balaglitazone was approved in the USA. Thereafter, in January 2006, DRL 11605 also commenced Phase I studies in Canada. For a while, there was hope.

Meanwhile, Bristol-Myers Squibb filed for regulatory approval of muraglitazar with the FDA. Muraglitazar was also a PPARα and PPARγ activator, and an analogue of ragaglitazar. It had initially been behind ragaglitazar in clinical development, but Bristol-Myers Squibb had pushed ahead with development even after the discontinuance of ragaglitazar. The application was put up to the FDA Advisory Committee in the USA. The committee voted in September 2005 to recommend its approval, but the FDA held back approval on the ground of safety concerns and required cardiovascular safety studies that were not commercially viable for Bristol-Myers Squibb to undertake. The writing on the wall for all further applications for approval of new diabetic drugs, particularly glitazones and glitazars, was quite clear.

The door finally shut on the PPARs in 2007 in a fairly dramatic fashion. The man instrumental in doing so was Dr Steve Nissen, the head of cardiovascular medicine at the Cleveland Clinic. Nissen had been very vocal in calling attention to the safety concerns of muraglitazar and had forcefully called upon the FDA to withhold its approval. In early 2007, he had asked GSK for access to the clinical trials on rosiglitazone but was refused. However, soon thereafter, GSK put all the clinical trials of rosiglitazone on its website because of an entirely different development. In 2004, the State of New York had sued GSK alleging that it had not published trials that showed suicidal tendencies in children and adolescents using paroxetine, an antidepressant. As part of the negotiated settlement in that case, GSK agreed to make all results of its clinical trials from end-2000 public and did so. Nissen heard of this and accessed their results sometime in April 2007. He identified forty-two trials with rosiglitazone, including thirty-five that had not been published. Nissen did a meta-analysis of all the trials and submitted an article to the respected *New England Journal of Medicine* reporting a statistically significant increase in the risk of heart attacks with the use of rosiglitazone. Rosiglitazone had become the top-selling diabetic drug and GSK had achieved peak sales of over 3 billion dollars. The prescriptions for rosiglitazone plummeted after Nissen's article and so did GSK's share price. Steve Nissen was declared one of the 100 most influential people in the world in 2007 by *Time* magazine.

The FDA was apparently fully aware of all the studies but had not come to a conclusion that rosiglitazone needed to be withdrawn. However, a 'black box' warning was issued. A black box warning is a prominent boxed warning on the labelling of a drug. It is the strongest warning that is issued by the FDA and is based on the occurrence of serious adverse events. There was a two-year Senate inquiry in the USA and pressure to withdraw the drug intensified, but the FDA stood its ground. However, it required GSK to initiate a study to investigate the cardiovascular effects of rosiglitazone in 2008. This study, named TIDE, was designed to evaluate the cardiovascular outcomes of long-term treatment with rosiglitazone and pioglitazone. It commenced, and a heated public debate ensued, on whether it was the ethical thing to do. The trial was scheduled to be completed in 2015, but bowing to public pressure, the FDA terminated it in 2010. Though rosiglitazone continues to be sold in the USA, it was withdrawn in Europe in 2010 and thereafter in many other countries.

For a while, pioglitazone seemed to be faring better than rosiglitazone. Diabetic patients are at increased cardiovascular risk and, soon after the approval of the drug by the FDA in 1999, Takeda sponsored PROact, a randomized clinical trial to assess whether pioglitazone improved macrovascular outcomes, including the incidence of heart attacks, strokes and bypass surgery. The results of PROact, published in 2007, indeed showed a reduction.

The problem for pioglitazone came from another quarter. When the drug was first approved for marketing, the possibility of an increased risk of bladder cancer was noted. The FDA requested Takeda to conduct a safety study in 2003 to investigate this risk and Takeda initiated a study accordingly. Subjects were drawn from the North Californian diabetes registry of Kaiser Permanente, a large health-care organization headquartered in California. It was designed as a ten-year study, with two interim analyses scheduled at the end of five and eight years respectively. The first interim analysis at the end of five years was published in 2011 and a 'weak association' between bladder cancer and the use of pioglitazone for two years or more was reported.

Even before the Kaiser Permanente study could report its first interim analysis, a French insurance company conducted a study on patients taking pioglitazone between 2006 and 2009 and concluded that there was a higher incidence of bladder cancer associated with pioglitazone treatment. As a consequence, the drug was banned in France and Germany. However, the European Medicines Agency did not find enough evidence to direct the withdrawal of pioglitazone and it continued to be marketed in other European countries and elsewhere.

To confound matters further, there was a numerically higher incidence of bladder cancer noted in the PROact study on macrovascular outcomes in the pioglitazone group, though it was not statistically significant. The study was extended as an observational study on patients who had been randomized earlier. Six-year results published in 2012 from the ongoing study seemed to indicate no risk of bladder cancer.

Though the jury is still out on bladder cancer risks of pioglitazone use, there is little hope that the FDA or the European Medicines Agency will consider approval of a new glitazone or glitazar without evidence of cardiovascular safety and the absence of carcinogenicity. Such evidence can be generated only through clinical trials that are so large and of such long duration that it is commercially infeasible to do so.

The many glitazones—over fifty of them—that followed balaglitazone and the glitazars that followed ragaglitazar have all fallen by the wayside. Some of the largest pharmaceutical companies in the world pursued the glitazars after us—Bristol-Myers Squibb with muraglitazar, Hoffmann-La Roche with aleglitazar and AstraZeneca with tesaglitazar. As a matter of fact, glitazars were considered such hot property that Merck entered into a global deal for muraglitazar with Bristol-Myers Squibb, agreeing to share the development costs, pay 100 million dollars upfront and make milestone payments of another 275 million dollars in return for co-marketing rights and royalties on sales. All these molecules had entered Phase III, but were eventually buried in the graveyard of the glitazars.

I have often thought ruefully about of what would have happened if ragaglitazar had not been discovered and overshadowed balaglitazone so much that its development was suspended by Novo Nordisk. Strangely enough, a wonderful diabetes drug that is now the largest-selling oral anti-diabetic also nearly suffered a similar fate. Metformin was first described and synthesized in 1922 and its anti-diabetic effects were reported in 1929. But it was so overshadowed by the discovery of insulin that it was forgotten. Some twenty years later, Eusebio Garcia, a physician in the Philippines, noted that metformin lowered blood sugar when he was trying to treat influenza with it. Finally, it was a French diabetologist studying the glucose-lowering effects of galegine, an alkaloid extracted from *Galega officinalis*, who spotted its structural resemblance to metformin and, recalling Garcia's report, experimented with metformin in the treatment of diabetes. He published his study in 1957 and called the drug Glucophage—glucose eater. It was first marketed a couple of years later by a small company. Like metformin, balaglitazone used a scaffold derived from a natural alkaloid and it was overshadowed by ragaglitazar, a potentially better drug. Sadly, the parallel ended there.

Metformin is very interesting as it has the effect of restricting the production of sugar in the liver through an entirely novel mechanism. The wonderful thing about it is that it does not cause hypoglycaemia, a potentially dangerous condition where the level of sugar is lower than what is needed and is sometimes the case when there is excessive production of insulin with sulphonylureas or when more insulin than is necessary is injected into the body. Equally important, it has a beneficial effect on obesity and is a mild insulin sensitizer. Quite extraordinarily, it took nearly forty years after its first introduction in Europe before it was approved in the USA in 1995.

The first in the next new class of anti-diabetics was Merck's Januvia approved in 2006. Sitagliptin is the generic name of Januvia and works in a different metabolic pathway to regulate sugar levels in the blood by inhibiting an enzyme called dipeptidyl peptidase-IV (DPP-IV). Saxagliptin, vildagliptin and linagliptin have followed. Takeda has also joined the bandwagon with alogliptin, which was approved in early 2013, even as I wrote these recollections.

Another interesting drug that was approved in 2005 was exenatide. It has properties similar to an incretin hormone in human beings—the glucagon-like peptide 1 (GLP-1). GLP-1 has an important role in glucose regulation and insulin secretion. Exenatide was first discovered in the saliva of a giant lizard found in the USA, called the Gila monster. What is commercially produced is the synthetic version. Exenatide was followed by liraglutide, commercialized by Novo Nordisk in 2010. Both these drugs are injectables.

These developments are very good as they offer additional options to treat diabetes, which remains a growing scourge. However, the central problem of overcoming insulin resistance without weight gain or other adverse effects remains. More than ever before, we need a better metformin. As indeed, we need new medicines for cancer, Alzheimer's, atherosclerosis and other stubborn diseases that have as yet not succumbed to modern medicine.

17 THE NEW BIOLOGY

Sir Walter Bodmer: *His Book of Man introduced
me to dazzling possibilities*

The turn of the millennium brought to momentous fruition the labours of a thousand scientists across six nations in reading the human genome. Announcing the completion of the Human Genome Project on 26th June 2000, the then US President Bill Clinton termed this learning of 'the language in which God created life' as a profound new knowledge that would 'revolutionize the diagnosis, prevention and treatment of most, if not all, human diseases'.

The dramatic moment announcing the sequencing of the human genome and its molecular composition was, of course, preceded by decades of painstaking research punctuated by brilliant flashes of insight. It was a pivotal marker of the most breathtaking advances of our understanding of DNA, the 'prime molecule of life', and the surrounding science of the new biology—cells, genes, proteins, enzymes and the like. Biology, the science of life and living organisms, is many centuries old. What was spectacular, however, was the new biology that developed at dazzling speed during my lifetime. If I had to date its beginning, I would choose 25th April 1953, when Francis Crick and James Watson first published their brilliant deduction of the double helix structure of DNA in *Nature*, which has been hailed by Sir Walter Bodmer as 'the most important milestone in our understanding of the living world since Darwin devised his theory of natural selection and Mendel discovered his laws of inheritance'. The citation of the Nobel Prize Crick and Watson won in 1962 was comparatively prosaic and read, 'For their discoveries concerning the molecular structure of nucleic acids and its significance for information transfer in living material.'

Around the time the Genome Project came to fruition, I decided to deepen our scientific capabilities and broaden the areas of our research, embracing the 'new biology' that had captured the imagination of drug researchers. I knew very little about the new biology and Dr. Reddy's did not have adequate molecular biology capabilities. Quite by coincidence, I had chanced upon a book—I think it was at a Borders shop—called the *Book of Man*. The title intrigued me and I bought it. It turned out to be one of the best buys I had ever made. I met the author, Sir Walter Bodmer, some years later when he visited CCMB at Hyderabad and he graciously inscribed my well-thumbed copy.

Among Bodmer's many extraordinary accomplishments, two have probably contributed to making the *Book of Man* so readable and rewarding. First, he has done more than most others in promoting the public understanding of science and all this experience illuminates the book. Second, he was one of the first to suggest the Human Genome Project and was president of the International Human Genome Project in the initial years, and his grand vision enriches the book. He wrote it when the Human Genome Project was still under way and what a marvellous tour of the evolution of modern genetics it has turned out to be!

The seeds of modern genetics were sown by a Moravian monk, Gregor Mendel, whose laboratory was the garden of his monastery. About 150 years ago, experimenting with breeding of the common pea, he reasoned that traits passed on to successive generations were controlled by two distinct 'factors'—later called genes—one from the male and the other from the female parent. Mendel became the abbot of the monastery in 1868. This elevation to management effectively ended his scientific work. Just a year later—and entirely independently—Johann Miescher, who was at the University of Tübingen in Germany working on pus cells on the bandages of wounded soldiers, chanced upon a strange substance in the nuclei of the cells and five years later separated its acidic and protein components. We know them now as deoxyribonucleic acid and ribonucleic acid (DNA and RNA). Nothing much came out of these discoveries, nor was the relationship between the two speculated upon for a long time.

Since then, much progress has been made. We now know that the essential component of our genes is DNA, which consists of three billion letters, each letter denoting a pair of substances that replicate twice within each one of our ten billion cells. As Bodmer so eloquently says, DNA is the 'true chemical of life' and in it is encoded 'the genetic language' that is 'read and translated into proteins from which tissues, nerve cells and hormones are constructed'. Eventually, they are 'transformed into organs, thought processes, memories, and even behaviour patterns'.

Coiled rods of DNA reside as chromosomes in the nucleus of each of our ten billion cells and contain all the hereditary information of a human being. All human beings have exactly forty-six chromosomes, organized into twenty-three pairs. All but one are distinctive pairs and denoted by numbers from one to twenty-two. The intriguing twenty-third chromosome has a pair of 'X' chromosomes in females, but an 'X' and 'Y' chromosome in men, the only difference that an unromantic geneticist would see between males and females in the human species. The totality of the DNA present in the twenty-three chromosomes in a human being is known as the human genome.

Cells are the smallest units of life and the sites of incredibly complex feats of chemistry. They are microscopic factories, synthesizing several thousand molecules of varying sizes and functions. The 'small molecules', of which there are at least 750 in a cell, are the sugars, amino acids and fatty acids. The large molecules, known as 'macromolecules' are more numerous—perhaps more than 30,000 in a cell—and are generally small molecules linked together in long chains to form carbohydrates, lipids and proteins.

Genes trigger the production of proteins, which are amino acids joined together in long chains. There are not that many amino acids—only twenty of them—but there are an enormous number of proteins, some small with just a few dozen amino acids and some with thousands. Proteins are essential for life processes, like insulin that aids our body to extract energy from the ingested food, especially carbohydrates, or erythropoietin, which is essential for the production of new red blood cells from progenitor cells. We know now that minute genetic differences explain why among people with the same disease some respond to certain drugs and others do not. We also know that more complex differences are responsible, at least partly, for some people being prone to a whole host of diseases such as cancer, Alzheimer's, atherosclerosis and diabetes.

Genes are responsible for happy inheritance, like the colour of the eyes or hair, but when they go wrong, the diseases they cause can also be inherited. Victor McKusick, who was at one time professor of medicine as well as professor of medical genetics at Johns Hopkins, authored *Mendelian Inheritance in Man* in 1966. Now available online and updated daily, it is a remarkable catalogue of about 4000 heritable diseases and related genes. Interestingly, McKusick suggested the mapping of all human genes as early as 1969 to understand birth defects. I was tickled that in an autobiographical note, McKusick had later said, 'In part, the proposal reflected the exuberant mind-set that followed the first moon landing.'

It is easy to see why the increasing understanding of molecular biology—the branch of biology that studies the structure and activity of macromolecules essential to life, particularly their genetic role—had become an integral part of drug discovery for several decades prior to the completion of the sequencing of the human genome.

It is one thing to bring new chemical entities to development by analogue research, but the path-breaking developments in molecular biology demanded that we assimilate the new knowledge. I scouted for talent all over the world. In the process, I met Uday Saxena, who had set up the programme in inflammation and atherogenesis at the research division of Parke-Davis at Ann Arbor, Michigan, and then moved on to become vice president of research at AtheroGenics, Georgia. He directed the programme at AtheroGenics which led to several molecules moving into late-stage clinical trials, including for atherosclerosis. He was prepared to set up shop in Hyderabad. Expanding capabilities in Hyderabad would have been the conventional thing to do but, in another twist to the tale, I asked Uday to stay back in Atlanta and set up a lab there for harnessing the new science that had unfolded.

That decision proved to be right because we were not only able to get going quickly, but were also able to get the best of talent available in the USA. Sivaram Pillarisetti, a molecular biologist and a leading researcher in atherosclerosis, joined us, and so did Ish Khanna, an accomplished chemist at Pfizer, who was one of the co-inventors of celecoxib.

Atherosclerosis is by far the most important cause of heart attacks and strokes. It is a condition where fatty deposits form plaque on the walls of arteries and interfere with blood circulation. Atherosclerosis starts early in life, indeed from childhood, progresses slowly and presents itself dramatically in middle age or later. There is no medicine as yet that will directly act on the plaque and reverse its build-up. Atherosclerosis is currently managed by lowering the 'risk factor' of low-density lipoprotein or LDL, the 'bad' cholesterol. This is inadequate, as almost half of all heart attacks and strokes occur in people with 'normal' levels of LDL.

At Norcross, Atlanta, Uday and his team worked on the idea that plaque build-up consists of three steps: inflammation, cell proliferation and thrombosis. They hypothesized that a protein, perlecan, could inhibit the process. In three years flat, they synthesized a molecule that promoted the expression of perlecan, and showed remarkable activity at all the three stages of plaque build-up, and also demonstrated the regression of plaque in animal models.

The discontinuance of ragaglitazar in December 2002 was a big setback but it did not hurt us financially as Novo Nordisk was footing the bill. We had learnt a good deal about clinical development and Dr Reddy's revenues were healthy. I therefore made a big decision to undertake early clinical development—Phase I and Phase II—of the new molecules from our discovery programme. As a result, we had a cancer molecule from our earliest research, a molecule to elevate HDL from our PPAR programme and the atherosclerosis molecule in clinical development.

Data from the trials for the cancer molecule did not warrant the continuance of the programme. PPARs had come under a cloud and eventually all progress in this programme was stalled. The atherosclerosis molecule discovered in Atlanta had an unacceptable safety profile in human beings in Phase I trials and the programme was discontinued.

In the meanwhile, we synthesized DRL 17822, another new molecule that held out great promise. The big question that surfaced was whether we could afford to press ahead with clinical development, when so much of expenditure incurred on the other molecules had not paid off.

The new molecule followed from Pfizer's discovery of torcetrapib, which attacked the cholesterol problem in an exciting new way. A protein called the cholesteryl ester transfer protein (CETP) is involved in transferring cholesteryl esters from high-density lipoprotein (HDL), the good cholesterol, to LDL, the bad cholesterol. Torcetrapib was designed to inhibit CETP, the idea being that if there is less of CETP activity, the less will be the transfer of cholesteryl esters from HDL to LDL resulting in higher levels of the good cholesterol and lower levels of bad cholesterol.

Other CETP inhibitors followed—dalcetrapib from Roche, anacetrapib from Merck and evacetrapib from Eli Lilly. Dr. Reddy's too got into the race and commenced clinical trials with DRL 17822.

Pfizer spent 800 million dollars on the development of torcetrapib and had to discontinue it in 2006 while in Phase III trials. Though the compound did its job of increasing HDL and lowering LDL, there was unexpected increase in blood pressure which probably led to increased mortality in the trial. Roche also discontinued dalcetrapib in 2012 as it failed to show any benefit in preventing heart attacks and stroke despite increasing HDL. It is unclear whether this disappointing result was because dalcetrapib did not increase HDL enough to prevent cardiovascular events such as heart attacks and strokes.

Merck's anacetrapib and Eli Lilly's evacetrapib are currently in late-phase development and have demonstrated increases of HDL up to 135 per cent as well as lowering LDL by about 35–40 per cent. Merck has reconfirmed its intent to continue with the development of anacetrapib, even after Roche's dalcetrapib was discontinued. Dr. Reddy's CETP inhibitor, DRL 17822, has completed Phase II and its efficacy and safety profiles match the published information on Merck's anacetrapib.

A fine balance needs to be struck between present costs and uncertain future profits. Discovery costs are accounted for as they happen. The profits from discovery are somewhere in the uncertain future, though when they do come they are substantial. R&D expenses soared, largely because of clinical development. I had made a mistake and had bitten off more than we could chew. Our profits were under pressure.

Prasad and Satish, who are very conscious of our responsibility to shareholders, made a careful analysis of the prospects. We discussed the matter among ourselves and with our board of directors. We came to the conclusion that we had no option but to restructure our discovery activity so that our other businesses were not hurt. The discovery research programme, along with the staff and facilities, was folded into Aurigene—a wholly owned subsidiary of Dr. Reddy's headquartered in Bengaluru. Aurigene was set up in 2002 and is in the business of providing contract research services for drug discovery to international clients. The idea was that Aurigene could plough the surpluses it earns from its contract research services into discovery research so that there was no pressure on the profits of Dr. Reddy's.

Aurigene has collaborated with some of the largest pharmaceutical companies in the world to develop new chemical entities, for biological targets of disease identified by the collaborators, to the stage where they can be considered for human trials. Aurigene has worked on over thirty-five programmes of this nature. The diversity of these programmes and the constant challenges they present have provided the team with a remarkable opportunity to sharpen their biology and product development skills. The company is now well positioned to take forward ambitious programmes in discovery. I have encouraged them to devote half their resources to their own path-breaking programmes.

I am invariably delighted when I spend time with the head of Aurigene, C.S.N. Murthy, as well as the scientists there and hear about their progress. They are delving deep into science and one of their own programmes is fascinating. It is based on the advances of the new biology in the area of immune response.

Our innate immune system is our defence mechanism against a number of diseases. It produces antibodies when it detects an invasion by foreign bodies, such as bacteria or viruses, to fight them off. Science has now taught us that the spread of certain diseases are marked by a suppression of the human immune system, partly explaining their unhindered progress. Thus, the proliferation of the human immunodeficiency virus (HIV) is aided by a 'switching off' of the body's immune system. Similarly, the spread of cancer cells is also aided by the switching off or the weakening of the immune system to an anergic state, where the defence mechanism is not energetic enough to fight the disease. The question that arises is whether one can 'switch on' or re-energize the immune system so that the body is better armed to fight cancers and infection.

The starting point is, of course, the identification of what causes the immune system to be compromised when faced by cancers or viruses. Several proteins and receptors have been identified as the culprits. One of them is CTLA-4 and there is invariably an increased level of this protein in patients afflicted with certain types of cancer. Ipilimumab, a monoclonal antibody that targets CTLA-4 and in effect neutralizes its ability to suppress the immune system, was discovered by Medarex, an American biotech company. Medarex was acquired by Bristol-Myers Squibb and it undertook the clinical development of the drug. Ipilimumab was approved by the FDA in March 2011 for treatment of certain types of melanoma, a deadly skin cancer. Bristol-Myers Squibb launched it with the brand name of Yervoy and priced it at 120,000 dollars a treatment. Clinical trials were conducted on patients with untreatable melanoma and it has been shown to prolong survival. Though more data is needed to understand the extent to which it prolongs survival and whether it works better in combination with other drugs, ipilimumab is a hugely significant breakthrough. It has demonstrated that immunotherapy works.

PD-1 is another protein that has been identified as a culprit in compromising the immune system. Bristol-Myers Squibb has a drug in development, also discovered by Medarex, which targets PD-1.

Aurigene has also discovered a compound that targets PD-1 and it may well have an advantage. Modulating the immune system can be a very delicate task. Just as subdued immunity allows diseases such as cancer and bacterial or viral infections to proliferate quickly, enhanced immune response can give rise to a whole set of new issues. Though the mAbs target diseases very well, they are long acting and often remain in the body for thirty to sixty days, sometimes causing severe problems. This was observed in clinical trials of antibodies to CTLA-4 as well as PD-1.

Scientists at Aurigene have started their own programme to overcome this problem. The idea, as many good ideas are, is simple: develop a 'peptide', an abbreviated protein that would have the same specificity as an antibody does, but would be metabolized in the human system in a short span of time, such as a few hours or days. Once metabolized, it would no longer be active. Aurigene now has a novel peptide therapeutic that has demonstrated excellent activity against PD-1 as well as safety in both cancer and infection settings in animal models. The next step is clinical trials. This is one example of the new biology at work at Aurigene. They are working on several other programmes too.

I am aware of the question that will inevitably arise. Why do I persist in going down the undoubtedly risky path of drug discovery despite the failures of the past? I need to answer this question.

18 AN UNFINISHED AGENDA

How do I give it one more push? *Pondering the future of discovery at the cafeteria of the research facility*

Failures happen more often than not in drug discovery, and every failure is an occasion for reflection. Every time I reflected, my resolve to pursue the quest for the discovery of new drugs only strengthened. I have narrated the failures and I must now explain why my resolve to succeed is justified. I think it is important to explain my optimism, lest the failures dishearten researchers and cause them to steer clear of drug discovery. That would be tragic, as the world needs Indian enterprise to engage actively in drug discovery research.

Though a new drug discovered by Dr. Reddy's has not yet been commercialized, our discovery efforts have not gone in vain. The discovery and licensing of ragaglitazar was a defining moment in my life. It was a validation of our scientific capabilities. Novo Nordisk is a world leader in diabetes and they would not have licensed a molecule and paid good money for it if they had not believed in its potential to be a useful treatment. It was a scientific milestone for the pharmaceutical industry in the country for it established that India could discover a first-in-class compound.

I call the discovery of ragaglitazar a milestone as few people associated India with drug discovery at that time. The first reaction to the news of a drug discovery would understandably have been greeted by scepticism, if not downright disbelief. For example, when David Pilling profiled me in the *Financial Times* in August 1999, he characterized our analogue research as being 'only one step up from outright piracy' and took no notice of the fact that we had discovered a first-in-class-compound in 1998 and licensed it to Novo Nordisk.

One of the major factors that contributed to the common misconception of Indian scientific capabilities was the opposition to the changes in the patent law which were in the offing at that time. It created the impression that the Indian pharmaceutical industry opposed the grant of patents to new medicines because they had no capability to develop them and therefore could benefit little.

Some of our political leaders added to the confused perception of Indian science in those days. Sometime in 1999, I was honoured for my contributions to the pharmaceutical industry by Pragna Bharati, an organization in Hyderabad. The chief guest was Dr Murli Manohar Joshi, then the minister for human resource development as well as science and technology. Dr Joshi made no secret of his antipathy to patents for medicines and I was mentally debating the propriety of making a reference to it in my speech while accepting the award. Dr Joshi spoke first and made the point that Indian children were clever even by global standards. One example he mentioned was the Stuyvesant High School in New York, where academic standards are very high and admission is entirely on merit. Even in this much-sought-after school, he said, seven to eight Indians gain admission every year. At least in this, he was right—Stuyvesant had very bright students and several Nobel laureates had been nurtured there, including Roald Hoffman who won the Nobel for his work in theoretical chemistry in 1981. I thought this was an opening to strike a personal note before I gave my acceptance speech, so after Dr Joshi finished his address and returned to his seat on the dais, I leaned across and told him that my daughter-in-law had studied in Stuyvesant.

I started my speech on an affable note, agreeing with Dr Joshi that Indians were bright, but went on to say that the message we give the world is that Indians are brainless when we oppose patents for medicines, more so after signing an international agreement that obliged us to grant them. I then spoke about the research going on at Dr. Reddy's and how we had obtained international patents for several promising discoveries and even licensed out some of them for substantial amounts of money. I said that Indian research should be recognized and incentivized with patents in our own country or we would remain laggards in science. It must have made some impact because Dr Joshi got up and said, 'We have given away our knowledge because our dharma says knowledge cannot be sold, but now I agree with Dr Reddy that we must profit from our knowledge.'

Dr Joshi was in the news at around that time for encouraging research in the therapeutic properties of cow's urine at CSIR, which came under his purview. The next year, I saw in the newspapers that scientists at CSIR had distilled cow's urine and claimed that the distillate enhanced the activity of antibiotics. CSIR then applied for a patent in the USA for this discovery. Dr Joshi appeared to have discovered the value of patents!

Ramesh Mashelkar was the director general of CSIR at that time. Mashelkar was a very capable scientific administrator and an indefatigable proponent of patents. It is no exaggeration to say that he has left an indelible imprint on the scientific establishments of the country. He is also a friend; when I met him around that time, the conversation veered to cow's urine. I said to him, 'Ramesh, it's all right for your minister to talk about cow's urine, but why are you doing that? You know full well that when you distil your urine or my urine or cow's urine, the distillate is water. What therapeutic value can it have?' Mashelkar said nothing, but a year or so later I read the news about a US patent having been granted to CSIR for the distillate of cow's urine. Dr Joshi was jubilant. To his credit, Mashelkar was diplomatic when he was asked to comment on it—he merely said it was a good effort but there was a long way to go before it could be developed into a drug.

The common view of the multinational pharmaceutical industry and the governments of developed nations seemed to be that the Indian pharmaceutical industry was unabashedly 'pirating' Western technology without being hindered by patents. The impact of patents, should they be introduced, on prices of new medicines was usually brushed aside by those who held this view.

One proponent of this view was Henry 'Hank' McKinnell, who was the president of Pfizer when he visited India; he was to become CEO in 2001. Ian Young, who was then managing director of Pfizer in India, invited me to meet McKinnell and we had lunch at the Belvedere at the Oberoi in Mumbai. The conversation was very general. Hank McKinnell was polite enough, but the meeting left me cold.

Some months later, when I was in Singapore in April 2001 in connection with our ADR issue and NYSE listing, I found McKinnell featured on the front page of the *Herald Tribune* for the wrong reasons. In early April, McKinnell had become chairman of PhRMA—the Pharmaceutical Research and Manufacturers of America—an association of large multinational pharmaceutical companies. The South African arms of the multinational companies had gone to court against a law passed in South Africa empowering the government to make parallel imports of AIDS drugs despite the existence of patents in the country. South Africa was facing an AIDS crisis and patented drugs priced at 1000 dollars *per month* were wholly unaffordable in a country where the average *annual* per capita income was 2600 dollars. The new law was enacted primarily to take advantage of lower prices of drugs in other countries such as India. Just a few months earlier, Cipla had made the dramatic offer to supply AIDS medication at an annual cost of 350 dollars per patient. The case was being heard in court. The international media was up in arms against the attitude of the multinational drug companies and the pressure tactics employed by the US government in their support. As chairman of PhRMA, McKinnell made strong statements against the dilution of patent monopolies in South Africa and earned the wrath of the international media. His theme was that drug discovery was a hugely expensive process and patent monopolies were the only way to make such investments worthwhile. He argued that drug discovery brought benefits to patients the world over, so no country ought to dilute patent protection for new drugs. One statement that he made in this context was that there was no drug discovery in the Third World. As it happened, all of McKinnell's protestations were of no avail and the South African companies bowed to public pressure later in the month and withdrew their case.

However much one disagreed with McKinnell's views, he was entitled to them. But I thought he had crossed the line with his assertion that there was no drug discovery going on in the Third World. When I came back to Hyderabad, I wrote to McKinnell reminding him of our meeting and congratulating him on his becoming chairman of PhRMA. I also politely told him that he was wrong in saying there had been no drug discovery in the Third World as Dr. Reddy's had discovered and licensed two molecules to Novo Nordisk. I offered to meet him as I was travelling to New York and give him an overview of the research that was happening at our facilities. A month later, McKinnell wrote saying he wished me luck but regretted that he had some prior commitments and could not meet me.

I thought to myself that Western companies had a point about patents. They could not afford to innovate if they did not have the benefit of monopolies. Any dilution of patents was therefore anathema to them. But their model of drug discovery is very expensive and their monopoly prices are often so high that their new drugs can only benefit people with insurance reimbursement or government-provided health care of the sort that exists in thirty-five developed nations with about 15 per cent of the world's population. This is most often not the situation in the less-developed nations with 85 per cent of the world's population. Of what use is drug discovery if only a few people in poor nations can afford to buy the new drugs and benefit from the advances in science? It is no answer to say that these people cannot afford to buy any medicines, new or old, so let us not ask the question.

In February 2013, *Science* magazine carried a study of the cost-benefit of intensifying anti-retroviral treatment for HIV patients. The study was conducted during 2000–11 for a population of about 100,000 people in the rural area of the KwaZulu-Natal province in South Africa. The life expectancy in 2003, the year before the anti-retroviral treatment was made available in the public health system, was about forty-nine years. By 2011, the life expectancy had increased to more than sixty years. The estimated economic value of the life-years gained far exceeded the 10.8 million dollars spent on providing anti-retroviral treatment during the study period. Another study published in the same issue of *Science* showed that the risk of contracting HIV by uninfected people in KwaZulu-Natal was reduced significantly over an eight-year period by increasing coverage of infected people with anti-retroviral treatment. All this was possible with treatment costs that ranged between 500–800 dollars per annum per person. Would this have been possible with drugs priced at 1000 dollars per month per person? One cannot say that innovation will not take place in the first instance without such prices, and that it would be available at rock-bottom prices after a delay of ten to fifteen years when patents expired and generics came into the market. By this time, a whole generation of patients in need of the medication would have died.

Large populations in the developing world, who had access to affordable medicine because of the lack of patent protection or lax implementation, might soon find that they are unable to afford the cost of new drugs. At the beginning of the twentieth century, the leading causes of mortality were communicable diseases: pneumonia, tuberculosis and diarrhoea. The war against communicable diseases has not been won—AIDS and SARS are grim and sobering reminders that we have a long way to go. But the leading causes of mortality now are non-communicable diseases led by cardiovascular diseases (CVD), which afflict 200 million people globally. Heart disease and stroke, the two principal CVDs, kill seventeen million people a year, compared to the three million who die from HIV/AIDS. About 80 per cent of CVD deaths and an even greater percentage of CVD-related disability is in low- and middle-income countries, and atherosclerosis is the root underlying cause. Diabetes is a huge and growing problem and I dread the growing burden of diseases like Alzheimer's, requiring intensive, long-term care which developing countries will remain ill-equipped to provide for a long time to come. New drugs for treatment of atherosclerosis, Alzheimer's and certain cancers are desperately required, as no effective treatment exists today. But how many people in the developing nations can afford 2–6 dollars (around 130–390 rupees) a day, which is the current cost of many new medicines for each chronic condition in America—the costs go up with multiple diseases—or the huge costs of some treatments for cancer? I was astounded that most new cancer drugs launched in the USA in 2012 were priced at 100,000 dollars or more per year of treatment.

Even the richest nations in the world are groaning under the weight of their health-care expenditure. There are many components of the cost of health care, but one of them is the cost of new drugs. It would be a mistake to live in denial by arguing that the cost of new drugs is only a small fraction of health-care costs. It is thus not just a question of poor versus rich nations. It is a global problem.

I am a votary of patents, but also a committed votary of affordable pricing. The only way to solve this conundrum is to search for lower-cost alternatives for drug discovery that will lead to lower prices of new drugs. The current model of drug discovery of Big Pharma in the West is simply not in a position to deliver the goods. It is just too expensive to be sustainable. This is where the opportunity lies and I firmly believe that Indian companies are well positioned to take advantage of it.

India has a traditionally frugal culture. That culture shows up not only in the way we innovate but also in what, and for whom, we innovate. So much so, it has become the stuff of case studies at universities in the West. Frugal innovation could be, or ought to be, an important advantage in drug discovery as well.

Sometime in 2004, a headline in an issue of *Scrip* magazine caught my eye. The headline was 'India will deliver on innovation' and the person who asserted this was Brian Tempest, the CEO of Ranbaxy at that time, who was speaking at the FT Global Pharmaceutical Conference in London. To support his thesis, he quoted from an analysis that demonstrated that the average Indian chemistry researcher was better educated, put in 40 per cent more working hours every week, and cost the company *less than 7 per cent* of his US counterpart. And who did this analysis? None other than Pfizer. People may dispute the numbers estimated, but it cannot be disputed that India has a significant cost advantage.

Cost advantages and making do with less are not sufficient for drug discovery. Most importantly, there should be scientific capability. I think there is now no doubt that India either has, or can access, the scientific capability to deliver new drugs. Dr. Reddy's itself has demonstrated that. We have forayed into both analogue research and target-based discovery and I am immensely proud of the results obtained by our scientists who have worked with unflagging zeal and a quiet confidence. They have proved that they are as much at the forefront of discovery as anybody else in the industry, anywhere in the world. Other Indian companies are also in the fray now and the Indian presence in discovery is here to stay.

The only thing left at Dr. Reddy's was to demonstrate results in research. I felt the purpose could not be served with traditional approaches and I thought up one that was unusual. I discussed my idea with the board of directors of Dr. Reddy's to make sure there was total transparency and no conflict of interest. I told them that I would like to continue with research in diseases where there are unmet needs, like

Alzheimer's, diabetes, CVDs and cancer. I also told them that since the approach I wished to try defied conventional logic and the outcomes were uncertain, I would not like to risk the funds of the shareholders of Dr. Reddy's in this venture, and I, therefore, intended to invest my personal money. The board of directors found no possible conflict of interest and had no objection to my going ahead.

I roped in three past presidents of discovery research at Dr. Reddy's—Venkat, Rajagopalan and Uday Saxena, as well as Ram Pillarisetti and Ish Khanna who had also worked earlier in Dr. Reddy's. I was looking for somebody who could handle all the commercial work. I asked Patrick Doyle, who had been with Novo Nordisk during the balaglitazone days, whether he knew anybody who might be interested and, to my surprise and delight, he volunteered. My team was complete and I formed a new company, Kareus Therapeutics, in 2009. Kareus is derived from my name and that of Uday's—**K. A**nji **RE**ddy and **U**day **S**axena. Just six people made up the whole company.

Kareus does not have an office and the six work out of their homes in three different continents. Venkat and Uday are in Hyderabad and Rajagopalan is in Bengaluru. Ish and Ram are in the USA and Patrick is based in London. Given the different time zones, I can truthfully say that Kareus works twenty-four hours a day! It does not have laboratories or any physical assets. Quite understandably, at first glance, it seems an insane idea. How can a 'virtual' company discover drugs that are hard to find in large laboratories?

I believe it can, as the skills are there. Uday and Ram are accomplished biologists, Venkat and Ish have extraordinary chemistry skills, and Rajagopalan is one of the most competent pharmacologists I know. Patrick handles the all-important commercial and corporate responsibilities. They know each other well and are bound together by their common passion for drug discovery. They have enormous collective experience and are well networked in the industry so they can contract with the most suitable facilities in the world for all their laboratory work—synthesis, screening, assays, animal pharmacology and everything else they need. They have no regular staff and do not waste any time with committees and meetings or management headaches. They can focus all their time on important things. There can be no leaner organization in drug discovery and it may well be the most cost-effective and productive outfit in the industry.

The diseases that the Kareus team has collectively identified are some of the most demanding and difficult ones to tackle, but these are the ones that will be the most rewarding if better treatments are found for them.

One of the diseases Kareus is working on is Alzheimer's disease, the most frequent form of dementia. Most people know that memory declines with age, but when this is accompanied by any one of several other symptoms, such as incoherence, confusion of time and place or an inability to identify objects, it could well be Alzheimer's. The disease develops when nerve cells in the brain, called neurons, die or no longer function normally. In the beginning, the brain copes with this and the symptoms are not obvious. As the disease progresses, the damage in the brain impairs a person's memory, behaviour and ability to think clearly. People with Alzheimer's lose their ability to converse and are prone to aggression and depression. When neuronal damage is severe, the decrease in cognitive functions is also so severe that it interferes with basic activities of daily life like walking or swallowing, and ultimately leads to death.

The disease was named after Alois Alzheimer, a German psychiatrist and neuropathologist, who was the first to describe it. Alzheimer called it 'a peculiar disorder of the cerebral cortex' when he presented its clinical symptoms and pathology at a lecture at Tübingen in November 1906, based on the treatment and autopsy of just one patient. That patient was Auguste Deter, and her story surely ranks as one of the most remarkable in medicine.

Auguste Deter was fifty-one years old in 1901 when she was admitted to a hospital in Frankfurt where Alzheimer worked. She exhibited peculiar symptoms, including short-term memory loss, delusions and hallucinations. Alzheimer was intrigued by this strange ailment and followed her case even after he moved to Munich. After Deter died, Alzheimer got her medical records as well as her brain transferred to Munich. He autopsied the brain and observed both 'plaques' and—for the first time—'tangles', that are typical of the disease.

Astonishingly, the medical records of Deter and the specimens of her brain were rediscovered ninety years later. There is a verbatim record of the questions that Alzheimer asked his patient and her responses to them. Extracts were published in the *Lancet* in 1997. Just this one unvarnished document is one of the most moving accounts of Alzheimer's that anybody can imagine.

The analysis of the remains of Deter's brain was repeated with all the advantages of modern science and published. Alzheimer's observations of plaques and tangles were confirmed. In February 2013, *Lancet Neurology* also featured the finding that Auguste Deter had a genetic mutation of presenelin 1—PESN1, the probable cause of the first diagnosed case of Alzheimer's disease. Despite the spectacular advances in science in the twentieth century that enabled the identification of the probable cause, Deter would have suffered a similar fate even if she had been born a hundred years later, as there is yet no cure.

The mutation in PESN1, or in one of two other genes, each one of them situated in a different chromosome, is a form of Alzheimer's that occurs earlier in life but accounts for less than 10 per cent of the incidence. What triggers the disease in old age, which is the case with the majority of patients, is still uncertain.

What we do know is that an adult human brain has 100 *billion* neurons. These neurons are all interconnected by what are called synapses and there are 100 *trillion* of them, constantly transmitting tiny chemical signals on the neural network. This is the cellular basis of all brain functions, including thoughts, skills, emotions and memories. Alzheimer's seems to develop when there are glitches in the neural network. When synapses fail and decrease, communications in the network are interrupted and eventually neurons die. The deterioration is mirrored by progression of the disease and fatality.

What causes these glitches with age in the network of the brain is unclear. The dominant theory, which developed in the early 1990s, is that deposits of a protein called beta-amyloid, or its fragments, accumulate as plaque in the spaces *between* neurons and disrupt communications. This theory is now known as the amyloid hypothesis. Another theory is that when a protein called tau is produced in excess, it creates twisted tangles of fibres *within* the neurons and blocks the transport of essential nutrients in it. Most people develop plaques and tangles as they age, but patients with Alzheimer's have far more of them.

The plaques and tangles of Alzheimer's are a solid wall that refuses to yield to the battering ram of modern science, though it has not been for want of trying. PhRMA released a report, 'Alzheimer's Research: Setbacks and Stepping Stones' in September 2012, detailing the efforts of its member companies, which are the largest multinational companies in the world. Its analysis discloses that in the thirteen years between 1998 and 2011, 101 compounds have failed. Three medicines have been approved, but only to treat symptoms of the disease, not the disease itself. Despite this, and the daunting prospect of finding a cure for Alzheimer's if one considers the complexity of the disease and uncertainty about what causes it, there is no evidence of a slackening of effort. PhRMA reports that ninety-three medicines are now in the research pipeline of its member companies.

The size of the problem and the costs of dealing with it are equally daunting. One in eight persons over sixty-five years of age in the USA and nearly half of the people over eighty-five years suffer from Alzheimer's disease. The cost of providing care to the estimated 5.4 million patients in the USA is enormous—200 billion dollars in 2012 with about 70 per cent of this cost being borne by Medicare and Medicaid. The physical and emotional toll on the caregivers in the family is also enormous. The projection is that the number of Alzheimer's patients will triple with an ageing population by 2050 and health-care costs will exceed a trillion dollars. As life expectancy in the less-developed world improves, the number of patients with Alzheimer's disease will increase at a faster rate. I shudder to think of the burden of this disease in the poorer nations, or the likely cost if there is a new drug that is discovered to treat Alzheimer's. It is perhaps time to think of new—and cost-effective—approaches to scale Alzheimer's defences.

Uday has done just that.

Recognizing that the brain's needs for energy are high—it accounts for just 2 per cent of body weight but 20 per cent of the total energy consumption—Uday noted the evidence of the marked energy deficiency in the brain that precedes the onset of Alzheimer's and persists during its progression. Uday therefore suggested that a drug targeting the known enzymes involved in the 'energy crisis' in the brain may be a promising new approach. As a matter of fact, one of these enzymes is already a target for Alzheimer's on which work is happening elsewhere.

After careful consideration, the Kareus team decided to pursue this approach and synthesize new drugs. Scientific reasons apart, I liked the approach as it held out the promise of resulting in a drug that would be simple to manufacture and use in therapy—important considerations when evaluating its suitability for use anywhere in the world, but more so in the less-developed countries.

However elegant the conception of a drug is in the abstract, it is an enormous effort to translate the idea into reality and come up with a physical entity. Then, one has to show evidence of activity and safety in animal models, before it becomes a clinical candidate fit for human trials. Most people would consider this to be a dream, and a wild one at that, for a 'virtual' company with six people to achieve, particularly for a disease that has defied a cure for over a century.

KU 046, the Kareus molecule intended for the treatment of Alzheimer's, has been synthesized. It has shown sufficient improvement in cognition and decrease in amyloid plaque formation over placebo and comparators in animal models. It has also shown sufficient safety. The FDA has approved the investigational new drug application for KU 046 and the first phase of human clinical trials is under way, even as I write. All this has happened in just about three years since Kareus was set up.

There is obviously a long way to go and, as always, the odds are against a new drug making it into the market. Kareus has therefore worked on a portfolio of ideas that may be useful in other diseases. One of the ideas that I have always been fascinated by is overcoming insulin resistance, the root problem of diabetes. Kareus has persisted in this direction and has worked on harnessing the potential benefits of the activation of an enzyme called AMP-kinase or AMPK. AMPK is an energy-sensing enzyme and we know that when it is activated, AMPK shuts down anabolic processes such as synthesis of glucose, fatty acids and cholesterol in the liver that consume energy and triggers catabolic processes such as glucose transport and fatty acid oxidations in skeletal muscle that produce adenosine triphosphate, or ATP, which transports energy within a cell. In addition, AMPK is believed to play a role in the regulation of insulin synthesis and its secretion in pancreatic islet β-cells. AMPK activation mimics exercise and the term 'exercise in a pill' reflects the potential utility of these agents in diabetes and obesity. All this is known and though efforts have been going on for more than ten years to develop a clinical candidate, there has only been failure to date. Despite this history, Kareus has developed a series of AMPK-activators that has shown promise. KU 5039 is the lead molecule and it is now undergoing regulatory toxicity studies. If acceptable safety is demonstrated, the molecule will progress to human clinical trials in the second half of 2013.

It would please me enormously if KU 5039 makes it to the market for all the obvious reasons. One not so obvious reason is buried in history. The idea central to the design of KU 5039 is that it will trigger the production of ATP. It was in 1929 that India's greatest biochemist, Yellapragada SubbaRow, who was from my home state of Andhra Pradesh, first isolated ATP and discovered its function, working with Fiske and Lohmann.

I had occasion to recall the extraordinary triumphs of SubbaRow over adversity in life and seemingly impenetrable problems in science when I had the privilege of delivering the SubbaRow Memorial Lecture at the

Central University of Hyderabad in 2002. Though I am digressing, I must recount the story of SubbaRow, for it made a profound impact on me.

SubbaRow was born in Bhimavaram in 1895, in what is now West Godavari district of Andhra Pradesh. His performance in school was abysmal. He often played truant and failed his matriculation examination twice. SubbaRow's father died and his mother sold her gold ornaments to continue financing her son's education, but it was the financial help from the man who would become his father-in-law that enabled him to study medicine at the Madras Medical College. Heeding Mahatma Gandhi's call, he took to wearing khadi and incurred the displeasure of his British professor, who failed him in the surgery examination. Consequently, SubbaRow was denied the bachelor's degree in medicine and surgery (MBBS) and was awarded only a Licentiate of Medicine and Surgery (LMS) certificate. SubbaRow got a teaching position at the Madras Ayurvedic College and immersed himself in this ancient science. During a chance meeting with a young American doctor, he learnt about the School of Tropical Medicine at Harvard University, which altered the course of his life. SubbaRow got admission to the school. Financed by the Malladi Satyalinga Naicker Charities in Kakinada, which incidentally still continues its philanthropic activities, he bought a passage to Boston in 1923, leaving behind his pregnant teenage wife.

Penniless in Boston, SubbaRow needed a job to survive. The only job he could find was that of a night porter at the Brigham and Woman's hospital, cleaning bedpans and bathrooms. His son, whom he had never seen, succumbed to illness in India. This tragedy made life in an alien and hostile environment even more difficult. SubbaRow, however, remained steadfast in his quest and obtained his diploma specializing in parasitology. He then got a position in the biochemistry laboratory of Cyrus Fiske at the Harvard Medical School, which was the launching pad of his research career.

Within a year or so of joining Fiske's laboratory, SubbaRow developed a method of estimation of serum phosphorus which even today is described in biochemistry textbooks as the Fiske–SubbaRow method. The method was published in the *Journal of Biological Chemistry* and a printer's devil forever altered the spelling of his name from the usual Subba Rao. This was followed by the discovery of phospocreatinine and ATP and their role in muscular activity. He was, however, denied a tenured professorship at Harvard, despite earning his PhD there in 1930. Frustrated, he left Harvard in 1940 and joined Lederle Laboratories, a division of American Cyanamid that is now a part of Pfizer.

The eight years that SubbaRow was with Lederle as director of research were marked by prodigious output. He synthesized folic acid and Vitamin B_9. Siddhartha Mukherjee in his fascinating, moving, and sometimes depressing, 'biography of cancer', *The Emperor of All Maladies*, provides a riveting account of SubbaRow's collaboration with Sidney Farber of the Children's Hospital in Boston and the discovery of aminopterin. It was an analogue of folic acid and the first drug ever that produced a remission in leukaemia, even if temporary. This drug led to an analogue, amethopterin, later known as methotrexate, which SubbaRow helped develop. It continues to be used to the present day as a chemotherapeutic agent. Another major discovery was diethylcarbamazine that found use as an anthelmintic drug in the treatment of filariasis. Aureomycin, the world's first tetracycline antibiotic, was discovered under his guidance. SubbaRow's contributions to the development of antibiotics were remarkable. C.W. Hesseltine of the US Department of Agriculture's fermentation laboratory at Illinois named a new genus of fungi *Subbaromyces*. When asked why

Yellapragada SubbaRow:
Memorial plaque at Lederle,
Pearl River, New York

he did so, he simply said, 'I wished to honour him as a great man who was responsible more than any other person for developing the broad spectrum antibiotics which still are the most useful antibiotics today.'

The greatest drug discoveries have often happened not in the largest and most impressive laboratories but in modest facilities. They have often been ascribed to chance and serendipity, but why does chance favour a few? The answer, I think, was provided by Louis Pasteur more than 150 years ago when he famously said that 'chance favours the prepared mind'. The essential prerequisite for a 'prepared mind' is a very high order of scientific competence, but I suspect that it helps greatly to have an equal concern for the human condition and a compulsive desire to better it.

Because of the enormous progress in science we now have a better understanding of medicine and are possessed of many tools to prise open solutions to stubborn problems. As Pasteur said, 'the veil is getting thinner and thinner' and never more so as now. Yellapragada SubbaRow and Paul Janssen have demonstrated how much of a difference the power of the prepared mind and an unswerving commitment to good science can make to the human condition. I am, therefore, not daunted by the enormity of the task at hand, or the slender resources that Kareus has to address it.

Around the time I started my career forty-five years ago, we were struggling to make the most basic drugs. At that time, few would have thought that India would emerge as the leading manufacturer of low-cost active pharmaceutical ingredients and generics for the world. We now have the opportunity to build on our experience for the benefit of humanity. I strongly believe that drug discovery is a noble, perhaps even a spiritual, pursuit. It is beyond bottom lines and investor relations. The mission is to improve the quality of life and life expectancy itself. This requires good science. But for science to be good, it has to result in affordable medicine. Indian enterprise is best positioned to deliver both.

That is my unfinished agenda.

19 GIVING BACK

The joy of hope
It takes so little to bring out a smile

Prof. Chaturvedi, a small shareholder of Dr. Reddy's, was a regular at our annual general meetings (AGMs). He invariably asked an unusual question which I usually deflected with a light-hearted response, much to the amusement of the gathering. I think it was at our AGM in 1995, a couple of years after our spectacular run of three bonus issues in consecutive years and the huge appreciation in the value of our equity shares, that Prof. Chaturvedi asked: 'The company is making good profits and you are getting wealthier every year, but what are you giving back to society?'

Giving back?

The question lodged itself in my mind, rather like a tiny speck of dust in the eye that refuses to get washed away.

I was not even sure what one did to 'give back'. Charity was an obvious way, and a good one too, but it seemed inadequate.

Offerings at places of worship perhaps? There is a temple dedicated to the goddess Bala Tripura Sundari across the road from our house at Tadepalli. Most people in the village made small contributions when they worshipped there. Chandramouli, the hereditary priest at the temple, was a pious man whose goodness rubbed off on those who spent time with him. The contributions helped him eke out a frugal existence and maintain the temple. But making such contributions was not giving back.

I thought about my father's effort in making Ayurvedic medicine, perhaps influenced by Chandramouli who knew a lot about Ayurvedic medicines and also made some. He went every month to the nearby city of Vijayawada to buy something that resembled dried lemons, scooped out the inside and made a pulp. My mother's job was to add some powder following my father's formula and make lumps of it, which took time and effort. My father then followed a set procedure to break up the lumps and make small round balls of it. He gave this away free to whoever needed it. My father thought it was something he needed to do and never considered it an expense. My mother never grudged the extra effort. Providing medicines and relief from ailments was certainly a very good thing to do, but this was my business.

As I was casting about for something suitable, I noticed a hospital on my way to work. The sign said Heritage Hospital: A Hospital for the Elderly. I thought this was a useful idea as many elderly did not receive adequate medical attention. I got in touch with K.R. Gangadharan, who ran the hospital, and invited him to my office. Gangadharan told me about his work. I asked him how he raised the money to set up the hospital. Gangadharan said that he had borrowed 2.5 million rupees from the Bank of Baroda. I thought he would be financially stretched and hard put to pay the interest of 18 per cent or about 450,000 rupees annually which the banks charged in those days. Gangadharan admitted he was having a hard time, but never asked for any assistance.

I wrote out a cheque for 500,000 rupees and insisted he take it. It was the first time I had done something like that. It seemed a worthwhile idea to support somebody who was putting in his own money and all his time to provide succour to some of those who needed it.

A year or so later, Gangadharan's wife, Nalini, came by to meet me. I had met her couple of times, but was not aware of what she did. It turned out that she was representing the Ashoka Foundation in India. Embarrassingly enough, I had not known about the Ashoka Foundation till then. Nalini told me about her work and I was very impressed. She mentioned that she had resigned from the Ashoka Foundation as she had been offered a job in the USA. I said it would be a good break for her. She told me her children also felt the same way and were excited about making their home in that country but she did not want to uproot herself from Hyderabad.

Nalini paused for a moment and said, 'If you set up a foundation, I would like to join it.' Just the one sentence and I responded equally briefly, 'If you come, I will start a foundation tomorrow.'

The next day, we started work on setting up Dr. Reddy's Foundation for Human and Social Development and Nalini Gangadharan became its executive director.

The foundation's first project, oddly enough, was a business project—Nalini organized a garbage business! I had heard of Exnora in Chennai. The name of the organization is derived from the concept that motivated its formation—**EX**cellent, **NO**vel and **RA**dical ideas to prevent environmental degradation involving those who were the cause of it. I was horrified by the garbage I saw on the on the streets of Mumbai and was apprehensive that Hyderabad would soon catch up with that city if nothing was done about it. Nalini was enthusiastic and soon organized 'street beautifiers' who collected garbage from houses in tricycle carts provided by the municipality and dumped it in municipal garbage bins for a nominal monthly fee from each of the households.

The scheme expanded rapidly to over twenty areas and I was told that some street beautifiers earned up to 8000 rupees each per month from their monthly fee as well as the sale of plastic waste for recycling.

Nalini did some other projects responding to civic needs. One of them was in a vegetable market called Monda Market in the city. It is among the largest in Asia and perhaps also ranks as one of the most crowded, dirty and chaotic retailing centres for vegetables anywhere. Nalini took on a task that had daunted the municipality—of cleaning up the place and bringing in some order. She persuaded the vendors to hawk their wares behind lines she drew in chalk to allow customers to walk through and coaxed them to clean up after they finished for the day, saying it would help business, and it apparently did. A survey estimated that on an average, each vendor's earnings grew by about 25 rupees a day and by 100,000 rupees a week for the market as a whole. Nalini continued with other projects with the twin objectives of bettering the environment of the city and encouraging micro-entrepreneurship.

In 1997, we celebrated fifty years of Independence. I was one of fifty persons who were asked to write an article by the Confederation of Indian Industry. I thought I should write about the many achievements of independent India and our hopes for the future when I chanced upon a *Newsweek* article that painted a dismal picture of India fifty years after Independence, with the destitute in Bihar faring worse than the poorest in sub-Saharan Africa. There were also unflattering comparisons with China and the Asian tigers. I was annoyed that *Newsweek* seemed to have no sense of the occasion. I comforted myself by focusing on the positive things that had happened. Among other things, I wrote of the immense wealth that had been created for the country by the companies born after Independence, like Reliance and Infosys. But I felt that successful businesses could step up their efforts to help people come out of poverty. I also believed that public scrutiny of such efforts by companies would be useful for several reasons. Among others, it would be an example for others and commitments made public would not be easily forgotten. I therefore suggested that business houses 'publish a second balance sheet on what they have done for the community in that financial year'. I was not preaching something I did not practise. I had already started including a report on the foundation's activity in the annual report of Dr. Reddy's and I am glad to say it continues to the present day.

However, the *Newsweek* article had found its mark and it hurt. The stark contrast between those who had acquired wealth and those who had not haunted me and provided the second trigger—Prof. Chaturvedi's being the first.

It occurred to me that I was a lucky one. Chance and fortuitous circumstance had time and again presented me with opportunities that I had grasped. The majority of the disadvantaged had never had the chance and those who did were ill-equipped to benefit. I thought that it would be wonderful if the foundation worked towards giving people a chance to grab an opportunity when it came by.

Nalini's next idea therefore excited me tremendously. Extreme poverty has many tragic consequences, particularly for children. Apart from malnutrition, disease, the lack of education and everything else that stares us in the face, some children are just abandoned. Others are forced to work, often in sweatshops and hazardous workplaces, in complete disregard of the statute that forbids it.

Most street children have nothing to look forward to except bondage, occupational ill health or delinquency. How does one give these children a chance?

Nalini had a plan, but it was a tough problem to tackle. Abandoned children had to be identified. Working children had to be brought out of their workplaces, often a fraught task, easier said than done. We needed help from the police.

I had kept a wary distance from the police since the days I rode a scooter without a headlight and I was unsure whether they would be supportive. Heart-warmingly, Dr C. Ramachandra Naidu, a senior police officer, was enthusiastic about the idea and it soon gathered momentum with a number of police officers getting involved. Children were brought out of hazardous workplaces and enrolled in bridge schools for a year with the objective of enabling them to gain admission in regular schools. Foster-mothers, often poor widows, were identified to care for abandoned children and send them to the bridge schools with small financial support from the foundation. Reflecting the whole-hearted involvement of the police, the project fittingly came to be called the Child and Police Project. I remember that the project started with about fifty children initially. About five years later, the annual enrolment had grown to around 5000 children.

It is to Nalini's credit that the programme succeeded. However, she would have been the first to acknowledge that this was possible only with the enthusiastic support of the police department in the city. The person who helped in getting the police involved was Shanta Sinha, chairperson of the M.V. Foundation, also headquartered in Hyderabad. Shanta was honoured with the Ramon Magsaysay Award in 2003, a fitting recognition of her pioneering and stupendous work to end child labour. Generous financial support came in from UNICEF, Balajyothi and other institutions. What touched me greatly were the donations made by individuals. Among others, many police constables, often caricatured as bumbling and callous or worse in Telugu films, not only

Courtesy of Dr. Reddy's Foundation

A residential bridge school: *The compassion of volunteers made a difference* put in considerable effort but also made financial contributions to the project. Diana Hayden from Hyderabad, who won the Miss World title in 1997, was a fervent supporter of the Child and Police Project. She donated 33,000 dollars from her prize money and Miss World Inc. made a matching contribution, perhaps at her instance. I am glad to say that as early as 1998, for every rupee that the foundation invested in its projects, four rupees came in from others. Surprised perhaps by the ballooning contributions, income tax authorities scrutinized the foundation's receipts. They were reassured soon enough. It helped that several income tax officers figured in the list of donors.

Nalini was always looking around for big donors, as the programme was growing rapidly. She talked to Plan International, an organization with global operations working towards bettering the lives of deprived children, which was the mission of the Child and Police Project too. Nalini introduced me to the programme officer of Plan International, Manoj Kumar, an interesting young man who had given up a promising career in banking to work in the social development sector. He impressed me with his quick intelligence and his commitment to the work he was doing. We hit it off and I asked Manoj to get in touch with me whenever he had a new idea. Manoj was, of course, brimming with ideas and keen to help in whichever way he could. He helped with funding some activities of the Child and Police Project—and this had an unexpected aftermath. But that comes later.

An idea that evolved during the constant interaction with the police was to host a global conference of chiefs of police from across the world to discuss how they could learn from each other in dealing with children at risk. Manoj said he would bring in the funds for the conference. The police as well as the home department of the state government invited a number of police chiefs in India and elsewhere. The conference, the first of its kind, was held in Hyderabad in 1999 and police chiefs from eight countries and from fourteen states in India attended it. Chandrababu Naidu, the then chief minister of Andhra Pradesh, was the chief guest and it went off very well.

While the Child and Police Project was growing and getting increasingly noticed, there was still work to be done. The families of the children who had stopped working felt the pinch as they were deprived of some income. Many of them had older children who had come of age but were jobless. If they were employed, it would augment the family income and the programme would then become deep-rooted. I pondered over where the opportunities lay for them and how unemployed young people could be better equipped to tap into these. For a while, it was my favourite question for colleagues, friends and acquaintances.

The winds of economic liberalization were blowing through the country and creating many opportunities for livelihoods, but they seemed to be passing by these unskilled and relatively unschooled youth, as indeed millions of young people who had completed school or college. At the same time, there seemed to be a huge shortage of manpower in all kinds of services in cities and towns—bedside attendants, shop assistants, waiters, mechanics and so on. These kinds of services did not pay very much, but the training needs were modest for such employment. It seemed to be a good starting point to launch the first training projects, with a tie-up of some kind with potential employers.

Nalini did a pilot programme in Balanagar, an industrial suburb of Hyderabad with just nine trainees. Hyderabad is an important IT hub and the first programme was one on computer literacy, with volunteer faculty from Satyam Computers. It was a good learning experience and validated the concept and the programme.

We were fortunate to find Raj Iyer, an electrical engineer and an alumnus of the Indian Institute of Management, Kolkata. After a fairly long innings in the corporate world, Raj decided to get into the development sector and joined the foundation as executive director to lead the training effort. He did a marvellous job in giving concrete shape to early ideas and taking them forward with enthusiasm. We needed a name for the programme and Manoj came up with with a suggestion— LABS, an acronym for Livelihood Advancement Business School. That sounded perfect and LABS it was. The happy coincidence did not escape me. Dr. Reddy's Research Foundation had its labs for drug discovery and Dr. Reddy's Foundation had its LABS for livelihoods!

The initial successes left no doubt that it was a programme with great potential. Even as the programme was taking off in my home state of Andhra Pradesh, the word spread to other states. Khivraj Motors, a dealership for Maruti cars in Chennai was among the first to help. It agreed to recruit personnel from the LABS training programme and generously offered space for LABS on Chennai's prime Mount Road. The government got involved too. The foundation struck a deal with the government of Andhra Pradesh to run pilot programmes. These programmes did well and soon both the rural and urban development ministries of the Government of India teamed up with LABS to scale up skilling and employment opportunities for unemployed youth across the country. In due course, LABS crossed the borders of the country in collaboration with Plan International and set up operations in Vietnam, Sri Lanka and Indonesia. When I last checked, LABS had proved to be the springboard for more than 200,000 young people finding livelihoods.

Even more heartening was the adoption of the LABS model by a

Onward and upward: *LABS imparted livelihood skills and built self-confidence*

number of business houses. I remember that a company in the BPL group provided training for refrigeration mechanics and Godrej, a competitor, employed them. The Rane group in Chennai set it up. Starting with a school in Pune in 2007, the Mahindras are doing it across the country in a big way with the Mahindra Pride Schools and Naandi, an organization I will talk about later, is implementing the programme for them. Forbes Marshall in Pune started its own programme and also named it LABS. I was particularly pleased that Naveen Jindal of the Jindal group, a young man who has made a mark in politics, implemented the programme in his constituency. LABS may have been started by us, but it soon rightfully belonged to everybody. When LABS started, I had a figure of one million livelihoods by 2010 as a target. I was told that this may well have been achieved if everybody's programmes were taken into account.

Numbers apart, it was wonderful to see the confidence that it instilled in the young people who had come out of it. An alumnus of LABS once asked to see me and I met him as I was curious to know about his experience. He said that he had done the LABS programme three years earlier and found a job as a data entry operator. When that business went bust, he borrowed money from a bank to start a cybercafe, a place where one could work on personal computers or surf the Internet for a fee. He had not only found a livelihood for himself, but was employing half a dozen people. He then told me, 'Sir, I am a managing director like you now.'

BBC once did a programme on LABS and shot footage of what was going on with some of those who had gone through the programme. I was also there. A girl asked me why I was sponsoring such programmes. I answered her honestly and said I did it for my own satisfaction. She did not look convinced and she asked me the same question again and I said the same thing. She was persistent and asked for the 'real reason'. I realized then that she suspected I was planning to enter politics. I was taken aback and wanted to erase the thought from her mind. So I thought I should point out that she too could do something good without joining politics. I said, 'I do not think that you will remain in this 2000-rupee job

Celebrating 200,000 livelihoods, 2007: *Jimson Jos (right), an early LABS alumnus, greets me as Anuradha looks on*

forever. One day you will rise higher and perhaps become the owner of a company. You will then do what I am doing now.' She looked thoughtful after that and did not ask me anything further.

The Child and Police Project as well as LABS were growing exponentially soon after the turn of the millennium. The University of Sussex did a study on the health of the Child and Police Project and recommended that it be spun off as a separate entity to sustain its focus and momentum. It was possible to do so as the project was receiving near-adequate funding by that time. Nalini spun it off as an independent entity in 2005 and left the foundation to head it. I am glad that she continues to work on this project with undiminished zeal and her trademark intensity. Raj Iyer now heads the Mahindra Pride School and continues to advance livelihood training admirably.

My daughter, Anuradha, has been overseeing the work of the foundation for about a decade now. Anuradha is a caring person and I am sure that the foundation will be all the better for her stewardship.

20 A NEW BEGINNING

Araku coffee, anyone?
A cup that cheers connoisseurs and growers

N. Chandrababu Naidu became the chief minister of Andhra Pradesh in 1995. Chandrababu had a vision for the state and was determined to realize it swiftly. His style of functioning was markedly different and often grabbed the headlines.

One of the things that caught the world's attention was his meeting with Bill Gates, the chairman and CEO of Microsoft Corporation. Chandrababu sought a meeting with Gates when he visited India in 1997. The American ambassador diplomatically suggested that he meet him at a cocktail party, but Chandrababu would have none of it and insisted on meeting Gates one-on-one. It was widely reported that he finally got a ten-minute slot, but he wowed Gates with a half-hour presentation on the advantages of Hyderabad over Bangalore and sold him the idea of setting up the first development centre of Microsoft outside the USA in Hyderabad. That Chandrababu had made his presentation with Microsoft's PowerPoint would not have escaped Gates.

Some months later, I received a call from the chief minister's office, inviting me to a Sunday breakfast meeting with him. I was in for a surprise. Chandrababu talked of his vision to create an institutional framework outside of government with a mission to improve the quality of life of the people of Andhra Pradesh. He thought this would put development on the fast track as it would be professionally managed and free of bureaucratic red tape. He talked of outsourcing poorly managed government projects to this organization to ensure revenues to it. He was also confident, based on assurances he had received, that a number of wealthy non-resident Indians in the USA hailing from Andhra Pradesh would generously support such an effort if it were led by credible business leaders. He then sprang the surprise. He said, 'Dr Reddy, I want you to be chairman of this organization. You will bring credibility to it.'

I was, of course, pleased with the confidence that the chief minister of my home state had in me but was most reluctant to accept the offer. I said I was busy with my business and needed to spend all the time I could find on drug discovery research. I pointed out that I had no experience working with the government and was apprehensive that funds would be a perennial problem. The list went on. Naidu had a ready answer for everything. I would be given a free hand, projects were available aplenty with adequate budgetary provisions for funding and a senior officer from the civil services would be posted on deputation to the organization to take care of the administration and liaising with the government. I was no match for the consummate negotiator that Chandrababu undoubtedly was. After all, even Bill Gates had succumbed to his persuasion.

The new organization was registered as public charitable trust on 1st November 1998 and named Naandi, which in Sanskrit means 'a new beginning'. I was named the founding chairman and three other trustees were also appointed. Each of us made a contribution of 5 million rupees to the corpus so that Naandi had adequate funding to get off the ground. An officer on special duty was seconded to it from the civil service and the office was set up. The board of trustees met several times and little else happened. No worthwhile projects were identified, nor did funds flow in from non-resident Indians.

About a year later, Chandrababu was the chief guest at the conference of global chiefs of police that was organized as part of the Child and Police Project of Dr. Reddy's Foundation. Chandrababu asked about the progress at Naandi. I was in a spot as I had nothing to report. He asked what the problem was. I told him the biggest problem was that we did not have a CEO with ideas who could effectively lead the organization. Chandrababu said nothing, but I could sense his disappointment and it left me very uncomfortable. Manoj moderated the whole programme and I could see that Chandrababu was paying attention to the proceedings. At the end of the formal function, as Chandrababu left the venue, he called me aside and said Manoj may be the person we were looking for to head Naandi. I wasted no time at all in talking to Manoj and was delighted when he agreed to be the CEO of Naandi.

Manoj joined Naandi in 2000 and it was indeed a new beginning. Anand Mahindra, now the chairman of Mahindra and Mahindra, Isher Judge Ahluwalia, the chairperson of the Indian Council for Research on International Economic Relations, and M. Rajendra Prasad, the chairman of Soma Enterprise, joined the board of trustees. They are all so well known that they need no introduction. As may be expected, they are terribly busy people, but they are also wonderful human beings who made the time to provide the vision, the drive and the steadying hand to make Naandi what it is today.

Naandi is doing a lot of significant work. I must recall some of it to acknowledge the generosity of the people who contributed so much of their knowledge and time, entirely free of cost, motivated only by the desire to serve communities in need. There have been many who have helped Naandi, but a few examples would be sufficient to explain why I am overwhelmed by the goodness of people who have done so. Equally, I must also acknowledge the generous financial contributions made by individuals and institutions, though they are not all mentioned here.

Irrigation for small farmers

Chandrababu not only conceived of Naandi and spotted the CEO, he also suggested the first project.

Andhra Pradesh is a major agrarian state and is served by gigantic irrigation schemes that supply water to hundreds of thousands of acres of land for cultivation. Apart from these major irrigation schemes, the government had also constructed about 1300 minor irrigation schemes known as lift irrigation schemes designed to serve small farmers. Water was pumped up or 'lifted' from rivers and distributed to farmers' fields. Chandrababu was concerned that many of these schemes were not in operation and thought that reviving them would be far quicker and more economical than investing in new irrigation projects. Chandrababu was aware that many of the schemes had become defunct as the farmers had not paid electricity charges in the hope that these would be waived. However, power supply was cut off and over time, disuse resulted in deterioration of the pumps and theft of the components that could be dismantled. The problem was not just one of repairing the pumps but also putting in place a system where the community served by the irrigation schemes would pay for their operation and maintenance, or these would soon become defunct again. Normally such work would be executed by the irrigation department of the government. But Chandrababu was also aware that the government was ill-equipped to involve farmers in keeping the systems running and paying for them. He wanted to outsource the work to Naandi. I agreed to take it up.

I knew nothing about lift irrigation or the problems involved. Neither did anybody at Naandi. The first task was therefore to find experts who would know how to tackle the situation. We found an unusual guru in Malcolm Harper, emeritus professor at the Cranfield School of Management in the UK. An Indophile and an authority on rural finance, Prof. Harper was the chairman of BASIX, a Hyderabad-based microfinance institution. He was familiar with the issues involved as BASIX had also worked on reviving some defunct irrigation schemes and had given loans for this.

Prof. Harper sat with the Naandi team to work out a revival plan. He recommended that Naandi undertake a pilot to revive four schemes in Mahboobnagar district of Andhra Pradesh. A critical step in the revival process was the repair and replacement of various electrical and mechanical parts of the huge pumps. They were typically in the range of 50–175 horsepower and each scheme usually had four or five of them. Most of these pumps were manufactured by Kirloskar & Co. and they recommended replacing all the pumps with new ones. We could not afford this. At this juncture I met Mr Cowlagi, a soft-spoken petrochemical engineer from Russia, who is an authority on pumps and a consultant to several large organizations. He had helped a small farmer in a village in Belgaum and seemed to be the man we were looking for. He agreed to get the pumps working, but on two conditions—one, that he would help us free of cost, and two, that we would not stop the revival with just four schemes.

I had a friend who used to joke that some of the best minds of our country were employed with the government, but most of them worked best after they left the government. Dr D.S.K. Rao was a former NABARD general manager who had gained international recognition as a trainer, researcher, author and adviser on agriculture, irrigation and microfinance. Having financed irrigation projects for governments and farmers when he was a banker, Dr Rao was the ideal person to help revive the very schemes that he had once funded. Andhra Pradesh being his home state, Dr Rao was happy to join hands with Mr Cowlagi and Prof. Harper.

Terms of revival were negotiated with the government, and I must say the government was responsive and reasonable. It agreed to pay the arrears in electricity charges on behalf of the farmers and most of the cost of repairs. The government was also willing to transfer the ownership of the pumps to farmers' cooperatives, as well as the governance of the scheme. The non-negotiable precondition for reconnection of electricity, however, was that farmers would pay the estimated cost of power for six months in advance and contribute a small percentage of the cost of revival. It was a struggle to get the pumps repaired and form the cooperatives. And then we hit a roadblock. How was one to persuade farmers to pay the electricity charges in advance, when the prevailing belief was that the government would eventually provide power free?

It was Prof. Harper and the women of the community who broke the ice under a tamarind tree one Sunday afternoon. Prof. Harper convened a meeting of a hundred-odd farmers. Many of their womenfolk were also there. Prof. Harper came up with a question.

'If a guest like me came to your house, would you give him a cup of tea?' he asked.

'Yes,' said a some voices, mainly those of women.

'But what would you do if there was no sugar at home?' Prof. Harper asked. There was silence.

'You could do one of four things,' he said. 'One, you could go to a politician and ask him to recommend the issue of free sugar from government stocks. Two, you could go to the ration office and stage a protest, demanding free sugar. Three, you could ask Naandi to supply you with free sugar for your guest; or four, you could go and buy some sugar from the shop. What would you do?'

There was laughter all around. 'Of course we would buy the sugar,' said a woman and the others chimed in with good-humoured comments. The ice was broken.

Courtesy of Naandi

Reviving lift irrigation schemes:
A problem-solving meeting in progress

Prof. Harper struck while the iron was hot. 'The electricity department is like a grocer's shop,' he told them. 'It sells electricity, just as a grocer sells sugar. It cannot give it free forever.' He pointed out that if farmers paid for the electricity, the water would flow and they could cultivate their land. 'Surely,' he said, 'this is not too high a price to pay for feeding your children when they are hungry.' The discussions became intense. Finally, the farmers under one scheme agreed to pay electricity charges in advance and the other three followed. Prof. Harper had flicked the right switches and power was reconnected.

It took nearly two years for Naandi to revive four schemes in the pilot phase. Chandrababu saw that it was successful and took the big decision to hand over these, as well as those revived subsequently, to farmers' cooperatives. Over the next two years, Naandi revived about sixty-five more schemes. In the next phase, another eighty-four schemes were taken up with government funding as well as generous assistance from the Sir Ratan Tata Trust. Eventually, about 150 schemes irrigating over 55,000 acres and serving the needs of about 20,000 small farmers were revived and handed over to farmers' coperatives.

Midday meals for schoolchildren

Manoj joined me on one of my morning walks on a chilly winter day, early in 2002. We talked of the progress Naandi was making towards reviving the first lift irrigation scheme in Mahboobnagar district. I could see that Manoj had enough problems on his plate.

Surprisingly, he was willing to take on more. The state government had asked Naandi if it could set up a kitchen to prepare and deliver cooked meals to children in government schools under what was known as the midday meal scheme. Manoj wanted to do it.

The midday meal scheme had been in operation for a long time. Most people remember it as the creation of M.G. Ramachandran, the charismatic film actor turned politician who became the chief minister of Tamil Nadu in the late 1970s. As a matter of fact, it had been introduced earlier by K. Kamaraj, a simple and sagacious Congressman in the Gandhian mould, who became the chief minister of Tamil Nadu in the mid-1950s, but it was MGR, as he was popularly known, who made it more nutritive and ordered its implementation in all government schools in 1982. It was a great success and over 100,000 poor school-going children had at least one square meal a day. Several other state governments had their own versions of the scheme. The Government of India took the cue rather belatedly and introduced the scheme nationally in 1995. It had a long name—The National Programme of Nutritional Support to Primary Education—but people simply called it the midday meal scheme. While some states supplied cooked food, many others distributed 3 kilos of foodgrains per month to each child who had attended 80 per cent of the classes. The scheme was, therefore, expected to improve both nutrition and attendance at school.

The intentions of the scheme were laudable, but the implementation came in for widespread criticism. There were reports of pilferage and substandard foodgrains. It seemed to be going the way of many other government welfare schemes. Reflecting public disgust, the People's Union for Civil Liberties filed a writ petition in the Supreme Court asking for directions that all governments should implement the many programmes announced for public good, and the midday meal scheme was one of them.

Justice was quick. The Supreme Court issued interim orders on 28th November 2001, directing all state governments to provide *cooked* food to all primary schoolchildren in government and government-aided schools. A deadline was fixed for implementation. Half of all the schools were to be covered in three months and the remainder in six. The media went to town with the news and reactions to it. State governments scrambled to implement the directions. In Andhra Pradesh, Chandrababu Naidu's government turned to Naandi for serving cooked food to children in the primary classes of schools in Hyderabad.

The first thing that occurred to me was that something could easily go wrong. What would happen if a lizard jumped into a vessel while the cooking was going on? The food could spoil, or the kitchen could catch fire. The way we cook, all kinds of disasters were possible. If something like that happened my neck would be on the block. It was not just my reputation at stake, there could well be repercussions on the company that bore my name. I told Manoj all this.

Manoj looked increasingly disappointed. His only response was that the midday meal was the only good meal that a poor boy or girl would get. We walked in silence for a while.

I broke the silence and told Manoj I needed to understand a few things. Manoj knew me well enough to instantly realize that I had decided that he should go ahead, or I would not have prolonged the conversation. His face lit up. I asked him who would be responsible for running the kitchen. Manoj said he had identified Sibu Joseph and Leena, a husband-and-wife team. Leena was in her mid-thirties and the mother of two. She had been brought up in a plantation in Kerala and had made Hyderabad her home. I paused the questioning for a moment, wondering if a homemaker was the right choice to manage an industrial-scale kitchen for 200,000 children. More details poured out. The vessels would be of stainless steel, procured from the supplier to the Taj Mahal Hotel, a popular vegetarian hotel and eatery with several branches in Hyderabad. The vessels would be steam-cleaned. The cooks would be properly clothed and trained in hygiene. Logistics for supplies and delivery were a problem, but not

Inauguration of the first kitchen: *Manoj Kumar (left) is a trifle nervous as Chief Minister Chandrababu Naidu does his bit*

insurmountable. About a 1000 schools and madrasas (Islamic schools, primarily serving the poor; nowadays they also impart modern education) had to be supplied freshly cooked meals every day and on time. Manoj had obviously done his homework before coming to me.

In less than forty-five days, the district administration of Hyderabad and the team at Naandi, with a couple of Good Samaritan volunteers pitching in, worked day and night to set up what was one of the largest kitchens in the country. I vividly recall the surprise of visitors who came for the inauguration of the kitchen. The sheer scale of operations to feed 200,000 children a day was impressive. Cooking was going on in huge shiny steel vessels and everything was spotlessly clean. The kitchen was inaugurated by the chief minister, Chandrababu Naidu. He went around and then told me, 'Dr. Reddy, you have surpassed all my expectations.' I, in turn, looked at Manoj and Leena and told them that the place gave me more satisfaction than any laboratory that I had built for my company.

Manoj told me that the Naandi kitchen at Hyderabad has served over 200 million meals in the first ten years without a single serious complaint. The meals are delivered to schools in the city on time, like the famous *dabbawallahs* do in Mumbai. A number of people have visited the kitchen, including David Miliband, a former minister of Britain's Labour Party, and they were all appreciative.

I doubt if Leena and Sibu Joseph thought that managing the Naandi kitchen was just another job. They were so dedicated that it seemed to be almost a spiritual engagement, a reflection of their Christian faith. Come to think of it, feeding the poor is a tradition in all religions. It is a tradition among Hindus. The Muslims in Hyderabad are well known for feeding the poor on certain festivals, and on other days too.

I remember a feature aired on TV9, a Telugu television news channel, some years ago. A small eatery in the Old City in Hyderabad served a simple meal of dal, a bit of curry and rice for 10 rupees a meal. Biryani, a traditional Hyderabadi rice preparation, was available for another 10 rupees for those who wanted it. This is certainly not a commercial proposition. When asked why he did it, the Muslim owner of the eatery said it was a 100-year-old family tradition started by his great-grandfather. They continued the tradition as they were financially well-off and did not feel like discontinuing it. There was this other story too. A person whose name sounded like he was from the Marwari community of Rajasthan stood outside the eatery with 200 rupees in his hand almost every day. If anybody did not have money for a meal, he would give 10 rupees to the owner to serve that person. He said that on some days he fed fifty people. There is no better charity than feeding the hungry.

The Naandi model is simple. It seeks one-time donations from corporates to set up a kitchen and then runs the kitchen with foodgrain supplied by the government under the midday meal scheme. The government also reimburses the cooking costs. Corporates have been generous in supporting this initiative. For example, Hindustan Zinc, a mining company taken over by the Vedanta group in 2002, supported the setting up of several kitchens in Rajasthan. I must say, however, that the midday meal kitchen set up with the support of Hindustan Zinc in the Kalahandi district of Odisha touches me the most. Kalahandi is one

Roasted in a trice: *A million meals a day needs some mechanization*

of the most unfortunate districts in the country. Blighted by drought, it has suffered at least one serious famine every decade for most of the twentieth century. In the 1980s, it gained notoriety when it became known that children were sold in Kalahandi as a consequence of a famine. The pictures were even more heartbreaking than the news. There was, however, a problem. Delivery costs in Kalahandi were expected to be very high as the schools were dispersed and access was difficult. I went to Anil Agarwal, Vedanta's chief, and told him about it. He agreed immediately to reimburse the transport costs and that arrangement continues till today.

Naandi now runs twenty-odd kitchens in the country and serves *a million meals a day* under the midday meal scheme. I think it has demonstrated that a difference can be made.

Naandi's work is increasingly influencing policy on child health and nutrition. A five-year programme called Project Bachpan (meaning 'childhood' in Hindi) was undertaken in the Bajna block of Ratlam district in Madhya Pradesh. It was a tripartite action-research programme of the World Bank, the government of Madhya Pradesh and Naandi to assess the impact of the project on the status of children in the entire block of Bajna, populated by the Bhil tribe with high rates of malnutrition. The programme delivered a package of interventions, including nutrition, health care and education. The evaluation at the end of the five-year period showed dramatic improvements in the health of children and its impact on the community.

In 2011, Naandi designed and undertook a massive survey to measure the nutrition status of over 100,000 children below five years of age, representing 20 per cent of India's child population. It was called the HUNGaMA survey, a smart acronym for hunger and malnutrition, which also means commotion in Hindi. Naandi's effort was funded by Avantha Foundation, Mahindra Group, Thermax Foundation and scores of ordinary citizens. It was also backed by the group of thirty-odd young parliamentarians from a dozen political parties who came together as the Citizens' Alliance against Malnutrition. This group was so enthused that it persuaded the then prime minister Dr Manmohan Singh himself to release the

Courtesy of Naandi

The HUNGaMA Survey, 2011: *Prime Minister Manmohan Singh said the survey was an 'extraordinary accomplishment'*

report on 10th January 2012. The prime minister was moved to call malnutrition a national shame and he committed himself to give the highest priority to its eradication.

The elimination of malnutrition among children is within our reach. We only need to grasp it.

Safe drinking water for all

Thanks to Manoj, I spoke to some farmers in Medak district of Andhra Pradesh, not far from Hyderabad. Water was the problem uppermost in their minds, but not just for irrigation. There was an even more urgent problem—they had no access to safe drinking water. It was no surprise as newspapers often carried woeful reports of communities without access to safe drinking water and I was quite aware of its impact on health. But listening to first-hand accounts of people suffering without safe drinking water was a powerful catalyst.

The problem continued to haunt me. I recalled staying at a hotel in Tokyo where a sign next to the wash basin read: 'The water in this bathroom is potable. However, we are also pleased to keep a bottle of mineral water in your room with compliments.' Surely, if luxury hotels in the world could supply potable water in bathrooms, it was ridiculous that millions in India did not have enough potable water to quench their thirst. It was not rocket science. If India could plan a mission to the moon, surely a solution could be found for providing safe drinking water for all.

My first thought was that perhaps we could develop the technology at one of our labs. As usual, I asked my friends for ideas. One of them, Dr Nair, told me over dinner in Chennai that there were already many technical solutions available to purify water. Dr Nair said reverse osmosis and ultraviolet light were in common use for water purification, but he was aware of a patented technology that held out the promise of being a better technical solution, with a business model that was sustainable.

Dr Nair told me that Dr Ashok Gadgil had invented a water purification system while working at the Lawrence Berkeley National Laboratory, which is located in the campus of the University of California at Berkeley. Dr Gadgil had an interesting background. He was a physicist who graduated from IIT, Kanpur, and had earned a doctorate at the University of California, where he was also teaching. The purification system consisted of the usual filtration to remove particulate matter and then passing the water through activated carbon to remove odour and colour, before reverse osmosis. The water was then subjected to purification with ultraviolet (UV) light, which would destroy the pathogens. The system itself was probably well known to water treatment specialists. However, the novelty of the invention seemed to be the way it was engineered. In conventional systems, water flowed around a jacketed UV lamp. Quite often, the available water was 'hard water' and this resulted in salt deposits on the jacket of the lamp. With use, the jacket was also fouled by biomass, compromising water quality and the system required servicing by experienced technicians. In Dr Gadgil's system, the *bare* UV lamp was suspended *above* the water, eliminating these problems.

Dr Gadgil had teamed up with Dr Tralance Addy, a former vice president of J&J, who had established Water Health International to serve the needs of communities without adequate access to safe drinking water. Their business model was to install the plants and charge a fee for the water supplied. This seemed to be a sustainable proposition, because it intended to be commercially viable. Dr Gadgil was keen to roll out the product in rural India and had got in touch with Dr Nair, hoping he would be able to get Dr Addy a reliable Indian partner.

I did not waste a moment. I called Manoj right in the middle of dinner and he was enthusiastic. In a fortnight or so, Dr Addy was in discussion with Manoj at Naandi's office in Hyderabad. Within days, a deal was struck.

Naandi's role was to identify villages where the water purification system could be installed, convince the communities to drink only purified water and, most difficult of all, persuade them to pay for it. Water Health International would establish an Indian subsidiary, install and operate the plants with people recruited and trained locally, and raise finances for the capital costs. The water was to be sold at 10 paise (about 3 cents) a litre, which would meet all expenses. Projected cash flows were sufficient to repay the loans.

In the next few months, sometime in 2006, the first plant was inaugurated in a village called Bomminampadu in Krishna district of Andhra Pradesh. It worked out very well and attracted quite a bit of attention. People started calling it the Bomminampadu model.

Manoj and his team worked tirelessly to implement the programme rapidly. In less than two years, the Bomminampadu model was replicated in 200 other locations in the state of Andhra Pradesh. Ironically enough, the rapid progress was the cause of a serious problem. Water Health International's finances were strained by the increasing demands of capital to install new plants. The revenues from the plants previously set up were insufficient to service their loans, in part because the revenues

An on-site review of a drinking water facility

from the commissioned plants took longer than anticipated to build up. The capital costs were high—over 2 million rupees for each plant. Water Health International had a cash flow crisis.

In the meanwhile, the demand for drinking water projects was growing. Communities, governments and philanthropists were willing to untie their purse strings, but all of them wanted a more efficient financing model.

Manoj found the solution. Tata Projects offered a similar water purification plant at half the cost or less. The financing costs plummeted and the payback period of the investment was acceptable to everybody. It provided a fillip for the next wave of growth for Naandi's safe drinking water programme.

I invited Dr Montek Singh Ahluwalia, the deputy chairman of the Planning Commission, to inaugurate a project in Nalgonda district of Andhra Pradesh. Nalgonda was in dire need of safe drinking water as the fluoride content of ground water was dangerously high there. Excessive fluoride in drinking water causes its accumulation in bones and that in turn results in disabling stiffness and pain in joints. The disease is called fluorosis and it was rampant in Nalgonda district. Montek graciously accepted my invitation. Not only was he impressed by the enthusiasm in the community, he also recognized the potential of Naandi's programme to meet rural drinking water needs across the country.

Montek's wife, Isher, however, was familiar with its potential even earlier and had championed the safe drinking water programme of Naandi as a member of its board. She took the initiative to take the programme to Punjab and Haryana. Both the state governments saw the potential of the scheme and supported Naandi to scale it up. Within a couple of years, Naandi had more than 400 projects of its own in four different states in the country, with support from several organizations—Frank Water, a charity in Bristol, UK, that funded clean water projects; AAPI Charitable Foundation in Illinois, USA; APMGUSA, a federation of medical doctors from Andhra Pradesh in the USA; and GPOBA, a

Courtesy of Naandi

Safe drinking water for all
Stainless steel inside . . . smiles outside

global partnership of donor agencies whose fund is administered by the World Bank.

The programme was growing very satisfactorily, but the demands on management and money were also growing worryingly. A solution came from an unexpected quarter. While I was on the board of the Global Alliance for Improved Nutrition, I had met Franc Ribaud, the chairman and CEO of Danone, and Bernard Giraud, its chief of sustainability. Paris-based Danone is a world leader in the food industry. The conversation turned to danone.communities, a 'social businesses network' sponsored by Danone to fund and develop social enterprises that worked towards reducing poverty and malnutrition. danone. communities had already forged a partnership with Mohammad Yunus's Grameen Bank in Bangladesh to help rural women become micro-entrepreneurs and sell fortified yoghurt in their communities. One thing led to another; finally, the safe drinking water programme of Naandi was spun off in 2010 as an independent organization, Naandi Community Water Services, in which danone.communities made a capital investment. I am delighted that they have drawn up an ambitious programme of expansion to increase the number of water purification plants, first to 2000, and then to 5000. Manoj, of course, remains deeply involved in this.

When Naandi started the drinking water programme, I had a seemingly fanciful aspiration in my mind that everyone in rural India would have access to safe drinking water by 2020. By the time the drinking water programme of Naandi was spun off in 2010, a million litres a day of safe drinking water were being sold, primarily in rural communities. I am hopeful that my aspiration will be realized, not only because of the plans of Naandi Community Water Services, but also because of the entrepreneurship that has grown around the programme. Manoj tells me that after Naandi started operating about thirty water purification plants in Nalgonda district, more than 500 individuals have become micro-entrepreneurs and have put up their own water purification plants in smaller villages. This should have made a visible dent on the problem of fluorosis in the district. Even more heartening is that Naandi has competition across the country. At least a dozen social enterprises with competent CEOs have been set up. They have attracted social capital and are operating on a significant scale. Many state governments are also pushing implementation of safe drinking water programmes.

Manoj and his team have every reason to be satisfied with the remarkable transformation that they have been instrumental in bringing about. Speaking for myself, I am delighted.

I had occasion to relate the Naandi safe drinking water story at a talk that I gave. My son, Satish, was also there. At the end of the story, I turned to him and told him that his antibiotic sales may soon plummet. The audience dissolved in laughter, but I think the message that safe drinking water is indispensable to good health was driven home.

Organic coffee

Soon after Naandi was founded, I called upon one of the most respected senior bureaucrats of the state, S.R. Sankaran. I asked him for his advice on what a good beginning for Naandi would be. Sankaran had no hesitation in saying that Naandi should not settle for low-hanging fruit and must attempt to solve long-standing development problems. He talked of the Araku valley, about 120 kilometres from the port city of Visakhapatnam in the north-eastern corner of Andhra Pradesh. Sankaran said the region was in dire need of development and this effort alone could well consume the lifetime of an organization. Sadly, Sankaran is no more but, inspired by him, Naandi continues to work in Araku.

Nestled in the Eastern Ghats of India at an average height of about 3500 feet, Araku valley is the most picturesque region of the state. Tracts of moist deciduous forests topped by dense, dry savannah at the higher elevations and the pristine waters of cascading waterfalls and gurgling streams sustain a rich diversity of flora and fauna. Nearly a hundred species of birds, over fifty species of butterflies and 150 varieties of plants are the bounty that nature has blessed Araku with. Unsurprisingly, the ecosystem is fragile and increasingly threatened by shifting cultivation, coffee plantations, plastic and worse.

The Araku valley is home to about nineteen aboriginal tribes who have largely preserved their tradition and culture, despite the concessions they have made to polyester saris and the tourists who come in droves and make some contribution to the local economy. The pristine beauty of Araku and its marvellous tranquillity are in stark contrast to the poverty and pestilence that afflict the tribal people. The benefits of modern science, good health, education and comfortable living have passed by the tribals, who eke out a living with traditional crafts, petty jobs generated by tourism, and subsistence agriculture. It is hard to 'educate' them about the need to preserve their environment when they don't have many options to do things differently. In fact, I am not even sure they need to be 'educated'—they probably know more about nature and how to preserve their habitat than most of us. What they need is a chance to better their lives.

Sankaran knew all of this and much, much more. 'Do something for their livelihoods,' he said, 'without destroying their environment and their heritage.'

Manoj threw his heart and head into the task. He and some of his team members made a number of trips to the Araku valley. Every time he came back, the story was grimmer. The government had not made much progress in providing basic services. The vicious cycle of poverty and sickness was not yielding to the efforts of the Integrated Tribal Development Agency of the government, despite all its efforts. Malnutrition and disease were rampant. Almost every child seemed to be out of school and every household had a tale of a woman who died at childbirth. The tribals were wary of people from the plains who more often than not, fooled or exploited them.

Finally, Manoj came up with a plan.

Drive through the hilly terrain of Araku with the windows down, and you will catch the faint aroma of coffee plantations mingling with the scent of the forest. Naturally, Manoj's plan centred on coffee. It involved organizing the farmers into cooperatives, improving growing practices and throwing in bits of other things. But what made it different was the focus on better marketing and generating larger revenues for the coffee grower. It was enormous effort and there was measurable progress.

The work began to get noticed. One of those who heard about it was Claude Avézard. Based in Dubai, he had come to Hyderabad and met Manoj through a common friend. He visited Araku and fell in love with the hills, the people and Naandi's work. He was an outstanding photographer and was the toast of the advertising world in Europe before he emigrated to Australia and then shifted to the Middle East. He had produced a stunning coffee-table book on the Arabian Peninsula, *Whispers from the Sands*, and he offered to do one pro bono for Naandi! During three visits to Araku, Claude captured the divine tranquillity of Araku and the charm of its people like nobody else could have done. *Whispers from the Hills* came out in 2004. I promptly took it to R.K. Krishna Kumar of the Tata Group, who was also vice chairman of Indian Hotels, a Tata company that owns the chain of Taj hotels. He generously gave 6 million rupees for 3000 copies of Claude's book and placed them in hotel rooms of the Taj across the country. The money came in handy for Naandi.

It was not an easy task to sustain the effort at Araku. Coffee is a commodity and the second most traded one in the world. The margins in the business are wafer-thin. Prices fluctuate, but are usually unremunerative for the small grower. The export markets are perhaps better, but it is difficult to break into them and a chain of intermediaries limit the benefits to the grower. Moreover, Araku was not known as a coffee-growing region. Though Naandi's work resulted in benefits to the small coffee grower and were appreciated, I wanted more.

Something radical needed to be done.

Manoj came up with a better idea. He argued that the only way to increase returns to the coffee growers was to transform his produce from being a commodity to something special that would command a premium price. What were conventionally seen as weaknesses could be transformed into advantages. The coffee growers in Araku were too poor to think of pesticides, so the coffee was truly organic. Yields being poor, the supplies of coffee were limited, adding to its appeal of being special. The coffee had a distinctive flavour. Naandi's trade practices would enable fair-trade certification, which would make Araku a preferred source for certain kinds of coffee buyers. The story of the people who produced the coffee would be the clincher. All this, Manoj said, added up to an ideal branding opportunity, and potentially a substantial premium in price over commodity coffee beans.

Fine organic coffee. Nature's flavours from Araku. I swirled the phrases around in my head and savoured them. More importantly, I saw the possibility of returns to the growers increasing five-fold. It was a heady thought.

Manoj set to work with vigour. The supply side was secured by building on the foundation already laid and small farmers, each one of them owning less than a hectare of land, were organized into a cooperative in 2007. Coffee planting was intensified and agricultural practices were improved. Dr Sunalini Menon, a Bengaluru-based internationally acclaimed coffee expert and director of Coffeelab, agreed to be a consultant to Naandi and the impact of her expertise is visible.

Araku Emerald was launched in December 2007 by Jairam Ramesh, Union minister of state for commerce, amid 4000 tribal growers. Jairam Ramesh was particularly pleased. He had advocated the production of organic coffee by tribal cooperatives earlier in the year. The story was picked up by the media and there was quite some interest in Araku coffee.

I knew, however, that to sustain the initial interest and transform it to consistent sales was a tall order. I knew nothing about branding aspirational products. A lifetime of commitment to making medicines affordable did not equip me to help Manoj think about this task. We needed wiser counsel.

I turned to Anand Mahindra for advice and took Manoj along to meet him in Mumbai early in 2008. Anand was clear that Araku was a good story and the benefits to the indigenous people would be substantial if we could position its coffee as a premium brand. Besides, the approach would be suitable for many other communities in India and abroad, so there would also be a larger benefit. But the task of building a pricey brand would be enormous. The world's coffee experts would need to be convinced that Araku coffee was special. Marketing, logistics and ensuring quality were all demanding tasks. An organization that would be capable of raising substantial amounts of capital and providing an environment where specialized professional talent could be recruited and retained was essential. All this was unlikely to be feasible in an organization like Naandi, which marched to an entirely different tune.

We, therefore, decided that the activity would be spun off as a separate enterprise. Araku Orignals Limited, a social enterprise company, was set up, promoted by Anand Mahindra, Rajendra Prasad and myself to establish Araku as a premier global coffee brand. All the supplies of coffee to the company were to be from the cooperative organized by

Naandi, which was considerably strengthened by investments from the Paris-based Livelihoods Fund in 2010.

Work gathered pace. The membership of the cooperative has now grown to about 25,000, making it one of the largest organic coffee-growing cooperatives in the world. Internationally known coffee tasters from Ireland, Norway, the USA and Japan have joined Sunalini Menon in annual 'cupping sessions', called Gems of Araku, from 2009 onward.

In three years, 350 tonnes of Araku coffee have been exported all over the world. Swank restaurants in the country are serving it too. Brand Araku is being built along with better livelihoods for the tribal growers in the valley.

The power of partnerships

I sometimes worry that Naandi is stretching itself too thin and Manoj is biting off more than he can chew. There are so many areas outside the stories that I have related where Naandi has worked.

Tuition after school hours: *Government primary schoolchildren, Nawab Saheb Kunta, Hyderabad*

For example, the Michael and Susan Dell Foundation as well as many other Indian corporates and institutions support Naandi's initiative to improve the learning of children in government schools. The outcomes, reflected in examination results as well as third-party evaluation, are very encouraging. I could go on.

How has all this been achieved? I think the most important factor has been the partnerships that Naandi has forged. The most important partnerships have been with the government, both in the states and at the Centre. There is no better way to achieve scale and impact than through a partnership with the government. The government has underwritten a substantial portion of the expenses of many of Naandi's projects—the midday meal scheme being one of the best examples.

Naandi has also forged partnerships with a number of institutions and corporates that have inspired its work and contributed generously. But some of the most touching contributions have come from individuals. Naandi, in fact, started a Power of 10 fundraising initiative

The Naandi board: *(L–R) Anand Mahindra, Isher Judge Ahluwalia, me, M. Rajendra Prasad*

where people employed in large organizations contributed 10 rupees deducted from their monthly pay. A minuscule amount individually, but substantial collectively.

Naandi's story is not merely its own. It is also the story of all those with whom Naandi has joined hands.

21 MARS IS THE LIMIT

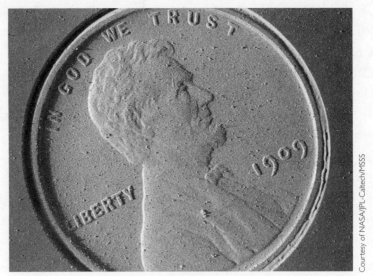

A penny for last thoughts: *Martian dust on the Lincoln penny.*
Curiosity's first full-resolution image

Hyderabad, 6 March 2013

I am idly surfing the net on my iPad in a hospital room. I chance upon the list of invitees to the State of the Union address of President Obama that the White House has put out a few weeks earlier. I skim through it and 'pancreatic cancer' catches my eye. I read it with more attention.

One invitee is a sixteen-year-old who has discovered a new method to diagnose pancreatic cancer, 28 times faster and 100 times more sensitive than the test currently available. Wait a minute, did I read right? Yes, it's a sixteen-year-old, Jack Andraka. I google him and find his TED talk. He is fresh-faced and sports a mop of hair that reminds me of the Beatles. His enthusiasm is infectious. Jack talks of the difficulty he had in finding laboratory space to pursue his research, till one of the 200 people he had mailed gave him a hearing and then the hospitality of his laboratory. He has developed a simple test to detect pancreatic cancer by estimating the level of a protein called mesothelin in blood. As against the 800 dollars of the conventional test, he thinks it will cost 3 cents. That's right, 3 cents! And it has the potential to increase survival dramatically as it can detect pancreatic cancer early, before it is too late for treatment to be effective.

I wonder who provided him with laboratory facilities. It can happen only in America! I google some more. It's a professor of pathology at Johns Hopkins with the distinctly Indian name of Anirban Maitra.

It will take time for Jack's test to be validated and the cost may be higher. But it is remarkable that Jack has obtained proof of concept. It seems to me that affordable medicine is lurking behind unexpected turns, waiting to be discovered by improbably young and incredibly talented scientists. I feel the familiar rush of exhilaration.

I get back to the White House list. 'Mars' catches my eye next. A person with the unusual name of Bobak Ferdowsi has also been invited. He was part of the Mars *Curiosity* rover team. It's not surprising that he caught President Obama's eye for he sported a Mohawk-style hairdo for the landing. I read on. Ferdowsi is the son of an Iranian immigrant. That explains his name, though in Hyderabad it is usually spelt Firdausi.

I had missed the telecast of the Mars Space Laboratory landing last August and *Curiosity* venturing out into the bleak Martian landscape. But it did not matter, for *Time* put it on the cover and provided great pictures and a graphic description. What a stunning achievement!

Curiosity carries a chemistry laboratory as well as a dazzling array of other instruments. Three of these have been provided by other countries—Canada, Russia and Spain. That is the way scientific collaboration should be, without borders. Come to think of it, that is the way it is in America. In which other country of the world will you find Andraka, Ferdowsi, Maitra and names from every part of the planet working at the frontiers of science? America will remain the knowledge leader of the world for a long time to come.

India is not too far behind though. *Chandrayaan-1*, India's moon orbiter, was launched in October 2008 and orbited the moon for nearly a year. The impact probe from *Chandrayaan* landed on the surface of the moon, with the Indian tricolour painted on its surface, on 14th November 2008, the birth anniversary of India's first prime minister, Jawaharlal Nehru, and the nation cheered.

India is scheduled to launch *Mangalyaan*, India's first Mars Orbiter, late this year. *Mangalyaan* is expected to cost around 4.5 billion rupees, about 74 million dollars. It will be a milestone for Indian science, and a truly affordable one. The nation could not have asked for more from its space scientists.

The moon is no longer the limit. Mars is.

My life in the pharmaceutical industry has run its course. As I look back for the last time, I am awed at its transformation from a technology beseecher to a technology provider and the world's premier producer of affordable medicine. The nation could not have asked for more from its pharmaceutical sector.

I could not have asked for anything more either.

AFTERWORD AND ACKNOWLEDGEMENTS

The last task that Dr Anji Reddy set for himself was writing his memoirs. I knew that it was not the first time he had considered this, but earlier attempts had soon given way to his many commitments. This time, however, it was different. It was his priority, he said. Though he knew the answer, he asked if I would assist him.

'Of course,' I said, matter-of-factly. I did not tell Dr Reddy that nothing could have been a greater privilege.

Dr Reddy laid out the plan. He would talk about his life for at least three days a week and I would record it. I would get it transcribed and periodically string it together for his review. I would then have to fill in the gaps and get the facts verified as needed. He would finish his part in six months or less and he wanted to see the first version of the book as soon as possible thereafter, but no later than nine months in all. Like most of Dr Reddy's business meetings, it was over in less than twenty minutes.

Dr Reddy was a marvellous storyteller. He told his story with gusto and laced it with anecdotes and laughter. He talked of how he strayed into chemistry and later decided to make a career in the pharmaceutical industry. He painted a vivid picture of the early years of Dr. Reddy's Laboratories and its subsequent growth. I was given a grand tour of the progress of science and medicine, each development a precursor to the next great advance, often with the minutiae that pinned it to memory. I was in thrall to his enthusiasm, his recall, and his optimism that leaps and bounds of scientific progress were imminent in India as much as elsewhere in the world.

249

Usually impatient with detail, Dr Reddy took the trouble to point me to his speeches and articles that would make my job easier. I got the notes he had made in his precise handwriting, probably when he had first thought of writing his autobiography many years earlier. He plied me with the books which had informed and inspired him. One of them was a handbook on Nobel laureates, which he had obviously read with care. Largely from memory, occasionally aided by the trusty Merck Index always on his table, he drew structures of chemical compounds and the schemes of processes he had developed decades earlier, to explain a point he was making. 'Don't you see the beauty of it?' he once asked with great enthusiasm as he looked up from his drawing—and saw that my eyes had glazed over. 'Even my grandchildren are not interested in chemistry,' he grumbled.

Dr Reddy was enjoyably engrossed in the whole process. He would call often, as soon as something struck him, when he came across an interesting titbit, or to share the news of an exciting development. Sometimes, the calls were from a hospital while he waited for a test or a procedure. Time took its toll. He came to office less frequently and tired more quickly, but he kept up with the calls and text messages. He suggested I see him at home. Sometimes, we met at his favourite spot under the pipal tree in his garden. On the first occasion I went there, he said, 'I may yet be enlightened, like the Buddha,' and laughed.

Finally, the book got done. It would not have been possible but for the unstinting help of many. If the list is long, it is because so many have done so much to ensure that Dr Reddy's last task came to fruition. Dr Reddy, always quick to appreciate the help he received, would have wanted to gratefully acknowledge every one of them. Sadly, I have to do so on his behalf, for he passed away on 15 March 2013, a week after he read the first version of his book.

Dr. Reddy's Laboratories achieved the milestone of a billion dollars of annual revenue for the first time in 2006. Dr Reddy immediately wrote a memo—reproduced in this book— to all the employees of the company. He conveyed his gratitude to each one of them. It would have been no different now, as his story in significant part is that of Dr. Reddy's Laboratories and the people who worked in it.

When I put together the initial transcripts, I asked Dr Reddy how he would like to begin his memoirs. He told me he had worked on his life story for a while in 2005 with Ravi Velloor. 'Ravi captured the spirit of my entrepreneurial journey very well,' Dr Reddy said. 'It was his idea to begin the book with the moon landing. I would like to start with that, if Ravi consents.' Ravi generously consented to that and more. Chapter 1 is entirely as Ravi wrote it, as are parts of chapters 2, 5, 6 and 8.

At some point, I asked Dr Reddy if he had thought about the title. He had obviously given it careful thought. 'Gauri Kamath wrote a feature in the *Economic Times* on what she called my philanthropic work,' he said. 'It was summed up very well as "The Unfinished Agenda" in the headline. It would sum up my work in discovery research equally well.' The *Economic Times* readily consented to the use of the headline in the title.

Years earlier, in 2005, Dr Reddy had written an article titled 'The Future of Medicine' for a special issue of *Business Today*. The use of extracts from the article in chapter 17 is gratefully acknowledged.

Over time, Dr Reddy noticed that the drafts given to him were getting better and said as much. I confessed that it was not my doing. My friend Vithal Rajan had helped in editing the transcripts. Vithal was captivated by Dr Reddy's conversational style, which reminded him of fireside lectures at a learned society. He insisted that it should be preserved in the book, without irksome footnotes and tedious explanations. Suchitra Shenoy read the manuscript with great diligence. The severity with which she pointed out distractions and needless complexity belied her sunny disposition, and the book is all the better for it. My sister Sudha Raghavendran patiently and painstakingly undid the damage I had unwittingly inflicted on the English language and more. Dr Reddy did not seem to be inclined to forgiveness at my confession. 'How can you rope in your family and friends to do your work?' he asked, with more than a hint of disapproval. But he appreciated the trouble they had taken.

I reached out to a number of people who are now with Dr. Reddy's Laboratories or had earlier been with it for information and help. The alacrity with which they responded to my requests was truly overwhelming.

Uday Saxena, A. Venkateswarlu and Ish Khanna, who worked closely with Dr Reddy in discovery research, dispelled the scientific haze I was stumbling in despite Dr Reddy's clear account of the discovery effort. So did C.S.N. Murthy, with regard to the progress being made at Aurigene. N. Ramesh Kumar helped ensure that I did not mangle the chemistry. I requested A. Shanavas to review the science, especially the biology. He not only did so meticulously, but also got rid of the errors that had crept in elsewhere. I am indebted to him. Joy Kumar Dutta pulled out scientific literature with unfailing efficiency and courtesy.

Luc Lamirault and Cristina Garlasu gave generously of their time to share their recollections of the early days in Europe and P. Muralidhar took the trouble of collating information on more recent acquisitions in the UK, Netherlands and Mexico. Viswanatha Bonthu, who has been with the company since the Cheminor days, and Anjum Swaroop helped dig out the details of events in the US that have long gone by. M. Srinivas Rao, a storehouse of knowledge about the US generics business, added to the information and brought it up to date. M.V. Ramana, whose unhurried calm cloaks a punishing work schedule, made the time to provide fascinating glimpses of the complexities of doing business in China and Russia and the changes that have occurred over time. M.V. Narasimham made sure that the financial figures were accurate. V.S. Vasudevan, who had worked with Dr Reddy even prior to the inception of Dr. Reddy's Laboratories and served the company for well over two decades, brought home the excitement of a start-up as only a participant could have.

Manoj Kumar put in considerable effort to chronicle the impressive achievements of Naandi and Nalini Gangadharan chimed in, recalling the satisfying course that Dr. Reddy's Foundation has run.

S.V.S. Chowdhury added to the photographs that Rajan had provided and Shilpi Lathia cheerfully completed the collection for this book. Rohini Mukherjee was responsible for choosing and providing the photographs that speak volumes about Naandi's work. *Business India* willingly agreed to the reproduction of its cover that featured Dr Reddy. Cristina Garlasu, Krishnan Ramalingam of Ranbaxy, Ritha Chandrachud of Merck & Co. and Jayendra Naidoo responded positively to our request for pictures and we are thankful. C. Seshagiri Rao chased down the image of the plaque installed in memory of Yellapragada SubbaRow at Lederle. B.V. Ramana of Rajan's School of Photography has done a wonderful job of digitally touching up all the photographs and restoring those ravaged by age and indifferent storage.

V.Ch. Kameshwara Rao and P. Jayanth worked with Dr Reddy for a long time. Kameshwara Rao had the uncanny knack of anticipating what Dr Reddy wanted and he did the needful unobtrusively. He was constantly by Dr Reddy's side when hospital visits caused 'interruptions' (as Dr Reddy put it) and his gentle interventions ensured that there was no pause in the progress of the memoirs. Jayanth did the hard work of transcribing a great number of hours of Dr Reddy's reminiscences and magically produced every single thing that Dr Reddy wanted, or I needed, from the recesses of his office or elsewhere. They, and T. Sambi Reddy who had worked with Dr Reddy from the very beginning, were a mine of information of the decades gone by. As indeed were the archives of the memories and history of the company painstakingly and imaginatively compiled by Indira Chowdhury of the Centre of Public History, Bengaluru.

Late in February 2013, Dr Reddy reviewed the typescript of the first version. He hid his disappointment at not being able to see it in book form. I mentioned it to Narendra Paruchuri of Pragati Offset, who knew Dr Reddy. Narendra's response was immediate and unequivocal. 'It has to be done,' he told me sternly. S. Rajan, then with the corporate communications department of the company, was galvanized into action by the urgency. He roped in Vivek Reddy of Priyadarshini Advertising to design the book with hastily assembled photographs. It turned out that Vivek's father had worked in IDPL and having heard about Dr Reddy's illness, he left Vivek with no option but to deliver. The book was designed in an incredibly short time and Narendra printed and bound it overnight. Both disrupted their busy work schedules to get the job done, entirely as a gesture of goodwill. Dr Reddy was deeply moved to finally have the book in his hands and was touched by the efforts of those who made it happen.

Mythili Mamidanna was more than helpful with her thoughtful suggestions. S. Chandrasekhar, Geetha Thoopal, Shankar Melkote and Pratap Ravindran, all of whom are voracious readers, very kindly read and commented on the manuscript. Dr Bala Chakravarthy, professor of strategy and international management at IMD, and Dr Karen Leonard, now professor emeritus of anthropology at the University of California at Irvine, did so too. Bala, who has done two case studies on Dr. Reddy's Laboratories, engaged in a helpful discussion on the structure and content of the memoirs. Karen was intrigued by the process of the writing of the memoirs and it was at her urging that this Afterword finds place in the book.

We are grateful to Udayan Mitra of Penguin Random House for agreeing to publish these memoirs and greatly appreciate his deft shepherding of the manuscript through the editing and production process. We are also grateful to his colleague Richa Burman who responded promptly to all our requests with patience and understanding, apart from doing far more than her fair share to make the book as readable as possible.

On a personal note, I am beholden to Satish, Prasad and Anuradha for their generous help and support which made my task a memorable and rewarding experience.

Raghu Cidambi
Formerly adviser to Dr Anji Reddy
and Dr. Reddy's Laboratories Limited

INDEX